NOPI

THE COOKBOOK

YOTAM OTTOLENGHI   RAMAEL SCULLY

WITH TARA WIGLEY

TEN SPEED PRESS
Berkeley

585MM × 685MM

835MM × 835MM

Contents

INTRODUCTION

If you happen to have any of my previous books—*Ottolenghi*, *Plenty*, *Jerusalem*, and *Plenty More*—you will notice right away that the dishes in this book are somewhat more complex. Therefore, most of the recipes here will be more challenging for home cooks. They are typically made up of a few distinct elements that need to be prepared separately, occasionally over a bit of time, before being put together on a plate at the very last minute.

I start with this disclaimer not in order to put anyone off—I think the food here is spectacularly delicious and I am massively proud of it—but because I want to make it clear that this is a restaurant cookbook: it features *restaurant food*. The vast majority of the recipes in my previous books were conceived in and for a home kitchen. The recipes here were created from a different frame of mind; that is, in an environment where a team of professional cooks labors for a few hours in preparation for a short pinnacle, the famous *service*, in which hundreds of dishes are served in short succession to a very large crowd. It is the complete opposite of the way we cook and eat at home.

The contrast between these two mindsets is, really, the story of this book. What Ramael Scully (or just Scully, from now on, as that's what everybody calls him) and I have attempted to do is to modify and simplify NOPI's recipes without losing their essential core. We tried to keep a degree of complexity that does justice to food that is by its very nature complex, at the same time as allowing a nonprofessional to feel that this is an undertaking that is doable at home, delicious, and gratifying.

The meeting of two distinctive worldviews also makes up the story of my relationship with Scully. I am telling it in detail here because it really is the story of the food you'll find in the following pages and how it came to be.

Random meeting

Many of life's most momentous moments stem from pretty random circumstances. My meeting with Scully is such a case. Well before I was even vaguely aware of the magical world of *rasam*, *sambal*, and pandan, I met Scully on an ordinary trial shift on an ordinary day in the kitchen of Ottolenghi in Islington: a big man with a congenial smile, baffling cultural heritage, and distinctive shuffling gait. Scully responded to what must have been the fifth online ad that Jim Webb, the head chef, had placed early in 2005, desperately looking for a senior *chef de partie*. His task would be to create a small menu of hot dishes served from the kitchen in the evening, alongside our familiar counter salads and cakes.

There was nothing unusual or particularly promising about this latest Aussie recruit; restaurant chefs tend to come and go quite regularly. Jim seemed to like him and that was good enough for me. Plus, with the chronic shortage of chefs in London, I couldn't really afford to be picky. And so Scully got the position and started training to run our evening service in the restaurant. After a few days, he seemed to be doing a decent job, though I can still remember a fleeting chat inside a walk-in fridge where Jim expressed certain concerns about Scully's experience and his efficiency during service. I suggested that we wait and see.

A few days later I got my first taste of Scully's food. He cooked, if my memory serves me right, portobello mushrooms braised in white wine, hard herbs, and, in typical Scully fashion, *tons* of butter, and topped with pearled barley with feta and preserved lemon. He also served the crispest pork belly that had ever entered my mouth, with a sweet and sharp compote of plums, rhubarb, chile, ginger, and star anise. I was hooked!

Everything that is brilliant about Scully's cooking was there in those two dishes: his ability to combine ingredients with virtuosity and flair (preserved lemon, rosemary, feta, and barley), his meticulousness in getting things *just* right (that heavenly crackling), his unreal generosity (a bottle of white wine in each of the dishes), his expertise in and understanding of both Mediterranean and Asian cooking, and his knack in blending them together thoughtfully, never willy-nilly, in a modern context.

Scully's food also fitted, almost perfectly (and I will explain this "almost" later), with the Ottolenghi way. The bold, surprisingly intense flavors that became synonymous with the name, the irreverent blends of ingredients, the vibrant colors on the plate, the generosity of spirit and big gestures, the curiosity and somewhat restless approach to food (always looking for the next ingredient, a fresh combination, or a radically different method): all these were features we unmistakably had in common.

Within a few weeks of joining, Scully was running the evening section at Ottolenghi, constantly creating new recipes and new flavors, many of which I had been oblivious to before; he was serving our customers dishes ranging from squid with quinoa, smoked cherry tomatoes, and prosecco to poppy seed tart with squash, goat cheese, and carrot jam. And with the food came stories: the *sambal* was a hybrid of his mother's recipes with those of his many aunties; the duck confit was salted and left in fat for three months because that's the way it was done at Bathers' Pavilion, the Sydney waterfront restaurant where Scully did his apprenticeship.

Scully's food reflected his rich and intricate background. He was born in Malaysia to a mother of Chinese and Indian heritage and a father with Irish and Malay blood. At the age of eight, he moved with his mother and sister to Sydney, where he went to school and later to catering school. When he came to us, Scully had very particular culinary baggage. His Malaysian flavors were, like Sami Tamimi's and my "Jerusalem flavors," the basic building blocks of his culinary world. He also had his years of training in the European tradition and his experience in formal restaurants. He was, just like us, an unusual hybrid. The dynamic that has evolved ever since—world Ottolenghi meets world Scully—has become the creative engine behind a large chunk of what we have been doing since Scully joined.

Taming Scully

First, Scully brought with him his very recent experience in the world of contemporary restaurants. After a few years of running Ottolenghi, with its focus on daytime dining and general sense of food inspired by the street or the home, Sami and I were less conversant in the old restaurant kitchen language. We needed a firsthand, up-to-date take on the theme.

Scully's first attempts at creating an evening menu for Islington showed his talent and enthusiasm for what I can best describe as "composition"; that is, putting together quite a few complex elements on a plate in an arranged, thought-through manner. There would normally be a piece of meat or fish, marinated for at least a day and cooked to perfection in a very particular stock, accompanied by a vegetable that had been braising slowly and was then mashed with some of Scully's favorite ingredients (miso, perhaps, or rehydrated dried chiles or an obscure Korean spice paste). A couple of other elements would no doubt be there: crisp vegetable pickle, maybe, or a caramelized nut and seed mix. A fruity salsa with fresh coconut could also work. Maybe even all three.

This was in extreme opposition to Sami's and my tendency to just "throw together" a few things on a large platter in a pretty effortless way: large chunks of roasted butternut squash with a drizzle of citrusy tahini and a dusting of za'atar would do us just fine. Scully would just *have* to add something else: five-spiced crispy shallots, maybe, or a drizzle of reduced passata with ginger and chile. He was also partial to liberal quantities of butter, various rich stocks, and salty, umami-heavy condiments such as kimchi or *ikan bilis* (salt-cured anchovies). Again, a far cry from our simpler favorites: yogurt, lemon, and garlic.

The years that ensued saw us in a constant state of negotiating to find a middle ground. A permanent Islington kitchen fixture would be myself or Sami engaged in one of our famous "tastings" with Scully to introduce a new dish to the menu (normally around 2 p.m., when the kitchen was already bursting at the seams with manic lunch service overlapping highly space-consuming

dinner prep). "Scully, this is marvelous but can we tone it down a notch? Lose an element or two? Wouldn't a plain salsa suffice?" And the answer: "Man, this is already super simple. I was actually going to slow-cook it for an extra twenty-four hours. Did you not see how David Chang does his kombu broth in five stages over three days?"

Scully's delight in slow processes—including meandering around Chinatown looking for any number of new ingredients while service is practically on its way, or vegging in bed with a pile of cookbooks by his side until inspiration finally hits—earned him our love and, occasionally, a fair bit of harmless exasperation. There's quite a lot Scully can get away with, owing to his disarming charm, big heart, and enormous talent.

Thanks to these exceptional qualities, collaborating with Scully has always been a breeze. In every single case we've managed to find a compromise, a dish that is a little lighter and simpler than Scully had in mind and a little heftier and more involved than what Sami and I wished for. This became the blueprint for the hot food we now serve at NOPI and at Ottolenghi in Islington and Spitalfields. In short, Scully showed us how to do "restaurant," we taught him how to do "Ottolenghi," and the result was this new hybrid set of dishes that are now the "Ottolenghi haute cuisine," and are featured in this book.

Scully's second big contribution to Ottolenghi and, similarly, a bit of a bone of contention at the outset, was a very fresh set of flavors, most of them Asian: curry leaves, yuzu, dried shrimp, lime leaves, glutinous rice flour, pandan leaves, galangal, *ketjap manis*, and many more. These were great additions to our repertoire and made complete sense because they were just as bold and colorful and rich as our sumac, preserved lemons, and pomegranate molasses. Yet they weren't part of our usual palate and I vigorously resisted turning the menu too "Asian" and losing the Middle Eastern/Mediterranean blend that was much more natural to Sami and to me. Much of the first few years of us working together were spent with me trying to curb Scully's "Asian tendencies." Slowly, however, I gave in. One dish in the first year (white pepper–crusted soft-shelled crab, with miso cucumber and wasabi mayonnaise, I believe it was), two the following year, then three, and, finally, as many as Scully wanted, really, when NOPI opened in 2011.

While haggling with Scully over the degree to which Ottolenghi would "go Asian," I secretly (I was keeping my cards *very* close to my chest, you see), developed my own love of all things to do with the Indian subcontinent and Southeast Asia. Through my physical and virtual travels and through friends and colleagues, one of whom was Scully himself of course, I was beginning to seriously enjoy my laksas and tamarind broths, my misos and yuzus, my tofus and peanut sauces. And so, gradually, my palate and the Ottolenghi repertoire naturally expanded eastward.

Our "grown-up" restaurant

The reason for NOPI was a somewhat self-indulgent one: a desire for what we called a "grown-up restaurant." We are not sure what made us think that the Ottolenghi delis weren't quite grown-up enough, but the reality was that Noam Bar, who formulated the vision, and the rest of the team—Cornelia Staeubli, Basia Murphy, Sarit Packer, Alex Meitlis, Scully, and me—were all ready for a fresh challenge: an all-day brasserie, a "proper" West End establishment serving the kind of food that we'd developed in Islington over the years, drawing in people seeking genuinely good food throughout the day with the quality of a serious restaurant but without any of the stuffiness and formality.

Easier said than done—*much* easier! The year that preceded NOPI's opening saw a painstaking process of getting details right—*all* the details!

Alex, mastermind of the Ottolenghi look, was translating Noam's ideas into a reality that included plenty of patina-laden brass, smooth-polished bloodshot marble, whitewashed brick, striking art, and the famous bathrooms, where a set of floor-to-ceiling concertina mirrors threw customers into a perplexing Wonderland and evoked a general sense of bewilderment and slight unease.

Cornelia and Basia were making sure that upstairs was quite the opposite. Everything—all the things you are not meant to notice when you sit comfortably in a restaurant enjoying a serene meal—needed to tick along in the nicest, smoothest, slickest, most predictable way. Waiters' probable journeys in strategic junctions were plotted and analyzed; training manuals perfected so that staff knew their stuff inside and out (grape varietals, the obvious distinction between farro and spelt—just between us, I am still not quite sure about that myself—and the very elusive art of laid-back etiquette). Reception had to operate in full harmony with the bar, shift managers, and downstairs office; the expeditor to be alert to the kitchen intercom and movement on the floor; table covers to be regularly stocked, wiped and changed; plates seamlessly cleared; bills to arrive on time; tables turned; guests called; guests seated; wines decanted; food served; kitchen informed.

Once we were open, at the top of the pyramid stood Basia, the general manager, who came from Ottolenghi in Islington and built up NOPI with infinite amounts of passion, commitment, and know-how. You didn't need to actually see Basia on the floor to recognize her mark, her boundless upbeat energy, clearly apparent in the movements of the waitstaff and in the smoothness and elegance of the operation. Basia was the embodiment of the restaurant in the first few years and the absolute key to its popularity. More recently she has been replaced by our very own Heidi Knudsen, a different kind of force of nature but with a similarly affirmative presence.

Since we never do things simply at Ottolenghi, NOPI's kitchen was designed from the start as a slightly peculiar, three-headed creature with responsibilities shared between Sarit (now running her own super-successful restaurant, Honey & Co), Scully, and me: an arrangement that generated a fair bit of confusion among our poor chefs. Even some exasperation, no doubt, when Scully's garnish of fried chile and baby cilantro was replaced by Sarit's fresh chile and pomegranate seeds and finally by my "Who needs a garnish at all?" Nevertheless, the aim was to create a strong structure that benefited from my experience, Sarit's management and food skills, and Scully's particular style and years of working at Ottolenghi.

Months before the restaurant was due to open, we would all get together once or twice a week at the back table of Ottolenghi on Motcomb Street and get to taste the progress of recent creations. In order to "sign off" on a dish, we'd all need to like it. Anyone who's ever worked with the Ottolenghi team can tell you how utterly impossible the task is of getting Noam, Cornelia, and me to unanimously agree on anything; adding all the others to the equation, the food really needed to be pretty spectacular to pass through our little committee. Scully and John Meechan, who worked with Sarit on desserts and bread, rose to the challenge and created some of NOPI's most iconic dishes: twice-cooked baby chicken, beef brisket croquettes, pig's cheeks, strained ricotta, and coffee financiers—they were all there.

On the day NOPI opened to the general public—February 17, 2011—we were all thoroughly exhausted and more than slightly anxious. Anyone who'd tell you that opening a restaurant is a trivial, cheerful kind of matter would be lying through their teeth. Even more difficult, though, is *running* a new restaurant; the real hardships start when the doors are finally open. It took a long while for the (proverbial, we assure you!) dust at NOPI to completely settle, probably a couple of years. Some key players had changed—Cornelia and Sami had become more involved in the kitchen once Sarit left, Basia was replaced by Heidi—but we think we can now say with confidence that we did manage to realize our dream of a "grown-up" restaurant, and that the vision that was set in motion in early 2011, or, actually, in early 2005, keeps on moving forward and expanding all the time.

Yotam Ottolenghi

COOKING NOPI AT HOME

As mentioned earlier, there's no denying that some of the dishes in this book are pretty involved. Even after all our adjustments and simplifications, this is still a restaurant cookbook, and certain recipes will remind the home cook why it's such a joy to eat *out* at a restaurant in the first place, where all the hard work is done by someone else. There was even a point when we were only half-joking about including a chapter called "epic," where the more complex recipes could go: the chicken pastilla, beef brisket, twice-cooked baby chicken, pig's cheeks, and a couple of others.

We've tried to balance the epic with other, more simple dishes (see "sides" page 71). Some of these aren't dishes we serve at NOPI. They are there, however, so that you can take one of the more involved dishes, pair it with a simple side, and have a complete meal as a result.

We have also compiled a list of meal suggestions (page 310) with some ideas for recipes that work well together to make a balanced meal. These will satisfy different appetites, both for food and for hard work in the kitchen. A list of ingredients (page 313) is there to help you navigate through the seas of unusual flavors we love to cook with. As we mention there, seeking out and cooking with new ingredients should always be fun and never intimidating. If you're not in the mood for something new or haven't got the time to go looking for it, we almost always offer alternatives that are readily available.

For both epic recipes and simpler ones, always keep in mind the rule we were told at school before taking an exam: first read through the text in its entirety. It is *really* useful to **read the whole recipe before you start** so that you can work out what can be done in advance, what needs to be done at the last moment, and so forth.

We also make a point of suggesting **alternative routes for different cooks**: more complicated cheffy options for those with a bit of time and an overall adventurous disposition; simpler alternatives, for those who are after an impressive result but want to get there pretty swiftly. Please don't hesitate to choose our shortcuts, ready-made alternatives, and quick substitutes; we use them all the time when cooking at home. Most dishes are rich and multifaceted enough to easily withstand at least one or two of those.

To cook NOPI dishes, we also highly recommend that you act a little bit like a chef and **do your *mise en place***—that is, getting ahead with all the chopping and weighing up of ingredients before you actually start to cook. You really don't want to be left trying to finely chop 2 green chiles when they are meant to be thrown into a pan 2 minutes after the diced onion has gone in.

Tool-wise, there are certain pieces of equipment that will make your life much easier when cooking our food, although none of them is absolutely essential. We'd recommend investing in a mandoline for those restaurant-thin julienned vegetables; a spice grinder will save you heaps of time and plenty of elbow work over the old mortar and pestle; a blender will enable you to make supersmooth soups and sauces; and, finally, an ice cream machine will also save you a fair bit of arm ache and will make you some pretty impressive desserts.

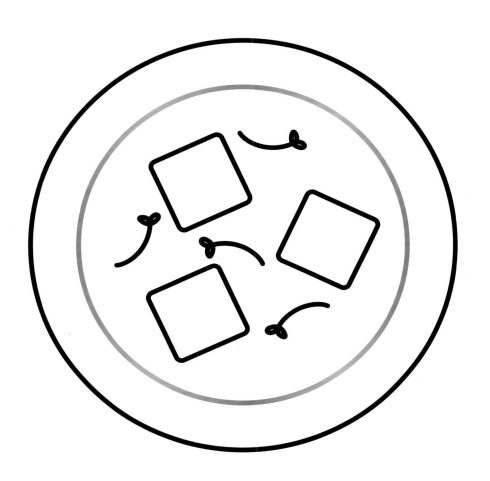

STARTERS

Roasted eggplant with black garlic, pine nuts, and basil

We'll be thinking we've done pretty much everything that can be done with a tray of roasted eggplant, and then a new ingredient comes along to shake things up. We discovered black garlic around the same time that NOPI opened, and quickly became hooked. It has an addictive mellowness and depth of fermented flavor: part balsamic vinegar gummy candy, part licorice allsort. Black garlic starts off as white garlic. Nothing is added to the cloves to make them change so fundamentally from one thing to another; they simply undergo a three-week heat process that transforms their natural sugars and amino acids. It's sold either as a whole bulb whose cloves you then need to peel, or in a small jar of slightly smaller cloves already separated and peeled.

This recipe benefits from being made a few hours before you want to eat it, for the flavors to really absorb and develop. The roasted eggplant wedges don't fully keep their shape once they're tossed in the garlic sauce, so don't worry if the result is slightly mushier than you'd expect: it'll be all the better to spoon on top of some toasted sourdough or pita bread.

With thanks to Gena Deligianni for this dish.

Serves 6

5 medium eggplants, trimmed
 (3 lb/1.4 kg)
1/2 cup/120 ml olive oil, plus
 extra to serve
2/3 cup/150 g plain yogurt
1/3 oz/10 g basil leaves

3/4 oz/20 g pine nuts, toasted
coarse sea salt and black pepper

Black garlic dressing
13/4 oz/50 g peeled black
 garlic cloves
11/2 tsp rose harissa
 (or regular harissa)

1 tsp pomegranate molasses
2 1/2 tbsp lemon juice
1/4 tsp urfa chile flakes (or a pinch
 of regular dried chile flakes)
1/2 tsp cocoa powder
31/2 tbsp olive oil

1 Preheat the oven to 425°F/220°C (390°F/220°C convection).

2 Cut each eggplant in half lengthwise, and then again widthwise. Cut each section into wedges about 11/4 inches/3 cm wide and 4 inches/10 cm long, and place in a large mixing bowl along with the olive oil, 1 tablespoon of salt, and a good grind of black pepper. Mix well, then spread the eggplants out on two parchment-lined baking sheets—you don't want them to be overcrowded—skin-side down. Roast in the oven for about 40 minutes, until well cooked and golden brown. Remove from the oven and set aside to cool.

3 Place all the ingredients for the dressing in the small bowl of a food processor, along with 1/4 teaspoon of salt. Blitz for about 2 minutes, until a very smooth paste is formed.

4 Place the eggplant in a large mixing bowl. Add the garlic dressing and use your hands to stir very gently: you want the eggplant to be coated without disintegrating completely. Leave for an hour or so, if there is time to spare. Spread the yogurt out on a platter or individual plates and arrange the eggplant wedges on top. Sprinkle over the basil leaves—tearing the large ones as you go—and the pine nuts. Finish with a drizzle of olive oil and serve.

CELERY ROOT PURÉE WITH SPICED CAULIFLOWER AND QUAIL EGGS

Ras el hanout is a North African blend of sweet and hot spices, finely ground. There's no definitive list of the spices that are combined—*hanout* means "shop" in Arabic, and every shop has its own "top-of-the-shop" variety—but it usually includes ginger, cardamom, allspice, nutmeg, cloves, black pepper, and cinnamon. Ready-made varieties are widely available and generally fine, but feel free to add to them for your own top-of-the-shop creation. We find that we often need to add a bit more cinnamon when using ready-made varieties.

The celery root purée works well as an alternative to hummus, if you want to make just this to snack on before a meal. With the additional elements, though, it's a substantial starter or even a little meal in itself, served with some warm crusty bread or white pita.

We like to fry the eggs here—the crispy edges of a fried egg work particularly well with the purée—but soft-boiled also works, if you prefer.

As with many of the dishes in this book, the main elements here can be made in advance, ready to be put together just before serving and, in this case, before the eggs are cooked. If you make the purée the day before, just cover it with plastic wrap—actually touching the surface of the purée—to prevent its forming a skin. It's better at room temperature rather than fridge-cold, so bring it out of the fridge at least half an hour before serving.

Serves 6

Celery root purée
1/4 cup/60 ml olive oil,
 plus 1 tbsp to serve
1 large onion, coarsely diced
 (5 1/2 oz/160 g)
2 cloves garlic, coarsely chopped
2 bay leaves
1 large celery root, peeled and cut
 into 3/4-inch/2-cm pieces
 (1 1/4 lb/600 g)
2 generous cups/500 ml
 vegetable stock

2 tbsp tahini
2 tbsp lemon juice
1/2 tsp ground cumin
1/2 tsp ground coriander
1/2 tsp sweet smoked paprika
coarse sea salt and black pepper

Spiced cauliflower
2 tbsp olive oil
1 large onion, thinly sliced
 (5 1/2 oz/160 g)
3 cloves garlic, thinly sliced
2 tsp ras el hanout

1 medium cauliflower, trimmed
 and coarsely grated
 (1 1/2 lb/650 g)
2 tbsp finely diced
 preserved lemon peel
3 oz/90 g almonds, skin on,
 toasted and coarsely chopped
2 oz/50 g parsley, coarsely
 chopped

Quail eggs
2 1/2 tbsp olive oil
6 or 12 quail eggs

1 First make the celery root purée. Place the olive oil in a medium saucepan over medium-high heat. Add the onion and fry for 5 to 6 minutes, stirring often, until soft and starting to caramelize. Add the garlic and bay leaves and cook for another minute before adding the celery root. Fry for 8 to 10 minutes, stirring often, so that all sides are golden brown. Pour over the stock, bring to a boil, then simmer over medium heat for about 15 minutes, until the celery root is cooked through. Remove from the heat, discard the bay leaves, and transfer to a blender or food processor. Blitz to form a smooth purée before adding the tahini, lemon juice, cumin, coriander, 1 1/2 teaspoons of salt, and a good grind of black pepper. Set aside until ready to serve. (You can make this in advance and keep it in the fridge—see headnote, page 7.)

2 Put the olive oil for the spiced cauliflower into a large sauté pan and place over medium heat. Add the onion and sauté for 5 minutes, until soft. Add the garlic and cook for another 2 minutes, then add the *ras el hanout* and cook for another minute. Pour over 7 tablespoons of water and stir for a minute before removing from the heat. Fold in the cauliflower, preserved lemon, almonds, half of the parsley, and 1 teaspoon of salt and set aside to cool.

3 When ready to serve, divide the purée among six plates. Drizzle 1/2 teaspoon of oil over each portion, spread the cauliflower on top, and sprinkle over the smoked paprika and remaining parsley.

4 To fry the quail eggs, place a large frying pan over medium heat and add the oil. When hot, crack each egg individually into the pan and fry for 30 to 60 seconds. Season each egg with a pinch of salt and a grind of black pepper, then place an egg or two on top of each portion of cauliflower and serve at once.

Fried baby artichokes with pink peppercorn aioli

However many large globe artichokes one has prepared over the years, the process never seems to get quicker or easier. It was head-over-heels, therefore, that Yotam fell for the tender baby globe artichokes of his fellow *Guardian* columnist Alys Fowler when visiting her vegetable garden in Birmingham's Highgate Park in the summer of 2014. The smaller the artichoke, the less fussy the preparation, and once the tough outer leaves are removed and trimmed, the inner pale leaves are so delicate and tender that you can even eat them raw. Use the more widely available larger globe artichokes if that's what you have, though: you'll just need a vegetable peeler, a small serrated knife, a bit of elbow grease, and a big bowl to collect the artichoke debris. Whether you have large or small, however, the dish only works when starting with raw hearts, so the ready-prepped varieties you can get in cans or jars need to be saved for another day.

The aioli lasts for up to 5 days in the fridge, so you can make it well before you want to eat it. The mix of flours and five-spice mix is also a great combination to have in mind for things that are to be dusted and fried: cubes of tofu, whole prawns, sliced shallots, and fish fillets all work well.

The fried parsley leaves that are mixed with the artichokes look absolutely fantastic but can be a bit challenging because they burn easily. You can simply do without them if you want to avoid the risk.

Serves 4

Pink peppercorn aioli
4 cloves garlic
2 thyme sprigs
1 tbsp olive oil
2 egg yolks
1/2 tsp Dijon mustard
1 tbsp white wine vinegar

1 tbsp lemon juice
2/3 cup/150 ml sunflower oil
1 1/2 tbsp pink peppercorns,
  lightly crushed

6 tbsp/50 g cornstarch
6 tbsp/50 g all-purpose flour
1 tbsp Chinese five spice
8 baby artichokes (2 1/3 lb/1.1 kg)
  or 4 globe artichokes

1 tbsp lemon juice
about 2 1/2 cups/600 ml sunflower
  oil, for frying
3/4 oz/20 g parsley leaves,
  pat-dried very well if rinsed
  (optional)
1 lemon, quartered, to serve
coarse sea salt and black pepper

1 Preheat the oven to 390°F/200°C (355°F/180°C convection.)

2 To make the aioli, place the garlic cloves in the middle of a square piece of foil with the thyme and olive oil. Wrap tightly and roast in the oven for 20 minutes, until the garlic is soft and fragrant. Remove from the oven, discard the thyme, and set aside to cool.

3 Place the egg yolks in the small bowl of a food processor with the mustard, vinegar, lemon juice, roasted garlic and its oil, 1/2 teaspoon of salt, and a good grind of black pepper. Blend until smooth and, with the machine still running, slowly pour in the sunflower oil. Add the pink peppercorns, stir to combine, and keep in the fridge until ready to use.

4 Place the cornstarch and all-purpose flour in a small bowl with the Chinese five spice, 1 1/2 tablespoons of salt, and a good grind of black pepper. Mix together and set aside.

5 To prepare the artichokes, use your hands to remove the tough outer leaves, then trim the tops off the artichokes with a serrated knife. Clean up each artichoke with your knife, smoothing it out by trimming off any rough ends. Cut through it vertically, then remove the hairy choke with the tip of your knife. Place the artichoke halves on a chopping board, cut side down, and slice into four 1/3-inch/1-cm slices: the two middle slices will have the stalk attached. Place them in a bowl, cover them with water, and add the lemon juice to prevent them from discoloring. Just before you are ready to fry the artichokes, drain them, pat them very dry, and roll them in the flour mixture.

6 Pour enough oil into a large sauté pan so that it rises 3/4 inch/2 cm up the sides and place over medium heat. Once hot, add the artichoke slices and fry for 5 to 6 minutes, until starting to turn golden brown and crisp: you will need to do this in batches so you don't overcrowd the pan. Use a slotted spoon to remove the artichokes from the oil and transfer to a paper towel–lined colander to drain. Sprinkle with 1/2 teaspoon of salt and keep somewhere warm until ready to serve.

7 Add a quarter of the parsley to the oil. (Careful! It will definitely spit.) Fry for 1 minute, until translucent, then remove with the slotted spoon to a paper towel–lined plate. Continue with the remaining parsley until it is all fried, then mix it with the artichokes. Divide among four plates and serve at once, with the aioli and a wedge of lemon alongside.

Burnt green onion dip with curly kale

Make just the dip if you want to keep things simple: it's delicious spread on bruschetta or at a barbecue, alongside some grilled ears of corn.

Slices of fried red chile and thin slivers of garlic are like old Ottolenghi friends. They've been together for many a year, sprinkled on top of various dishes of roasted eggplant or with grilled broccoli in the salad that has become our signature dish. They're on stage again here—providing heat and crunch and the supporting act to a mellow, creamy dip. Use lacinato kale, if you like, instead of the curly kale.

Instead of green onions you can use big fat Catalonian Calçot onions, if you can find them; they are wonderfully meaty, so are particularly happy to be grilled. One important point to remember: there's no such thing as overcharring your onions, so hold your nerve at the grill, whichever variety you are using. The more burnt they are, the better and more smoky they will taste. If you're having a barbecue, it is well worth grilling the onions outdoors; if you're using a grill pan indoors, make sure your kitchen is very well ventilated indeed.

Serves 6

Green onion dip
1 head garlic
2 tbsp olive oil
5 1/4 oz/150 g green onions (12 to 14),
 ends trimmed, then sliced in half
 lengthwise (3 3/4 oz/110 g)

1 1/2 tbsp sunflower oil
2/3 cup/150 g cream cheese
1/2 cup/110 g sour cream
coarse sea salt and black pepper

Kale
6 tbsp/90 ml olive oil
6 cloves garlic, thinly sliced

3 large red chiles, seeded and
 thinly sliced
1 1/4 lb/550 g curly kale, washed,
 tough stems removed, cut
 widthwise into 1 1/2-inch/4-cm
 slices (1 lb/450 g)
2 tbsp lemon juice

1 Preheat the oven to 425°F/220°C (390°F/200°C convection).

2 To make the green onion dip, slice off the top quarter of the head of garlic and discard. Place the garlic in the center of a square of foil with 1 tablespoon of the olive oil and a sprinkle of salt. Wrap up the garlic, place it on a baking sheet, and roast for 30 minutes, until soft. Set aside and, when cool enough to touch, squeeze out the garlic cloves, discard the skin, and, using the flat side of a sharp knife, crush to form a purée. Set aside until ready to use.

3 Place the green onions in a bowl and brush with the sunflower oil. Sprinkle over 1/4 teaspoon of salt and a good grind of black pepper. Place a small grill pan over high heat and ventilate your kitchen. When the pan is smoking hot, add the green onions and grill for 5 to 6 minutes, turning halfway through, until black and burnt all over. Set aside to cool, then finely chop. Transfer the onions to a bowl and add the cream cheese, sour cream, the remaining tablespoon of olive oil, the roasted garlic purée, and 1/4 teaspoon of salt. Mix well and set aside until ready to use.

4 Put the oil for the kale into a large sauté pan and place over medium-high heat. Add the garlic and chile slices and fry for 4 to 6 minutes, stirring constantly, until crisp and golden brown. Add the kale, along with 1 1/2 teaspoons of salt and a good grind of black pepper, and cook for 3 minutes—you might need to do this in two or three batches—stirring often, until the kale is cooked but still retains a bite. Remove from the heat, add the lemon juice, and serve warm on a large platter or individual starter plates, with dollops of the green onion dip spooned on top.

Burrata with blood orange, coriander seeds, and lavender oil

Customers come to NOPI for this dish alone. We sell about 1,000 each month! Burrata, which means "buttered" in Italian, is a fresh cheese made from mozzarella and cream. The outer shell is pure mozzarella while the softer inside is a mixture of mozzarella and cream, which starts to ooze out when a ball is pulled apart. Burrata is second to none and worth seeking out, but a buffalo milk mozzarella can be used as an alternative.

Burrata is commonly paired with tomatoes but, when playing with flavors for this before NOPI opened, Scully walked past a man sitting on a bench in Finsbury Park eating a blood orange. A citrus spark was struck, lavender was in season, Yotam introduced the coriander seeds, and the dish was born!

Bittersweet blood oranges have a short season in late winter but many alternatives have been served at NOPI: white peaches, clementines, pink grapefruit, roasted red grapes, pickled pears, and kohlrabi. Regular oranges, for those who want to keep things simple, also work very well.

Serves 4

2 tbsp olive oil
1½ tsp clear runny honey
¾ tsp dried lavender

½ small clove garlic, crushed
1 tbsp coriander seeds, toasted
2 blood oranges (11 oz/320 g), or 2 medium oranges

4 burrata balls (15½ oz/440 g)
⅕ oz/5 g basil or micro-basil leaves
coarse sea salt

---

1 Place the oil in a small saucepan with the honey, lavender, garlic, and ¾ teaspoon of salt. Bring to a simmer over medium-low heat and remove at once. Stir well and set aside until completely cool, then add the coriander seeds.

2 Use a small, sharp serrated knife to trim the tops and tails off the oranges. Cut down the sides of the oranges, following their natural curve, to remove the skin and white pith. Slice into 8 rounds, ¾ inch/1 cm thick, and remove the seeds.

3 Divide the orange slices among four plates, slightly overlapping, and place a burrata ball alongside. Spoon the coriander seeds and lavender oil over the cheese and orange slices, top with the basil leaves—tearing them as you go—or the micro-basil, left whole, and serve.

GRILLED ASPARAGUS WITH ROMESCO SAUCE AND APPLE BALSAMIC

When asparagus season comes around each year, it can—given how perfect the vegetable is simply steamed and served with butter—be hard to think of new things to do with it. We were delighted, therefore, with this fresh combination of flavors which, surprisingly, does not mask the delicate taste of asparagus.

The romesco came from Andreu Altamirano, originally from Catalonia. It's more rustic and textured than other romesco sauces but, from someone with so many different colors in his mohawk hairstyle, we'd expect nothing less.

If you have time to let the sauce marinate overnight, then do so, but don't let this stop you if you don't have the time.

Serves 6

Romesco sauce
1 dried ancho chile (1/3 oz/10 g), soaked in water for 30 minutes, drained, seeded, and coarsely chopped
1 1/2 oz/40 g whole almonds, toasted
1 3/4 oz/50 g crustless sourdough bread, cut into 1 1/4-inch/3-cm cubes

3 medium plum tomatoes, cut into 1/2-inch/1.5-cm wedges (7 oz/200 g)
1 tbsp Valdespino sherry vinegar or another good-quality sherry vinegar
5 tsp/25 ml olive oil
1 medium red chile, seeded and coarsely chopped

2 1/4 lb/1 kg asparagus, woody ends trimmed (1 3/4 lb/800 g)
2 1/2 tbsp balsamic vinegar
1/4 cup/60 ml apple juice
1 tsp superfine sugar
1 tbsp olive oil
1/3 oz/10 g sliced almonds, toasted
coarse sea salt and black pepper

1 Place all the ingredients for the romesco sauce in a small bowl, along with 1 teaspoon of salt and a good grind of black pepper. Stir well, cover, then leave in the fridge to marinate for 4 hours or, preferably, overnight. Transfer to a food processor and blitz to form a paste. Place in a small pan and warm through just before serving.

2 Bring a medium saucepan of salted water to a boil and add the asparagus. Blanch for 1 to 2 minutes, until al dente, then drain and refresh under cold water. Set aside to dry.

3 Place the balsamic vinegar, apple juice, and sugar in a small pan and place over high heat. Cook for 4 to 5 minutes, until the mixture has reduced by half and has a thick, sticky consistency.

4 Place a ridged grill pan over high heat. Toss the asparagus with the olive oil and 1 teaspoon of salt and put them on the grill pan. Grill for 2 minutes, turning halfway through so that both sides get scorched. Spread the romesco sauce on individual plates and place the asparagus on top. Drizzle the balsamic reduction on top, sprinkle over the slivered almonds, and serve.

PURPLE SPROUTING BROCCOLI WITH SKORDALIA

This was a hit when it first appeared on the menu at NOPI. It was winter, the sky was gray, and this was the dish to lift spirits. Garlicky, smooth, and silky olive oil mashed potato is called skordalia in Greece. It's almost a synonym for comfort food, and the broccoli is here to stave off the winter blues and colds. Serve as a stand-alone starter or a side to either the chicken livers (page 169) or confit duck (page 177).

Serves 4

1¼ lb/550 g purple sprouting broccoli or broccolini, leaves and woody ends trimmed (12 oz/350 g)

2¼ lb/1 kg large red or gold potatoes
1 head garlic
7 tbsp/100 ml olive oil, plus extra to serve
1 medium red chile, thinly sliced on an angle

3 long strips of shaved lemon peel
1½ tbsp lemon juice
1 lemon, quartered, to serve
coarse sea salt and white pepper

1 Preheat the oven to 425°F/220°C (390°F/200°C convection).

2 Bring a large pan of water to a boil and add the broccoli. Blanch for 3 to 4 minutes, until cooked but still retaining a bite. Refresh under cold water, then drain and set aside to dry.

3 Arrange the potatoes, unpeeled, on a large baking sheet. Slice off the top quarter of the garlic head and discard. Wrap the head in foil, along with 1 tablespoon of the olive oil and a pinch of salt. Place alongside the potatoes and roast for about 45 minutes, until the potatoes are cooked through and the garlic cloves are completely soft.

4 Place the chile in a small saucepan with the lemon strips and the remaining olive oil. Cook over medium heat for 5 minutes, until the chile has taken on some color, and then set aside to cool. Use a slotted spoon to fish out the chile and lemon strips, discarding the strips but keeping the chile and the oil, separately.

5 Peel the warm potatoes and press them through a potato ricer—twice if you want them completely smooth—or use a masher, and then place in medium saucepan. Unwrap the garlic and squeeze out the cooked cloves, adding them to the mash. Whisk the mash well over medium heat while you pour in all but 1 tablespoon of the strained oil, along with the lemon juice, 3 tablespoons of water, 1½ teaspoons of salt, and ½ teaspoon of pepper. Whisk until smooth and silky—you might need to add a tablespoon or two more water to the mash if it is still too thick—then cook for another minute, stirring constantly with a spoon. Set aside somewhere warm until ready to serve.

6 Place a ridged grill pan over high heat. Toss the cooked broccoli with the remaining tablespoon of oil, along with a pinch of salt. When the pan is hot, add the broccoli and grill in batches for 3 minutes, until the stems start to color.

7 Divide the mashed potatoes among four plates and top with the broccoli. Sprinkle over the fried chile and serve at once, with a final drizzle of oil and a wedge of lemon alongside.

BUTTERNUT SQUASH WITH GINGER TOMATOES AND LIME YOGURT

Roasted wedges of squash and roasted slices of eggplant: these are two bad boys that have been around the Ottolenghi delis and NOPI restaurant for a very long time. Any new player has to have very good credentials to gain the respect of the old-timers and get a shot on the menu. The combination here of sweet roasted squash with lime-fresh yogurt and gingery oven-dried tomatoes was deemed to cut the mustard.

Ready-made crispy fried shallots can be found in Asian food stores. If you want to make your own, see the instructions on page 110. They're a nice addition but, with the crunch already provided by the cashews, the dish can stand well without them, if you prefer.

Serves 4

1 medium butternut squash, trimmed, unpeeled, halved lengthwise, seeds removed, then cut widthwise into 1-inch/2.5-cm slices (1³/4 lb/800 g)
3 tbsp olive oil
6 large plum tomatoes, halved lengthwise (1lb 1oz/500 g)

1¹/4-inch/3-cm piece of ginger, finely grated (1 oz/30 g)
1 red chile, seeded and finely diced
2 cloves garlic, crushed
2 packed tbsp dark muscovado sugar
coarse sea salt and black pepper

Lime yogurt
scant ¹/2 cup/120 g Greek yogurt

¹/4 tsp ground cardamom
Finely grated zest of ¹/2 lime, plus 1¹/2 tsp lime juice

To serve
¹/5 oz/5 g cilantro leaves, coarsely chopped
1 oz/30 g cashew nuts, toasted and coarsely chopped
¹/3 oz/10 g crispy store-bought fried shallots (optional)

1 Preheat the oven to 465°F/240°C (425°F/220°C convection).

2 Mix the squash with 2 tablespoons of the olive oil, 2 teaspoons of salt, and a good grind of black pepper. Spread out on a large parchment-lined baking sheet and roast for 35 to 40 minutes, until golden brown. Set aside to cool.

3 Reduce the oven temperature to 340°F/170°C (300°F/150°C convection).

4 Place the tomato halves on a parchment-lined baking sheet, skin side down. Sprinkle with ¹/4 teaspoon of salt, drizzle with the remaining tablespoon of oil, and cook for 80 minutes, until softened.

5 Place the ginger, chile, garlic, sugar, and ¹/4 teaspoon of salt in a medium bowl. Mix to form a paste, then spoon this on top of the tomatoes. Cook for another 40 minutes, until the tomatoes are caramelized, and set aside to cool.

6 Place all the ingredients for the lime yogurt in a small bowl, with ¹/2 teaspoon of salt and a good grind of black pepper. Mix well and keep in the fridge until ready to serve.

7 Spread the squash out on a large platter and layer the tomatoes in between. Drizzle over the lime yogurt, sprinkle with the cilantro, cashews, and shallots, and serve.

BABY CARROTS AND MUNG BEANS WITH SMOKED LABNEH AND CRISP PITA

Yotam did a simpler version of this for *Plenty More*. The signature Yotam-rather-than-Scully signs were there: cilantro, lemon zest, and white wine vinegar. None of the pink peppercorns that mark Scully's work, like the "sold" stickers in an art gallery. Chunks of feta were also dotted on top, instead of the smoked labneh here.

You'll need to start 24 hours before to make the labneh, but if you are short on time, the process can be reduced to about 6 hours by squeezing the yogurt from time to time as it is hanging in the fridge. This helps the liquid drain faster than it would if left to hang by itself. The smoked labneh can be made in advance and kept in the fridge, sealed, for at least a week. We spoon it over *shakshuka* before serving it for breakfast. You can also use it for salads or roasted vegetables and alongside oily fish.

You might want to revert to the feta if you don't have the time to make and smoke labneh, but do give it a try when you can. It's fun to do and you won't need any fancy equipment. Parchment paper and a wok or large pan with a tight-fitting lid into which you can fit a wire rack (the sort you place in a baking sheet when you are cooking bacon, and so on) are all you need. A timer is also useful, as the smoking time needs to be exact: if you smoke the labneh for too long the taste can be very strong. Horrible, in fact!

Serves 4

Smoked labneh
1 cup/300 g Greek yogurt
2 tbsp olive oil
1³/4 oz/50 g oolong tea (or lapsang souchong)
1 tbsp caraway seeds
1 tbsp pink peppercorns
shaved zest of 1 lemon
1/3 oz/10 g thyme sprigs
coarse sea salt and black pepper

Crisp pita bread
2 pita breads
2 tbsp/30 g unsalted butter, melted
2 tsp za'atar

Mung beans
1/2 cup/120 g mung beans
4 tbsp/60 ml olive oil
1 medium red onion, finely diced (3¹/2 oz/100 g)
2 cloves garlic, finely diced
2 tsp caraway seeds, lightly toasted

1/2 tsp fennel seeds, lightly toasted
1¹/2 tbsp superfine sugar
1/3 cup/80 ml Valdespino sherry vinegar or another good-quality sherry vinegar
1/3 oz/10 g mint leaves, coarsely chopped

Carrots
1¹/2 lb/650 g baby carrots, scrubbed clean (or equal weight of regular carrots, cut into 3- by 1/3-inch/8- by 1-cm pieces)
1 tbsp olive oil

1 For the labneh, mix together the yogurt, 1 tablespoon of the olive oil and 1/4 teaspoon of salt in a small bowl. Transfer to a clean square of muslin or cheesecloth, draw up the sides and hang it inside a tall narrow pitcher, tied to the handle, so that the cloth is not touching the bottom of the pitcher. Leave in the fridge for 24 hours for the excess water to drain out. If you are short on time, squeeze the cloth from time to time to help release the liquid.

2 Once the yogurt is drained, line a wok or medium pan, for which you have a lid, with two layers of foil. Add the tea, caraway seeds, pink peppercorns, lemon zest and thyme, along with 2 tablespoons of water. Place over high heat and reduce the temperature to medium after 8 minutes, when the mixture starts to smoke. Place a wire rack on top of the pan and place a sheet of parchment paper on top, with small holes around the edge. You can use a hole puncher to make these holes or else make crosses with a small, sharp knife. Remove the labneh from the muslin and place the whole thing, slightly flattened, on top of the parchment. Put the lid on and smoke for 5 minutes. You'll need to ensure that no smoke escapes from the wok or pan, so use more foil or a kitchen towel if you need to, securing the seal. Remove from the heat but keep the lid on, and leave to stand for 5 minutes, making sure no smoke at all escapes. Transfer the smoked labneh to a small container, set aside to cool, then pour over the remaining tablespoon of oil. Store in the fridge, seated, until ready to use.

3 Preheat the oven to 250°F/120°C (210°F/100°C convection).

4 Slice open the pita breads, spread them out on a parchment-lined baking sheet, rough side up, and brush with the melted butter. Sprinkle over the za'atar, along with 1/2 teaspoon of salt. Place in the oven and bake for 1 hour, until the bread has dried out but not taken on any color. Remove from the oven and set aside to cool.

5 Rinse the mung beans and place them in a medium saucepan. Cover with plenty of water, bring to a boil, and cook for 20 to 25 minutes, until just cooked. Drain, rinse, shake dry, then transfer to a bowl with 1/2 teaspoon of salt and set aside.

6 Place 1 tablespoon of the olive oil for the mung beans in a small saucepan over low heat. Add the onion and garlic and sauté for 8 to 10 minutes, stirring from time to time, until soft and translucent. Add the caraway and fennel seeds and sauté for another minute before adding the sugar. Stir for a minute, then pour over the vinegar. Cook over medium heat for about 3 minutes, until reduced by half. Remove from the heat and stir in the remaining 3 tablespoons of olive oil, along with 1 teaspoon of salt and a good grind of black pepper. Pour this mixture over the mung beans and set aside until ready to use.

7 Place the carrots in a large saucepan of salted water. Bring to a boil and cook for 5 to 7 minutes, until just cooked but still retaining a bite. Drain, refresh under cold water, and set aside to dry. Put the olive oil for the carrots into a large sauté pan and place over medium-high heat. Add the carrots, along with 1/2 teaspoon of salt and a good grind of black pepper, and sauté for 7 to 10 minutes, until golden brown. Remove from the heat and keep somewhere warm until ready to use.

8 To serve, stir the mint into the mung beans and divide the beans among four plates. Arrange the carrots on top and serve, with spoonfuls of labneh on top and the crispy pita bread alongside.

TRUFFLED POLENTA FRIES

Polenta comes in two guises: regular and quick-cooking (also called instant). It's the regular variety that gives polenta its high-maintenance reputation: all that stirring! However unfounded the reputation may be—it requires no more effort than making a risotto—we tend to use the quick-cooking variety, without finding any compromises to the dish. We still cook it for a relatively long time, though, before leaving it to dry out: this prevents these fries from splitting when deep-fried and gives them a serious crunch.

These rich, impressive, and slightly addictive pre-dinner nibbles are great to make for friends, as they can be prepared well in advance ready for their polenta dusting and frying. If you don't want to fry, you can bake them in a hot oven instead, in which case you won't need to dust them with polenta; just brush them lightly with olive oil and roast on a parchment-lined baking sheet at 465°F/240°C (425°F/200°C convection) for about 25 minutes.

You'll make more aioli than you need for the polenta fries, but it will keep in the fridge for up to 5 days. It's great spread on sandwiches, used as a dip, or served alongside any roasted fish or grilled meat. We suggest serving the fries with either the aioli or a store-bought tomato chutney. Strictly speaking, though, there's no official rule to suggest that it would be unreasonable to serve them with both, lightly swirled together.

Serves 4 to 6

Aioli (optional)
10 cloves garlic
1 cup/250 ml sunflower oil
2 thyme sprigs
1 bay leaf
2 black peppercorns
2 egg yolks

2 tbsp Dijon mustard
2 tbsp white wine vinegar

1½ cups/250 g instant polenta,
   plus ⅓ cup/60 g for dusting
7 tbsp/100 g unsalted butter,
   fridge-cold and cut into
   ⅓-inch/1 cm dice

2⅔ oz/75 g Parmesan, finely
   grated
¾ tsp truffle oil
about 4½ cups/1 liter sunflower
   oil, for frying
1¼ cups/300 g store-bought
   tomato chutney (optional)
coarse sea salt

1 Preheat the oven to 360°F/180°C (320°F/160°C convection).

2 If you choose to make it, start with the aioli. Place the garlic cloves, sunflower oil, thyme, bay leaf, and peppercorns in a small ovenproof saucepan. Cover with foil and roast in the oven for 20 to 25 minutes, until the garlic is tender. Set aside to cool, then remove and reserve the garlic; also reserve the oil but discard the thyme, bay leaf, and peppercorns. Place the egg yolks, mustard, vinegar, and roasted garlic cloves in the small bowl of a food processor with ½ teaspoon of salt. Blend to form a smooth paste and, while the machine is still running, slowly add the garlic-infused oil to form a thick mayonnaise. Store in the fridge until ready to use.

3 Fill a medium saucepan with 4½ cups/1 liter of water and place over medium heat. Bring to a boil, then slowly pour in the polenta, whisking constantly. Reduce the heat to low and cook for 3 minutes, stirring very frequently, until the polenta is smooth and thick. Add the butter a few cubes at a time, stirring until each batch is incorporated before adding the next, followed by the Parmesan and 1 tablespoon of salt. Mix well and cook for another 5 minutes, stirring continuously, until the mixture no longer sticks to the sides of the pan. Remove from the heat, stir in the truffle oil, then transfer to a parchment-lined baking pan measuring 8 by 10 inches/20 cm by 30 cm. Use a wet spatula to spread the polenta evenly, so that it is ¾ inch/2 cm thick. Lay another sheet of parchment paper on top and press down lightly. Set aside to cool before transferring to the fridge. Let set for 2 hours or overnight.

4 Flip the polenta out of the pan onto a chopping board and cut into about 30 batons, each measuring 4 inches/10 cm long and ¾ inch/2 cm square. Spread the remaining instant polenta on a plate and roll the batons through, one by one, so that they are dusted on all sides.

5 Pour the sunflower oil into a medium sauté pan and place over high heat. When hot, carefully add a quarter of the batons and fry for 3 to 4 minutes, until golden brown. Using a slotted spoon, transfer to a paper-towel lined plate, sprinkle lightly with salt, and set aside while you continue with the remaining fries. Serve at once, with either the aioli or tomato chutney alongside.

Sharp and spicy watermelon soup

The starting point for this was Scully's desire to do something with the watermelon rind that normally gets thrown away. The urge to conserve met his passion for pickling and the result—pickled watermelon rind, inspired by our Twitter pal Maunika Gowardhan—was a complete revelation.

We encourage you to make pickled rind in advance next time you have a watermelon, and keep it chilled for at least a week, possibly more, before making the soup using the flesh of a fresh watermelon and the mature pickle. The pickled rind lasts for many weeks in a sealed jar in the fridge. It's delicious with cold meats or worked into various salads, such as the Watermelon and Feta Salad on page 55.

Ajwain seeds have a very distinct taste, slightly bitter and pungent but as welcoming as thyme. It's worth seeking them out and having a jar on the shelf, as they work well lightly crushed and sprinkled on top of roasted root vegetables or in legume-based dishes. If you can't find any, use celery seeds instead.

If you want to bulk this soup out, serve it with some rice or roti bread.

Serves 6

1 large watermelon, seedless if possible (7 lb/3.2 kg)

2 tbsp sunflower oil

1/2 tsp ajwain seeds or celery seeds

1 tsp black cumin seeds

1/2 tsp fennel seeds

1 black cardamom pod

2 bird's-eye chiles, seeded and finely chopped

5 cloves garlic, finely chopped

1 1/4-inch/3-cm piece of ginger, peeled and finely chopped (3/4 oz/20 g)

1/4 tsp ground turmeric

3/4 oz/20 g cilantro, leaves and stems coarsely chopped (or baby cilantro, as an alternative)

coarse sea salt

Pickled rind

3/4 cup/200 ml cider vinegar

1 cup/250 ml rice vinegar

4 1/2 tbsp/60 g superfine sugar

1/2 tsp whole cloves

1 tsp yellow mustard seeds

1 medium cinnamon stick

1 tsp black peppercorns

1 Using a vegetable peeler, shave off the dark green outer skin from the watermelon and discard. You want to leave the firm white rind intact, so don't shave down too deeply. Use a large, sharp knife to cut the watermelon in half, and then each half into 3 or 4 wedges. Next, slice between the white rind and the red flesh. Cut the flesh into 1 1/4-inch/3-cm cubes and remove any seeds. Set aside three-quarters of the cubes, covered, in the fridge, and transfer the remaining cubes to a blender. Blitz until liquefied—you should have 2 3/4 cups/650 ml of watermelon juice—and place in the fridge until ready to use. Cut the white rind into strips—1 1/2 to 2 inches/4 to 5 cm long and 1/10 inch/3 mm wide; set aside in a large bowl.

2 Pour 4 1/2 cups/1 liter of water into a medium saucepan and add 3 tablespoons of salt. Bring to a boil, stir to dissolve the salt, then remove from the heat. Set aside to cool and then pour it over the watermelon rind. Store in the fridge, covered, for 24 hours. Drain the rind, rinse it under fresh water, and set aside.

3 Place the cider vinegar, rice vinegar, sugar, cloves, mustard seeds, cinnamon, and pepper in a small saucepan with 3/4 cup/200 ml of water. Bring to a boil, then simmer over medium heat for 2 minutes to dissolve the sugar. Set aside to cool and then pour over the rind. Set aside until ready to use. It will be ready to eat after just 1 hour, but you can leave it at this stage in a sterilized jar for months in the fridge. The longer the rind gets pickled, the softer it will be and the more intense it will taste.

4 To make the soup, put the oil into a large saucepan for which you have a lid, and place over medium-high heat. Add the ajwain, black cumin, and fennel seeds,

along with the cardamom and chiles, and cook for 1 to 2 minutes, stirring frequently, until fragrant. Add the garlic and ginger and stir for another minute before adding 6 1/2 ounces/180 g—just over half—of the pickled rind (just pick out the rind, without the pickling liquid), the turmeric, and 1 teaspoon of salt. Reduce the heat to medium and cook for 3 to 4 minutes, until the mixture starts to brown slightly. Pour over the watermelon juice, along with 3/4 cup/200 ml of water and 1/4 cup/60 ml of the pickling liquid. Bring to a boil over high heat and cook for 2 minutes, skimming the surface. Reduce the heat to medium-low and simmer for 4 to 5 minutes, covered, until the rind is tender. Add the reserved watermelon cubes, increase the heat to medium-high, and simmer rapidly for 4 minutes, stirring gently, until the flesh starts to soften. Remove the pan from the heat, carefully stir in the cilantro, and serve.

Pea soup with rolled goat cheese croutons

It was during his time at Bathers' Pavilion in Sydney that Scully was taught how to make a "restaurant-style" pea soup. Or, as Scully puts it, where it was "drilled into him" by the restaurant's French-Canadian head chef, Serge Dansereau. Before starting at Bathers', Scully thought soups were something you just made to use up the leftover vegetables in the bottom of the fridge. It was Serge who taught him how to preserve the soup's vibrant green color and how to get a shiny, glossy, creamy soup by cooking the starches out of the potatoes in the pan and keeping an eye on their color so that they don't get overcooked.

You can make the soup and prepare the croutons ahead of time. Take the croutons up to the point where they are left in the fridge to firm up, and panfry them when you're ready to serve. You can let the soup cool naturally and reheat it before serving, but if you want to preserve the vibrant green color the soup has when first blended, speed up the cooling process by placing it in a container inside another larger container full of ice water.

Sorrel is hard to find outside its spring and early summer season, so use tender arugula or watercress as an alternative. They won't have sorrel's distinctive astringency but are still nice ways to freshen up the soup.

Serves 6

2 tbsp olive oil
3 tbsp/40 g unsalted butter
3 shallots, coarsely chopped
  (4½ oz/130 g)
2 cloves garlic, coarsely chopped
1 large leek, trimmed, green and
  white parts cut into ⅓-inch/
  1-cm slices (9 oz/250 g)
2 medium potatoes, peeled and
  cut into ¾-inch/2-cm dice
  (14 oz/400 g)

4½ cups/1 liter vegetable stock
1lb 1oz/500 g fresh or frozen
  shelled peas
coarse sea salt and ground white
  pepper

Goat cheese croutons
4½ oz/120 g soft rindless goat
  cheese
1 tbsp Dijon mustard
1 tsp lemon thyme leaves
3 slices crustless white bread,
  ½ inch/1.5 cm thick (5¼ oz/150 g)

1 egg, lightly whisked
5 tsp whole milk
⅓ cup/60 g instant polenta
¾ cup/200 ml sunflower oil,
  for frying

To serve
½ cup /120 g crème fraîche
2 oz/60 g sorrel leaves, shredded,
  or young arugula or watercress

1 Place the olive oil and butter in a large saucepan over medium heat. Add the shallots and garlic and sauté for 4 to 5 minutes, stirring from time to time, until soft and transparent. Add the leek, cook for another 2 to 3 minutes, then add the potatoes. Mix well and cook for 5 minutes before pouring in the vegetable stock. Increase the heat until the liquid comes to a boil, then return the heat to medium and simmer for 12 minutes, until the potatoes are soft but still holding their shape. Add the peas, return to a boil, and continue to simmer for 2 minutes. Remove from the heat, add 2 teaspoons of salt and ½ teaspoon of white pepper, then use a jar or immersion blender to blitz until completely smooth. Strain in batches by pressing through a fine-mesh sieve: you want the texture to be completely smooth. Discard the paste that won't pass through and set the soup aside.

2 To make the croutons, place the goat cheese in a small bowl and stir to form a smooth paste. Add the mustard and thyme, along with ½ teaspoon of salt and a pinch of pepper, and mix well to combine.

3 Use a rolling pin to flatten out each slice of bread to form a rectangle 4 inches/10 cm wide, 5½ inches/14 cm long, and 1/16 inch/2 mm thick. Slice each rectangle in half lengthwise, so that you have

6 rectangles, and spread 2 teaspoons of goat cheese over each piece. Starting with the longest side, roll each of the rectangles into a tight cylinder so that it looks like a long cigar.

4 Mix together the egg and milk in a wide, shallow bowl and place the polenta in a separate wide, shallow bowl. Brush each cylinder with egg wash, then roll it in the polenta. Continue with the remaining cylinders and set aside in the fridge for at least half an hour to firm up.

5 When ready to serve, place the sunflower oil in a large frying pan over medium-high heat. When hot, add the bread cylinders and fry for 2 to 3 minutes, turning often so that all sides are golden brown: if you need to, do this in batches so as not to overcrowd the pan. Transfer to a paper towel–lined plate to drain while you continue with the next batch, then slice each cylinder in half, widthwise, on an angle, to form 12 long croutons.

6 Warm the soup just before serving and divide among six bowls. Spoon the crème fraîche on top and sprinkle over the sorrel. Serve at once, with the croutons alongside.

Jerusalem Artichoke Soup with Hazelnut and Spinach Pesto

This soup was first served at NOPI topped with quickly pickled shimeji mushrooms. We've gone for a different garnish here but, if you want to reinstate the mushrooms, place 2/3 cup/150 ml of rice vinegar in a small saucepan with 2 whole star anise, 1 small cinnamon stick, 1 teaspoon of pink peppercorns, 1/2 teaspoon of whole cloves, 2 tablespoons of sugar, 7 tablespoons/100 ml of water and 1 teaspoon of salt. Bring to a boil, then reduce the heat to low and simmer gently for 5 minutes. Remove from the heat and set aside to cool, then add 7 ounces/200 g of shimeji mushrooms. Spoon on top of the soup just before serving. Any leftover mushrooms are delicious as part of a mezze spread.

Serves 6

Hazelnut and spinach pesto
1 3/4 oz/50 g blanched hazelnuts
1 tbsp hazelnut oil
2 tbsp olive oil, plus extra to serve
1 oz/30 g baby spinach
1/3 oz/10 g tarragon
finely grated zest of 1 lemon
1 tsp white wine vinegar
1 small clove garlic, crushed

1 or 2 green bird's-eye chiles, seeded

1 tbsp olive oil, plus extra to serve
2 tbsp/30 g unsalted butter
2 shallots, thinly sliced
  (3 1/2 oz/100 g)
1 medium leek, trimmed, washed, halved lengthwise, and then thinly sliced, white part only
  (4 oz/120 g)

2 cloves garlic, crushed
2 1/2 lb/1.2 kg Jerusalem artichokes, peeled and sliced 1/32 inch/1 to 2 mm thick (about 2 lb/950 g)
1 cup/250 ml dry white wine
2 cups /500 ml whole milk
3 cups/700 ml vegetable stock
1/3 oz/10 g chives, finely chopped, to serve
coarse sea salt and black pepper

1 Preheat the oven to 320°F/160°C (280°F/140°C convection).

2 First make the pesto. Spread the hazelnuts on a baking sheet and roast for 15 minutes. Remove from the oven and, once cool, coarsely chop. Set aside 1 ounce/30 g to serve and place the remaining 3/4 ounce/20 g in the small bowl of a food processor with all the remaining pesto ingredients and 1/4 teaspoon of salt. Add 2 1/2 tablespoons of water and blitz to form a smooth and runny paste. Set aside until ready to use.

3 Place the olive oil and butter in a large saucepan over medium-high heat. Add the shallots and sauté for 3 minutes, stirring once or twice. Add the leek and garlic, along with 1 1/2 teaspoons of salt and a good grind of black pepper, and cook for another 3 to 4 minutes, until soft but without color. Add the Jerusalem artichokes and cook for 12 minutes, stirring from time to time, until beginning to soften and caramelize. Pour over the wine, bring to a simmer, and cook over medium heat for 3 to 4 minutes, until reduced by a quarter. Add the milk and stock and bring to a boil. Skim the surface of any impurities, then reduce the heat to medium. Simmer for 50 minutes, stirring every few minutes, until the artichokes are cooked through and completely soft. Remove from the heat and purée in a blender until completely smooth, adding a bit more stock if you need to thin it out.

4 To serve, ladle the soup into bowls and drizzle with the pesto. Sprinkle with the chives and remaining hazelnuts and serve with a final drizzle of olive oil.

Baby squid with almond tarator and lime relish

Serves 6

Tarator
2²/3 oz/75 g crustless sourdough bread, torn
1/2 cup/120 ml whole milk
1 large head garlic
5 tbsp/75 ml olive oil3 oz/90 g blanched almonds, toasted
2 tbsp Pedro Ximénez sherry vinegar or another good-quality sweet sherry vinegar

Spice paste
1/4 tsp cumin seeds
1/4 tsp coriander seeds
1/4 tsp fennel seeds
1/4 tsp dried chile flakes
1/4 tsp black peppercorns
1/4 tsp ground cardamom
1 1/2 tsp superfine sugar
1 large clove garlic, crushed
1 1/4-inch/3-cm piece of ginger, peeled and minced (3/4 oz/20 g)
2 tsp tamarind paste
2 tsp sunflower oil

Lime relish
3 limes
1 tbsp olive oil
1 red chile, seeded and finely chopped
1/3 oz/10 g cilantro leaves, finely chopped

1lb 5oz/600 g baby squid, cleaned, rinsed, and patted dry
2 tbsp olive oil
coarse sea salt

1 Preheat the oven to 360°F/180°C (320°F/160°C convection).

2 To make the tarator, place the bread in a bowl, pour over the milk and set aside for half an hour. Slice off (and discard) the top quarter of the garlic head. Wrap the head in foil, along with 1 tablespoon of the olive oil and 1/4 teaspoon of salt. Roast in the oven for 50 minutes, until completely soft. Squeeze the soft cloves into a food processor along with the oil. Add the remaining 4 tablespoons/60 ml olive oil, the soaked bread and milk, the almonds, sherry vinegar, and 1 teaspoon of salt. Blitz to form a coarse paste, gradually adding 7 tablespoons/100 ml of water as you go. Transfer to a small saucepan, ready to be warmed through before serving.

3 To make the spice paste, put the cumin, coriander, and fennel seeds into a small frying pan along with the dried chiles and peppercorns. Place over medium heat and toast until fragrant, then transfer to a spice grinder or a mortar and pestle. Add the cardamom, 1/4 teaspoon of salt, and the sugar and grind to a powder. Add the garlic, ginger, tamarind, and sunflower oil and continue to grind or pound until a paste is formed. Transfer to a large bowl and set aside.

4 To prepare the lime relish, slice the ends off the limes and use a small serrated knife to cut around the limes to remove the peel and pith. Holding each lime over a bowl, cut between the membranes to remove one segment at a time. Continue until all the segments have been removed, then transfer to a sieve to drain. Transfer the lime pieces to a bowl along with 1 1/2 teaspoons of lime juice and the remaining relish ingredients. Mix well and set aside.

5 When ready to cook, place the squid in a bowl with the olive oil and 3/4 teaspoon of salt and mix well. Place a grill pan high heat and, once hot, add a quarter of the squid. Cook for 2 to 3 minutes, turning once, until cooked through. Add the cooked squid to the bowl of spice paste, mix together, then continue with the remaining batches, wiping the grill pan clean after each.

6 Warm through the tarator and divide it among six plates. Spoon the squid on top and serve at once, with the lime relish spooned on top or alongside.

Seared scallops with pickled daikon and chile jam

This is a complex yet elegant dish. To simplify it, you can leave out the chile jam and mix together a little sweet chile sauce, sunflower oil, Thai fish sauce, lime juice, and cilantro, using this to dress the scallops and leaves. Still, we would make the jam: it's completely addictive. Scully's mother and nine aunties (yes, all on his mother's side!) all have their own versions, each placing a different emphasis on the sour, spicy, sweet, and salty levels. Scully's order of preference, having played around with all the family recipes and consulted the authority on Thai cooking that is David Thomson, is sweet, then sour, then salty, then spicy.

The recipe makes enough to fill a medium jar (14 ounces/400 ml), but you can double the recipe if you like to keep a larger jar in the fridge. It will last for a month or more and is really versatile—it's as delicious with cold meat as it is spread in a cheese sandwich or spooned alongside some plain rice. Two disclaimers: first, don't be put off by the smell of the dried shrimp in the pan. It's not the ingredient's strongest selling point, we know, but the resulting taste more than makes up for it. Second, sorry about all the garlic peeling. And, no, twenty-four cloves is not a typo!

Serves 4

Chile jam

2 cups/500 ml sunflower oil

30 Thai (red) shallots, thinly sliced
(7 oz/200 g)

24 cloves garlic, peeled and thinly
sliced (2¾ oz/80 g)

¾ oz/20 g galangal, thinly sliced

⅓ oz/10 g long dried red chiles,
seeded

1¾ oz/50 g dried shrimp, rinsed
and patted dry very well

3½ oz/100 g palm sugar, coarsely
grated if starting with a block

1½ tbsp fish sauce

⅓ cup/80 ml tamarind pulp water
(see page 316)

Daikon

⅔ cup/150 ml rice vinegar

2 tbsp superfine sugar

2 tsp pink peppercorns

3 whole cloves, gently crushed

1 red chile, seeded and finely
chopped

½ daikon, peeled and julienned
(5½ oz/160 g)

coarse sea salt and black pepper

1 Granny Smith apple, cored, very
thinly sliced lengthwise
(5 oz/140 g) and soaked in water
with 1 tsp lemon juice

6 round red radishes, thinly sliced
(1¾ oz/50 g)

1 oz/30 g red baby chard leaves
(or mâche)

3 tbsp olive oil

12 jumbo sea scallops
(1 lb 3 oz/540 g)

---

1 To make the jam, pour the sunflower oil into a large saucepan and place over medium-high heat. Add the shallots and fry gently for 6 to 7 minutes, until golden brown. Use a slotted spoon to remove the shallots and transfer them to a paper towel–lined plate to drain while you continue frying. Add the garlic and fry for 2 minutes, until golden brown. Transfer to the paper towel–lined plate and add the galangal and chiles to the pan. Fry for just 1 minute, then remove. Finish with the shrimp: these will need just 30 seconds in the oil before being removed. Set everything aside to cool, then transfer to a food processor. Add 6 tablespoons/90 ml of the frying oil and blitz well until a smooth paste is formed. Return the paste to a medium saucepan along with the sugar, fish sauce, and tamarind water. Place over low heat and cook for about 15 minutes, stirring from time to time, until a jam-like consistency is formed. Don't be alarmed by the amount of oil in the jam: it works on the plate, soaked up by the scallops, and also helps give the jam a long shelf life. Cool before storing in a jar in the fridge.

2 To pickle the daikon, place the rice vinegar, sugar, peppercorns, cloves, and chile in a medium saucepan with ¾ cup/200 ml of water and 2 teaspoons of salt. Place over medium heat and cook for 2 to 3 minutes, stirring from time to time, until the sugar and salt have dissolved. Remove from the heat and set aside to cool. Add the daikon and leave in the fridge for at least 4 hours or, preferably, overnight.

3 Just before you are ready to serve, drain the apple slices, pat them dry, and place them in a large bowl. Drain the daikon and spices, discarding the liquid, and add both to the apple along with the radishes, chard, 1 tablespoon of the olive oil, ¾ teaspoon of salt, and a good grind of black pepper. Mix gently and set aside.

4 Put the remaining 2 tablespoons of olive oil into a large frying pan and place over high heat. Mix the scallops in a small bowl with ½ teaspoon of salt and some black pepper. When the pan is hot, add the scallops and cook for 4 to 5 minutes, turning once halfway through, until golden on both sides and starting to caramelize. Remove from the pan and serve at once, with the salad and a teaspoon of chile jam alongside.

SEA TROUT AND BULGUR TARTARE WITH PRESERVED LEMON SALSA AND JERUSALEM ARTICHOKE CHIPS

Kibbeh nayyeh is a popular dish served in Lebanon, often as part of a mezze spread. It's a mix of either raw lamb or raw beef—minced or, traditionally, pounded in a stone urn until puréed—with fine bulgur and spices. Here we replace the meat with finely diced fish. We love the earthy flavor of trout, but salmon fillet also works well. As always with fish, but even more so when serving it raw, get the fillets as fresh as you possibly can.

Making your own Jerusalem artichoke fries, as we do in the restaurant, is impressive as well as being delicious. If you are looking for a shortcut, though, just buy a bag of root vegetable chips.

Citrus-infused olive oils—lemon, lime, orange, mandarin—are a lovely way to finish off a dish and give it that final extra edge. We love to drizzle them over a creamy cheese like burrata (see page 17), and also over white fish. If you make a bottle, you'll be reaching for it all the time to spruce up a plain spaghetti supper or a legume-packed lunch. To make the oil, shave one or two long strips of zest off whichever citrus fruit you are using, avoiding the bitter pith, and place in a small pan with olive oil. Bring to a simmer over medium heat, removing it from the heat as soon as it starts to sizzle. Set aside to cool and infuse, then discard the zest strips and either store or use right away.

Serves 4

Tartare

1³/₄ oz/50 g bulgur

14 oz/400 g skinless, boneless
   sea trout or salmon fillet, cut by
   hand into ¹/₅-inch/5-mm dice

1 red chile, seeded and finely diced

4 small shallots, finely diced
   (2¹/₂ oz/70 g)

¹/₂ tsp cumin seeds, toasted and
   finely ground

³/₄ tsp coriander seeds, toasted
   and finely ground

³/₄ tsp ground allspice

2 tbsp olive oil

1¹/₂ tbsp lemon juice

coarse sea salt and black pepper

Salsa

2 oz/60 g pitted green olives,
   coarsely chopped

2 small preserved lemons, flesh
   discarded and skin finely diced
   (about 1 oz/30 g)

¹/₃ oz/10 g parsley, finely chopped

3 tbsp olive oil

Jerusalem artichoke chips

3¹/₂ oz/100 g Jerusalem
   artichokes, scrubbed well,
   thinly sliced with a mandoline
   and stored in water with 1 tsp
   lemon juice

1¹/₄ cups/300 ml sunflower oil

To serve

1 tbsp lime-infused olive oil or
   olive oil (see headnote, page 43)

1 To make tartare, rinse the bulgur well and place it in a small bowl. Cover with ¹/₃ cup/80 ml of cold water and stir in ¹/₂ teaspoon of salt. Set aside for 30 minutes, until the liquid has been absorbed but the bulgur still has a bite. Drain any excess water and set aside to dry before transferring the bulgur to a large bowl along with the remaining tartare ingredients except the lemon juice. Add 1 teaspoon of salt and a good grind of black pepper. Mix well, cover, and store in the fridge until ready to use, but for no longer than 1 hour. Just before serving, stir in the lemon juice.

2 Place all the ingredients for the salsa in a small bowl with a grind of black pepper. Mix well and set aside.

3 Drain the Jerusalem artichokes and pat them dry very well with a clean kitchen towel. Pour the sunflower oil into a small sauté pan and place over high heat. Once hot, add half the artichokes—you don't want to overcrowd the pan—and fry for 2 minutes, until golden brown and crisp. Transfer to a paper towel-lined plate, sprinkle lightly with salt, and set aside while you continue with the remaining batch.

4 To serve, place a 4-inch/10-cm round cookie cutter 1¹/₄ inches/3 cm deep, in the center of each plate and spoon in the tartare. Remove the mold to leave the tartare in a round shape and spoon the salsa on top or alongside. Place some Jerusalem artichoke chips on top of the tartare, finish with a drizzle of lime oil, and serve.

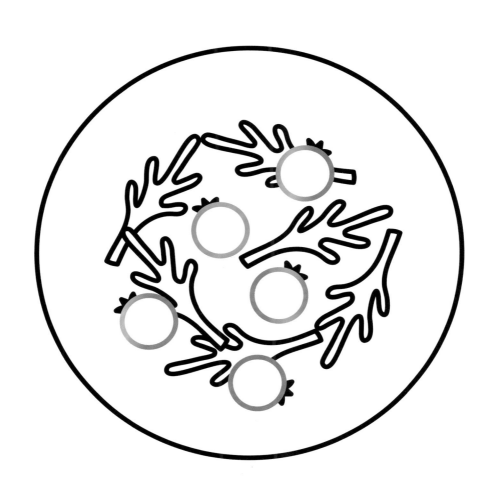

SALADS

THREE CITRUS SALAD WITH GREEN CHILE, STEM GINGER, AND CRUNCHY SALSA

The combination of sweet fruit and sharp leaves, along with the contrast in texture between the fruit and the crunchy, punchy salsa, makes this a very unusual salad. There's enough of a wow factor for it to be a stand-alone starter, but it also works well with some simply grilled mackerel or salmon, or leftover cold chicken.

Don't worry if you don't have all three citrus fruits suggested: so long as you keep the total weight for the fruit the same, the dish works well with a mixture of just two. When pomelo is not in season and you want to maintain the contrast of colors, substitute some white grapefruit.

Stem ginger—fresh ginger preserved in sugar syrup—is typically used in baking, at the ready to be diced and mixed into cakes, cookies, and trifles, or the syrup drizzled over ice cream. But the warmth of the preserved ginger and the sweetness of the syrup can also bring a lot to savory stir-fry dishes or salads. Stem ginger in syrup can be hard to track down outside of the U.K.; look for it online and in Asian markets. You can also make your own. To do so, peel a 4-inch/10-cm piece of ginger (3½ oz/100 g) and cut it against the grain into ⅓-inch/1-cm slices. Place the slices in a pan and pour in enough cold water to cover. Bring to a boil and then simmer for 10 minutes. Drain, replace the water, and repeat the process twice more. Drain for the last time, and then return the ginger to the pan along with 6⅓ oz/180 g sugar, 1¼ cups/300 ml water, and a pinch of salt. Bring to a boil, stir until the sugar dissolves, and then reduce the heat to medium-low. Simmer for 1 hour, until the syrup is thick and golden and the ginger is soft. Pour into a sterilized jar, cover with a lid, and let sit for 24 hours before using. It will keep for up to a year in the fridge.

Serves 8

Almond salsa
3 oz/80 g almonds, skin on
5 green chiles, seeded
and thinly sliced
3 oz/90 g stem ginger, finely diced
2 tbsp coriander seeds, toasted
for 1 minute and lightly crushed
1 tbsp fennel seeds, toasted for
1 minute and lightly crushed

1½ tbsp poppy seeds
3½ tbsp Valdespino sherry
vinegar (or another good-quality
sherry vinegar)
⅓ cup/80 ml olive oil
coarse sea salt and black pepper

2 oranges (about 1 lb/500 g)
1 pink grapefruit (14 oz/400 g)
1 large pomelo (2 lb/1 kg)

1 small head radicchio or another
similarly bitter leaf, base
trimmed, cut into ⅓-inch/
1-cm wedges (4½ oz/130 g)
1 Belgian endive, base trimmed,
cut lengthwise into 8 wedges
(3 oz/90 g)
1¾ oz/50 g tender/baby leaf
watercress

1 Preheat the oven to 320°F/160°C (280°F/140°C convection).

2 Start with the salsa. Spread the almonds on a small baking sheet and place in the oven for 20 minutes, until well toasted. Remove from the oven and, once cool enough to handle, coarsely chop. Transfer to a bowl along with all the remaining salsa ingredients, ¼ teaspoon of salt, and a good grind of black pepper. Mix well and set aside.

3 Take the oranges and use a small, sharp knife to slice off the ends. Now cut down the side of each orange, following its natural curve, to remove the peel and white pith. Cut widthwise into ⅕-in/5-mm rounds, and then slice each round into quarters. Prepare the grapefruit in the same way, but slice each round into sixths. Put both into a large bowl.

4 Use a sharp knife to peel away the pomelo skin. Divide the fruit into segments and use the knife to remove and discard all the pith and membrane. Break the fruit segments into ¾-inch/2-cm chunks and add to the rest of the fruit, along with half the salsa and the radicchio, endive, and watercress. Mix gently, arrange on a large platter, spoon over the remaining salsa, and serve.

Raw brussels sprout nests with oyster mushrooms and quail eggs

Brussels sprouts? Raw? We know that this requires a double leap of faith for some, but trust us here. With the sweet dressing, earthy mushrooms, and thin slices of cheese, this is an unusual and delicious winter starter or salad. Plated up like a nest, with the quail eggs perched inside, it looks pretty as a picture as well. Use a mandoline, if you have one, to slice the sprouts as thinly as you can. Take great care, though, as you'll be cutting very close to the blade.

Instead of the red wine vinegar and lemon juice suggested on the following page, we use verjuice at the restaurant. Made from semiripe and unfermented wine grapes, verjuice has a distinctive taste—part tart, part sweet—that we love. It's a common ingredient in Australia, so has always been a Scully staple, but it's still relatively hard to get hold of in the U.S. and Britain. Shops are beginning to stock it, though, so keep an eye out and buy some if you see it. If you use verjuice (rather than red wine vinegar and lemon juice), you'll need to simmer 3/4 cup/ 180 ml in a small pan over medium heat for about 10 minutes, until just 2 tablespoons of liquid remain.

When this is served at NOPI, the quail eggs are poached rather than soft-boiled. We've simplified the method here so that they can all be soft-boiled at once, but you can poach them individually if you want to.

Serves 4

7 oz/200 g oyster mushrooms, cleaned of any dirt and pulled into halves, if large

4 tbsp/60 ml olive oil, plus extra to finish

1¹/2 tbsp lemon juice

1¹/2 tsp red wine vinegar

1¹/2 tsp maple syrup

12 quail eggs

8 oz/250 g brussels sprouts, tough outer layers removed, thinly sliced

³/4 oz/20 g parsley, finely chopped

2 oz/60 g mature Manchego or aged pecorino, shaved into thin slices using a vegetable peeler

coarse sea salt and black pepper

1 Preheat the oven to 375°F/190°C (340°F/170°C convection).

2 Mix the mushrooms with 1 tablespoon of the olive oil, ¹/4 teaspoon of salt, and some black pepper. Spread out on a parchment-lined baking pan and roast for 15 minutes, until lightly golden. Remove from the oven and set aside to cool.

3 To make the dressing, place the remaining 3 tablespoons of oil in a mixing bowl with the lemon juice, vinegar, maple syrup, ¹/4 teaspoon of salt, and some black pepper. Whisk well to combine, and set aside.

4 Fill a medium saucepan with water and bring to a boil. Set a bowl full of ice water alongside. Once the water is boiling, use a slotted spoon to carefully lower in all the eggs. Cook for exactly 2 minutes, then transfer the eggs to the bowl of ice water to halt the cooking. Set aside until cool, then peel and sprinkle with a pinch of salt and some black pepper.

5 Place the sprouts, parsley, Manchego, and mushrooms in a mixing bowl. Add the dressing and toss gently—you don't want the cheese to break too much. Spread the salad out on four plates, making a little well in the middle. Top with the quail eggs, breaking some of them in half as you go. Finish with a drizzle of olive oil and serve.

WATERMELON AND FETA SALAD WITH MARINATED OLIVES AND PRESERVED LEMON

Two options here: one to make things simpler and the other to make things more complex. For those wanting an extra bit of work, top the salad with 2¹/₂ oz/70 g of pickled watermelon rind, which we recommend making well in advance. Instructions for making it, along with why we love doing so, are on pages 31 and 32. The rind adds a welcome astringency to the dish, but with the preserved lemons and olives already there, the salad is delicious without. Those wanting to simplify matters can bypass the olive-marinating stage—just buy some olives that are already marinated in herbs and spices and add 3¹/₂ tbsp of olive oil to them.

Serves 4 to 6

Marinated olives
3¹/₂ tbsp olive oil
1 medium red chile, thinly sliced
  into rounds
1 small clove garlic, skin on and
  lightly crushed
3 thyme sprigs
1 rosemary sprig

1¹/₄ oz/35 g preserved lemon peel,
  julienned (the skin from about
  2 small preserved lemons)
25 black Kalamata olives, pitted
  (3¹/₂ oz/100 g)
coarse sea salt and black pepper

1 small watermelon (3¹/₂ lb/1.6 kg)

To serve
3¹/₂ oz/100 g feta, lightly crumbled
  into ¹/₂-inch/1.2-cm chunks
2¹/₂ oz/70 g pickled watermelon
  rind, drained (optional; see
  headnote)
¹/₂ oz/15 g basil leaves
¹/₃ oz/10 g mint leaves

---

1 Place the olive oil for the olives in a small saucepan over medium heat with the chile, garlic, thyme, rosemary, and preserved lemon, along with ¹/₄ teaspoon of salt and a grind of black pepper. Warm gently for 4 to 5 minutes, then remove from the heat. Set aside to cool, then pour over the olives. Set aside until ready to use—the olives can be used right away, but their flavor will intensify if you keep them marinating for 24 hours before serving.

2 Quarter the watermelon, cut out the red flesh and set the skin—with the white rind attached—aside. Cut each section of red flesh widthwise, into ¹/₃-inch/1-cm thick slices, then cut each slice into smaller triangles, about 2¹/₂ inches/6 cm long and 1¹/₄ inches/3 cm wide.

You will need 1 lb 5 oz/600 g of flesh (discard the seeds if you like) for the salad, so anything in excess of this can be set aside for snacking. If you are pickling the watermelon rind, see page 32 for instructions on what to do next.

3 When ready to serve, spread the fresh watermelon wedges out on a large platter or individual plates and sprinkle the feta on top, along with the pickled watermelon rind. Spoon over the olives and their marinade, discarding the garlic, rosemary, and most of the thyme. Finish with the basil and mint leaves, tearing them as you go, along with a few sprigs of thyme, and serve at once.

FRENCH BEANS WITH FREEKEH AND MISO

However long we've been working together, some ingredients will always belong to Yotam and others will always show Scully's hand at work. *Freekeh* and miso are two such ingredients—the smoky grain is Yotam's and the umami-rich miso belongs to Scully. Like so many strong opposites, they pair together perfectly.

Nanami togarashi is a many-flavored Japanese spice mixture that blends red chiles, *sansho* pepper, roasted orange peel, black and white sesame seeds, seaweed, and ginger. It's a lovely mix to have around—we rarely eat noodles, tempura, or a bowl of donburi rice without adding a sprinkle. You'll find it in Japanese or gourmet stores or online, but if you can't get hold of any, cayenne pepper can be used instead.

Serves 6

2¹/2 oz/70 g freekeh
7 tbsp/100 ml olive oil
1 small onion, finely diced
  (2¹/4 oz/65 g)
1 medium celery stalk,
  finely diced (1²/3 oz/45 g)
2 cloves garlic, crushed
1 bay leaf
1 cup/250 ml vegetable stock

4 shallots, peeled, halved
  lengthwise, and cut into ³/4-inch/
  2-cm wedges (8 oz/250 g)
1 tsp nanami togarashi or
  ¹/2 tsp cayenne pepper
8 oz/250 g shiitake mushrooms,
  stalks removed
7 oz/200 g shelled edamame
  beans, fresh or frozen
12 oz/350 g French green beans,
  trimmed
¹/3 oz/10 g tarragon leaves,
  roughly torn

1 oz/30 g pea shoots
1 tbsp nigella seeds
2 tbsp lemon juice
coarse sea salt and black pepper

Miso dressing
5 tbsp/75 ml sake
¹/3 cup/80 ml mirin
1 tbsp superfine sugar
2¹/2 tbsp white miso paste
finely grated zest of 1 orange

1 Preheat the oven to 360°F/180°C (320°F/160°C convection).

2 Rinse the *freekeh*, soak it in fresh water for 5 minutes, then drain and set aside.

3 Pour 2 tablespoons of the olive oil into a medium saucepan for which you have a lid, and place over medium heat. Add the onion, celery, garlic, and bay leaf and sauté for about 8 minutes, until soft. Stir in the *freekeh* and pour over the vegetable stock. Bring the liquid to a boil, then reduce the heat to medium-low and simmer, covered, for 15 to 20 minutes, until the *freekeh* is cooked through and there is no more liquid in the pan. Remove and discard the bay leaf and set aside.

4 Mix the shallots with 3 tablespoons of the olive oil, the *nanami togarashi,* and ¹/4 teaspoon of salt. Place on a parchment-lined baking pan and cook in the oven for 30 minutes until cooked and golden brown. Remove and set aside to cool.

5 Mix the mushrooms with the remaining 1¹/2 tablespoons of oil, ¹/4 teaspoon of salt, and a generous grind of pepper. Spread out on a separate parchment-lined baking pan and roast in the oven for 20 minutes until golden. Remove and, when cool enough to handle, slice the mushrooms ¹/3 inch/1 cm thick.

6 Bring a small pot of salted water to a boil and blanch the edamame for 2 minutes. Remove with a slotted spoon and refresh under cold running water. Add

the French beans to the boiling water and blanch for 4 minutes, then drain, refresh under cold running water, and leave to dry with the edamame.

7 To make the dressing, mix the sake, mirin, and sugar in a small saucepan. Place over medium heat and bring to a simmer, stirring to dissolve the sugar. Simmer for about 8 minutes, until you have a scant ½ cup/100 ml of liquid left in the pan. Stir in the miso, return to a boil for 2 minutes, until thick and caramelized, and then remove from the heat. Stir in the orange zest and set aside to cool.

8 Place the *freekeh*, shallots, mushrooms, beans, dressing, and ½ teaspoon of salt in a large bowl. Mix well, then add the tarragon, pea shoots, nigella seeds, and lemon juice. Give everything a final gentle stir, transfer to a large platter or individual plates, and serve.

FRENCH BEANS WITH FREEKEH AND MISO

TOMATOES WITH WASABI MASCARPONE AND PINE NUTS

This is all about the tomatoes, so get as many different varieties as you can: red, green, yellow, baby plum, cherry, and vine. They also look great if they are not cut in uniform fashion; smaller tomatoes should be halved, while larger ones should be cut into wedges or sliced.

You can prepare all the elements for this in advance—the wasabi and herb-filled mascarpone, the pickled shallots, the chopped tomatoes, the toasted nuts. Just keep them separate and put the dish together just before serving.

This developed from a dish Sarit Packer created with Scully for the breakfast menu when NOPI first opened, when the wasabi mascarpone was served with smoked salmon and scrambled eggs. Yotam brought in the tomatoes, and the dish was reborn and shifted onto the summer lunch menu. It works well as part of a spread of salads or alongside some simply cooked fish or meat.

Serves 6

9 oz/250 g mascarpone
1 tbsp wasabi paste
1/3 oz/10 g chives, finely chopped
1/3 oz/10 g tarragon, finely chopped

1 green onion, thinly sliced (3/4 oz/20 g)
2 shallots, thinly sliced widthwise (3 1/2 oz/100 g)
2 tbsp Pedro Ximénez sherry vinegar or another good-quality sweet sherry vinegar
1 tbsp olive oil

2 1/4 lb/1 kg mixed tomatoes, cut into a mixture of slices and wedges, 1/3 inch/1 cm thick
3/4 oz/20 g pine nuts, toasted
1/5 oz/5 g mixed basil leaves (plain, purple, and micro basil, or just plain basil), to garnish
coarse sea salt and black pepper

1 Place the mascarpone, wasabi, chives, tarragon, and green onion in a bowl with 1/2 teaspoon of salt and a good grind of black pepper. Mix well and keep in the fridge until ready to use.

2 Place the shallots in a separate bowl with the sherry vinegar, oil, and 1/2 teaspoon of salt. Mix well and keep in the fridge until ready to use.

3 To serve, divide the mascarpone among six plates and spread it out to form a thin layer. Place the tomatoes on top, followed by the pickled shallots. Sprinkle with the pine nuts, then scatter over the basil leaves, tearing the larger ones as you go. Season with a scant 1/2 teaspoon of salt and a good grind of black pepper and serve.

Mixed cauliflowers with golden raisins, ricotta, and capers

Most people return from their travels with pictures of their friends and kids grinning or the view from their hotel room. Chefs, on the other hand, return with endless snaps of food. After a trip to the epic Berkeley Bowl market in California, Yotam's snaps of golden and purple cauliflowers piled high became the inspiration for this dish, which is all about the color. Use purple or golden varieties if you can find some, but if not, the combination of lime-green romanesco florets against the regular white looks just great.

Hugh Fearnley-Whittingstall perfectly described the glamorous romanesco as "the cauli that looks as it if were designed by Vivienne Westwood, with its sculptural, swirling, lime-green whorls." Also known as romanesco broccoli, its texture is crunchier than the white variety. Its high season is between October and November, so if you can't get hold of it, just use more white cauliflower instead.

1 Preheat the oven to 425°F/220°C (390°F/200°C convection).

2 Toss the regular cauliflower florets with 2 tablespoons of the olive oil, 1 teaspoon of salt, and a good grind of black pepper. Spread out on a parchment-lined baking sheet and roast for about 25 minutes, until tender and golden brown. Remove from the oven and set aside to cool.

3 Bring a medium pan of salted water to a boil and add the romanesco florets. Blanch for 5 minutes, until tender. Drain, rinse under cold water, and set aside to dry.

4 Finely chop half the capers and place in a small bowl with the ricotta, 1 tablespoon of the olive oil, ½ teaspoon of salt, and a grind of black pepper. Mix well and set aside in the fridge until ready to use.

5 Place the raisins in a small saucepan with a 5 tablespoons/75 ml of the vinegar and ¼ cup/60 ml of water. Bring to a boil over medium heat, then simmer for about 8 minutes, until the liquid has evaporated and the raisins have swelled. Remove from the heat and set aside to cool.

6 Place the remaining 2 tablespoons of vinegar in a small bowl along with the mustard, ½ teaspoon of salt, and a good grind of black pepper. Whisk together, then add the remaining 2 tablespoons of olive oil and 1½ tablespoons of water, stirring as you pour, until well combined. Set aside until ready to serve.

7 Pour enough sunflower oil into a small saucepan so that it rises ⅕ inch/5 mm up the sides. Place on medium-high heat and, when hot, add the remaining unchopped capers. Fry for 1 minute, until they open up like flowers and are golden and crisp. Remove from the pan using a slotted spoon and set aside on a paper towel–lined plate (you can re-use the oil).

8 Divide the ricotta mixture among six plates (or use one very large platter) and arrange the cauliflower and romanesco on top. Drizzle over the mustard dressing, scatter with the pine nuts, golden raisins, and fried capers and serve.

LENTIL AND PICKLED SHALLOT SALAD WITH BERBERE CROUTONS

Berbere is a hot spice mix popular in Ethiopian and Eritrean cooking. There are lots of spices in the mix—cloves, fenugreek, cumin, coriander, allspice, nutmeg—but the dominant ingredients are chiles, garlic, and ginger. It's widely available, but if you can't find it, use hot smoked paprika instead. Don't worry if you can't get hold of a black radish: the contrast with the red looks great, but just use double the number of red, if that's what you have.

Make more croutons than you need for this: they keep well in a sealed container for up to 5 days and are lovely to have on hand to sprinkle on any soup—lentil or otherwise—or a salad that can handle a bit of a crunchy kick. This dish has got enough substance to be a stand-alone light lunch but also works well on one large platter as part of a mezze spread.

With thanks to Gena Deligianni, from the early days of NOPI, for this dish.

Serves 6 to 8

10½ oz/300 g Puy lentils

8 shallots, thinly sliced
(10½ oz/300 g)

5 tbsp/75 ml olive oil

2 tbsp Valdespino sherry vinegar
or another good-quality sherry
vinegar

5¼ oz/150 g crustless
sourdough bread, roughly torn
into ¾-inch/2-cm chunks

1½ tsp berbere spice or 1 tsp hot
smoked paprika

1 oz/30 g cilantro leaves, whole
or coarsely chopped

¾ oz/20 g arugula, coarsely
chopped

1 large golden beet (or red beet),
washed, skin left on, sliced ⅛
inch/3 mm thick (5¼ oz/150 g)

½ large black radish, washed, skin
left on, sliced ⅛ inch/3 mm thick
(3 oz/90 g) (optional)

10 small red radishes, washed,
skin left on, sliced ⅛ inch/3 mm
thick (3 oz/90 g)

coarse sea salt and black pepper

Dressing

1 tbsp Valdespino sherry vinegar
or another good-quality sherry
vinegar

1 tbsp lemon juice

1½ tsp Dijon mustard

1½ tsp orange blossom honey
or another floral variety

3 tbsp olive oil

1 Rinse the lentils and place them in a medium saucepan. Cover with water, bring to a boil, and cook for 15 to 20 minutes, until cooked but still retaining a bite. Drain, rinse under cold water, and set aside until completely dry.

2 Preheat the oven to 360°F/180°C (320°F/160°C convection).

3 Place the shallots in a mixing bowl with 3 tablespoons of the olive oil and ½ teaspoon of salt. Spread them out on a parchment-lined baking sheet and roast in the oven for about 12 minutes, until they are soft but have not taken on any color. Remove from the oven, sprinkle with the sherry vinegar, mix well, and set aside to cool.

4 Place the sourdough pieces in a small mixing bowl with the remaining 2 tablespoons of olive oil and the *berbere* spice. Mix well, spread out on a parchment-lined baking sheet, and roast for 12 to 15 minutes, until crusty and light golden-brown. Set aside to cool.

5 Place all the ingredients for the dressing in a small bowl with 1½ teaspoons of salt and a good grind of black pepper. Mix well and set aside.

6 Just before serving, place the lentils and pickled shallots in a large bowl with the cilantro, arugula, beet, both radishes, and half the croutons. Pour over the dressing, mix well to combine, transfer to a large platter, sprinkle the remaining croutons on top, and serve.

Red quinoa and watercress salad

This first accompanied a potted crab dish served at NOPI, dotted with quail eggs. The sharp flavors of the salad work very well with most fish and seafood—potted or otherwise—or alongside grilled meat. It's also punchy enough to be a stand-alone starter to a meal.

If you can find it, black quinoa also looks great here, either by itself or in combination with the red. The black variety needs a bit more cooking than the red—an extra 5 minutes—so get it going in the pan beforehand, if you are using both. If you can't find either red or black, the more widely available white quinoa (which needs a couple of minutes less cooking than the red) is also an option.

Serves 4

5 small shallots, sliced 1/3 inch/ 1 cm thick (2²/3 oz/75 g)

1/2 tsp superfine sugar
1 tbsp sumac
3 tbsp red wine vinegar
7 oz/200 g red quinoa, rinsed
2 tbsp lemon juice

1 tbsp Dijon mustard
2 tbsp olive oil
5¼ oz/150 g young watercress leaves, tough stalks removed
coarse sea salt and black pepper

---

1 Place the shallots in a small bowl with 1 teaspoon of salt. Mix well and set aside for 5 minutes before adding the sugar, sumac, and vinegar. Mix again and set aside for another 30 minutes.

2 Bring a small pan of water to a boil and add the quinoa. Return to a boil, and then cook for 11 minutes. Drain, refresh well under cold water, and then set aside until completely dry.

3 To make the dressing, place the lemon juice and mustard in a bowl with 1 teaspoon of salt and a good grind of black pepper. Mix continuously as you slowly add the olive oil.

4 Strain the shallots and put them into a large mixing bowl along with 1 tablespoon of the pickling liquid. Add the quinoa and watercress and pour over the dressing. Stir gently, so that everything is combined, and serve.

BLACK RADISH, RED ENDIVE, AND APPLE SALAD

Fresh and crunchy, sweet and sharp, this salad works both as a great meal opener alongside a number of richer dishes—the beef and bone marrow pie (page 190), for example. The contrast of colors looks great here—the red endive, the black radish, the white of the freshly sliced apple—but the salad works just as well, flavor- and texturewise, with the more monochrome alternatives suggested.

Serves 4

Dressing
2/3 cup/150 ml cider vinegar
2 tbsp runny honey
3 tbsp lemon juice
2 small cinnamon sticks

3 tbsp olive oil
coarse sea salt and black pepper

2 small Cox or Pink Lady apples (8 oz/250 g)
6 red or white Belgian endives, trimmed, leaves separated, and core removed (10½ oz/300 g)

7 oz/200 g black radish or black or white turnip, sliced 1/16 inch/ 1 to 2 mm thick on a mandoline
½ oz/15 g parsley, coarsely chopped

1 Start with the dressing. Place the vinegar, honey, lemon juice, and cinnamon in a small saucepan. Bring to a boil, then reduce the heat to medium and simmer for 10 to 15 minutes, until the reduction is thick and syrupy and there is 3½ tablespoons left. Remove from the heat and set aside to cool before removing the cinnamon stick and whisking in the olive oil, along with a scant ½ teaspoon of salt and a good grind of black pepper.

2 Quarter and core the apples just before serving, then slice them thinly (1/16 inch/1 to 2 mm), lengthwise. Place in a large bowl and add the endive, radish, and parsley. Pour over the dressing, toss everything together and serve.

SIDES

CRUSHED NEW POTATOES WITH CAPER BERRIES, PINK PEPPERCORNS, AND ROASTED GARLIC

This is a side dish that really delivers on flavor, needing little more than some simply cooked meat or fish alongside. It's common to put all the effort into the main thing on a plate and let the sides provide the supporting act. It often works well, though, to switch the balance around: pull out the stops on the starch, for example, and keep the main ingredient on a plate very simple.

Caper berries are large brined berries from the caper bush, which come with their stem attached. They are milder than the smaller caper bud, with a slightly lemony flavor. They are widely available, but use regular capers if that's all you have.

Pink peppercorns—sweet, fruity, and with just a little heat—are almost as much about how completely pretty they look on a dish as how good they are to taste. Few fava bean or braised artichoke salads now escape our kitchen without some lightly crushed pink peppercorn confetti. They are also lovely stirred into mayonnaise served with some salmon or trout.

Serves 4 to 6

1 head garlic, cloves separated
  and peeled
1/3 cup/80 ml olive oil
1 bay leaf
1/3 oz/10 g thyme sprigs
1/3 oz/10 g rosemary sprigs

2 1/4 lb/1 kg new potatoes,
  unpeeled
3/4 oz/20 g mint, whole stalks
  and leaves, plus 1/3 oz/10 g mint
  leaves, finely shredded
2 oz/60 g caper berries, stems
  removed and cut in half if big,
  or 2 oz/60 g regular capers,
  rinsed and left whole

5 tsp/25 g unsalted butter
finely grated zest of 1 lemon
2 tbsp lemon juice
3/4 oz/20 g parsley leaves, finely
  chopped
2 tsp pink peppercorns, lightly
  crushed
coarse sea salt

1 Preheat the oven to 375°F/190°C (340°F/170°C convection).

2 Place the garlic cloves in a small ovenproof frying pan or in a small baking pan with the olive oil, bay leaf, half the thyme, and half the rosemary. Place in the oven and roast for 15 to 20 minutes, basting the garlic once or twice during cooking. Remove from the oven and, once cool, strain the oil into a large frying pan. The garlic cloves need to be set aside but the thyme and rosemary can be discarded.

3 Place the potatoes in a large saucepan along with the whole mint stalks and leaves and the remaining thyme and rosemary. Add a tablespoon of salt, cover with water, bring to a boil, and cook for 15 minutes. Drain, discard the mint, rosemary, and thyme, and cut the potatoes in half.

4 Place the pan with the garlic oil over high heat. Once hot, add the potatoes and fry for 8 to 9 minutes, stirring from time to time, until they start to break apart and are golden brown all over. Add the capers, roasted garlic cloves, and butter. Cook for a further minute before adding the lemon zest and juice, parsley, shredded mint, 1 1/2 teaspoons of salt, and the pink peppercorns. Stir everything gently together, cook for a final minute, and serve.

FONDANT RUTABAGA GRATIN

As with the Crushed New Potatoes on page 73, this is a side dish that can either support a larger act—the Confit Duck Leg on page 177, for example, or the Lamb Rump on page 155—or work as a show-stealing side. The gratin is complete and substantial enough to also work as a stand-alone main course for supper, if you like.

Don't balk at the amount of butter needed here, please. Something doesn't get to be called fondant without a certain amount of the golden stuff in the equation.

As seen on page 77, we serve these as individual portions at NOPI, in the same small copper pans that the baked cheesecakes (see page 213) come in. We've converted it to rustic one-dish fare for the home cook, but for something a bit more elegant, divide the gratin among four 5-inch/12 cm ramekins, soufflé dishes, or copper pans.

Caerphilly is a hard white mild cow's milk cheese originally produced in South Wales. It has a crumbly texture and a clean, tangy taste. Other crumbly cheeses—Cheshire, Wensleydale, a young Lancashire, or Cornish Yarg, for example—are all good alternatives.

If you want to get ahead and prepare this in advance, take it up to the point where the gratin is due to go in the oven and just bake it half an hour before you are ready to serve.

Serves 4

Herb crust
1 oz/30 g fresh white
  bread crumbs
1 1/2 tsp thyme leaves
1 tbsp tarragon leaves,
  coarsely chopped

finely grated zest of
  1/2 small lemon

10 tbsp/140 g unsalted butter
1 large rutabaga, peeled and
  cut into 1/3-inch/1-cm dice
  (2 1/4 lb/1 kg)

1 medium Savoy cabbage,
  thinly sliced (11 oz/320 g)
2/3 cup/150 ml vegetable stock
4 1/4 oz/120 g Caerphilly,
  roughly crumbled into
  1/3-inch/1-cm pieces
1 1/4 cups/300 ml heavy cream
coarse sea salt and black pepper

1 Place all the ingredients for the herb crust in a small bowl. Mix well and set aside.

2 Melt 7 tablespoons/100 g of the butter in a large sauté pan over medium heat. Add the rutabaga, along with 1/2 teaspoon of salt and a good grind of black pepper. Reduce the heat to low and cook, uncovered, for about an hour, spooning the butter over the rutabaga from time to time and turning it once or twice until the rutabaga is completely soft and caramelized. Remove from the pan, drain away any excess butter, and set aside.

3 Return the pan to medium heat with the remaining 3 tablespoons/40 g of butter. Stir in the cabbage, along with 1/2 teaspoon of salt and a grind of black pepper, then pour over the stock. Cook for 10 to 15 minutes, until the cabbage is soft and there are about 3 tablespoons of stock left in the pan. Drain in a colander and set aside.

4 Preheat the oven to 425°F/220°C (390°F/200°C convection).

5 Spread the cabbage out over the bottom of a rectangular ovenproof dish measuring 8 by 10 inches/ 18 cm by 25 cm wide by 3 inches/7 cm deep (or use individual ramekins). Sprinkle over half the cheese and spread the rutabaga pieces on top. Pour over the cream, then crumble the remaining cheese on top. Place in the oven and bake for 15 minutes. Scatter over the herb crust and cook for a further 10 to 15 minutes, switching the oven to a broil for the final 2 minutes if the bread crumbs need some help to become golden. Keep a close eye out if you do this, as the crumbs can quickly burn. Serve at once.

BABY CARROTS AND PARMESAN WITH TRUFFLE VINAIGRETTE

We use Belper Knolle cheese for this dish at NOPI; it's a Swiss cheese made from the raw milk of the Simmental cow. Scully discovered it on one of his many trips to Borough Market in search of something new. Talking with the producers of Belper Knolle—Jeurg and Mike of Jumi Cheese—Scully knew he'd found it. The distinct taste of the cheese comes from the thirteen weeks it spends wrapped around a garlic clove before black pepper is added. Cheese fanatics like Scully can go on similar cheese-seeking journeys to find Belper Knolle, but for those looking for a substitution, aged pecorino or Parmesan work well.

We love to showcase the baby carrots here—so perfect in their miniature completeness—but, if you can't get hold of any, just cut regular carrots into batons about 3 inches/8 cm long and 1/3 inch/1 cm wide. As with the cauliflower salad on page 60, this is a dish that loves a clash of color. If you're using regular carrots, find as many different colored varieties as you can: a mix of orange, yellow, and burgundy looks great.

This works well as either a stand-alone starter or as a side with some roast beef or pork.

Serves 4 to 6

Truffle vinaigrette
1 tsp Dijon mustard
1½ tbsp lemon juice
2 tbsp olive oil

1½ tbsp truffle oil, or less, if you prefer
coarse sea salt

2¼ lb/1 kg baby carrots, trimmed and scrubbed

2¾ oz/80 g Parmesan or Belper Knolle (see headnote), broken by hand into small pieces
½ oz/15 g tarragon leaves
⅓ oz/10 g parsley, coarsely chopped
2 tsp nigella seeds

1 Start with the vinaigrette. Place the mustard and lemon juice in a small bowl with ½ teaspoon of salt. Whisk together as you slowly pour over both oils, until combined.

2 Bring a large pan of salted water to a boil, add the carrots, and cook for 4 minutes, until just cooked but still retaining a bite. Rinse them briefly under cold water to halt their cooking and set aside to dry before transferring to a large mixing bowl. Add the cheese, herbs, nigella seeds, and 1½ teaspoons of salt. Pour over the dressing, mix together, and serve.

CRUSHED JERUSALEM ARTICHOKES WITH TARRAGON

Esme, who works in our test kitchen developing and testing recipes, is an unfailingly jolly person. Testing, tweaking, and re-testing recipes, going back to the drawing board, calling quits on a recipe that has been tested three times: there are very few things that cause Esme to sigh. Apart, that is, from when Jerusalem artichokes are in season and we are going for round four on a dish that requires another batch of 21 ounces/600 g to be peeled. There is no getting away from the fact that some kitchen jobs just *are* simply chores to be done, and peeling a pile of these knobbly tubers is one of them. The plus side, of course, is that the result tastes very good indeed: sweet, vaguely mushroomy, creamy, and nutty. Jerusalem artichoke season is October to March, so go and grab them while they are around.

Serves 4

1 lb 5 oz/600 g Jerusalem artichokes, peeled, cut into 1/3-inch/1-cm dice (15 oz/420 g) and stored in cold water, with the juice of 1/2 lemon

2 tbsp olive oil
4 small shallots, thinly sliced (2 oz/60 g)
7 tbsp/100 ml vegetable stock
5 cloves garlic, crushed
2 tbsp dry white wine

2 tbsp lemon juice
1/3 oz/10 g tarragon leaves, coarsely chopped
1/5 oz/5 g parsley leaves, finely chopped
coarse sea salt and black pepper

1 Drain the Jerusalem artichokes well and pat dry with a clean kitchen towel. Place a medium saucepan over medium-high heat and add the olive oil and artichokes. Sauté for about 8 minutes, until they are almost cooked and starting to caramelize, but still retain a bite. Add the shallots, along with the vegetable stock and 3/4 teaspoon of salt, and cook for another 8 minutes. Reduce the heat to medium and add the garlic stir and for another minute, then pour over the wine. Cook for 2 minutes, add the lemon juice, and cook for a final minute. Remove from the heat and stir in the herbs along with a good grind of black pepper. Lightly crush the Jerusalem artichokes with a potato masher or fork and serve.

CARDAMOM AND CLOVE RICE

This works well alongside a range of meat, fish, and vegetable mains. The Lamb Meatballs (page 147), Smoked Lamb Cutlets (page 152), Chicken Livers (page 169), Lemon Sole (page 124), Five-Spiced Tofu (page 214), and Spiced Chickpea Patties (page 223), to name just a few.

<u>Serves 4</u>

1 tbsp olive oil
10 whole cloves

10 cardamom pods,
  lightly crushed
8 oz/250 g basmati rice,
  well rinsed

scant 2 cups/430 ml boiling water
coarse sea salt and black pepper

1 Place the oil and spices in a medium saucepan for which you have a lid. Place over medium-high heat and cook for 2 minutes, stirring continuously, until the cardamom starts to turn golden. Add the rice, along with 1¼ teaspoons of salt and a good grind of black pepper, and continue to cook and stir for 1 minute. Pour over the boiling water and reduce the heat as low as it gets. Stir once, cover, and leave to cook for 12 minutes without removing the lid. Remove from the heat, uncover the pan, and quickly place a clean kitchen towel on top. Return the lid to the pan again and set aside for 10 minutes. Fluff up the rice with a fork—any stuck to the bottom will now come off easily—and serve.

FARINATA

_____

These Italian flatbreads are quite large, so each can serve two people. Cut them up to serve on separate plates, or just pile up the two large farinata on one sharing plate for people to pull at as they go. They go particularly well with the King Prawns (page 101), Spiced Buttermilk Cod (page 112), Celery Root Purée (page 7), Five-Spiced Tofu (page 214), Achar (page 217) and Urad Dal Purée (page 221). They're also delicious as they are, as a pre-dinner snack to have with drinks. Use good-quality olive oil if you can here: you'll really taste the difference.

Serves 4	7 oz/200 g chickpea flour	¼ cup/60 ml olive oil
		coarse sea salt

1 Place the chickpea flour in a large bowl and slowly add a scant 2 cups/450 ml of water, whisking constantly, until well combined. Set the batter aside for 20 minutes.

2 Preheat the oven to 465°F/240°C (425°F/220°C convection).

3 Whisk 2 tablespoons of the olive oil into the batter, along with 1 teaspoon of salt. Place a 10-inch/25-cm heavy-bottomed ovenproof skillet over high heat with 1 tablespoon of oil. Once the oil starts to smoke, pour in half the batter: it should be about ⅛ inch/4 mm thick. Leave on the heat for 30 seconds, until it starts to bubble, then transfer the pan to the oven for 10 minutes until the farinata is cooked through: it should be browned and crispy on both sides but soft in the middle. Remove from the oven and, using a spatula, transfer the farinata to a plate. Keep warm while you repeat with the remaining tablespoon of oil and half of the batter, then serve.

STICKY SESAME RICE

This is particularly good with a lot of the main fish dishes: the Sea Bream (page 109), Gurnard (page 121), and Panfried Mackerel (page 135), in particular. It's also good with the Lamb Fillet (page 149) and the Five-Spiced Tofu (page 214).

A top tip from Scully's mum, if rice has stuck to the bottom of the pan: immediately pour in boiling water and return the pan to the stove on high heat for 5 minutes. Rice released, no scrubbing needed.

Serves 4

2¹/2 tsp mixed black and white sesame seeds (or just white)

1¹/4 cups/240 g Thai sticky rice, soaked for at least an hour, preferably overnight, and drained well

1/2 tsp toasted sesame oil
1 tsp soy sauce (optional)
coarse sea salt

1 Put the sesame seeds in a small frying pan and toast over medium heat for 3 to 4 minutes, until golden brown. Remove from the heat and set aside.

2 Place the rice in a medium saucepan for which you have a lid. Pour over 1²/3 cups/400 ml of water, add 1/2 teaspoon of salt, and place over high heat. Once the water comes to a boil, reduce the heat to medium-low, cover the pan, and simmer for 15 minutes, until the rice is cooked through. Remove from the heat, add the sesame seeds and oil, and fluff up with a fork. Return the lid and set aside for 5 minutes before serving, with the soy sauce drizzled on top.

LIMA BEAN MASH WITH ROSEMARY AND GARLIC

This is a highly comforting alternative to mashed potatoes. It works well with dishes like the Lamb Rump (page 155), Confit Duck Leg (page 177), Quail (page 204), Scallops (page 129), and Soft-Shell Crab (page 141). It's also delicious as a dip or spread on bruschetta for a snack.

Serves 6

14 oz/400 g dried lima beans, soaked overnight in plenty of cold water with 1 tsp baking soda

¼ cup/60 ml olive oil, plus extra to serve

2 rosemary sprigs

1 clove garlic, crushed

coarse sea salt and black pepper

1 Drain the beans and place them in a large saucepan with 9 cups/2 liters of water. Bring to a boil, then simmer over medium heat for anywhere between 20 minutes to over an hour—the cooking time can vary hugely—until the beans are completely soft. Drain the beans, retaining the cooking liquid, and set both aside.

2 Put the olive oil and rosemary into a small pan and place over medium heat. Simmer gently for 3 to 4 minutes, until you can smell the rosemary. Remove from the heat, discard the rosemary, and set aside.

3 Place the beans in a food processor with the infused oil, garlic, 2 teaspoons of salt, and a good grind of black pepper. Blitz to combine and, with the machine still running, pour in about ⅔ cup/150 ml of the reserved cooking liquid. If you want a softer mash, add a little bit more of the liquid: about ¾ cup/200 ml in total. Continue to blitz for a minute, until a smooth, runny mash is formed. Serve warm, with a final drizzle of oil on top.

GREEN SALAD WITH SUMAC, RED ONION, AND ALLSPICE

The leafy greens, sweet dressing and sumac-sharp onions all make this salad a natural pairing with hearty dishes, to cut through their richness: Twice-Cooked Baby Chicken (page 167), Chicken Pastilla (page 172), Quail (page 204), Grape Leaf Beef Pie (page 190), King Prawns (page 101), Persian Love Rice (page 229), and Pearl Barley Risotto (page 227), to mention just a few.

If you want some added crunch here, shallow-fry some roughly torn pieces of pita and/or some chopped almonds in a mix of olive oil and butter. Fry for about 5 minutes, stirring constantly, until the pita is crunchy and golden brown. Drain on a paper towel–lined plate and toss them into the salad just before serving.

Serves 4

½ medium red onion, sliced into rounds ⅛ inch/3 to 4 mm thick (3 oz/90 g)
1 tsp sumac
2 tbsp olive oil
1½ tbsp Valdespino sherry vinegar, or another good-quality sherry vinegar
1¼ tsp superfine sugar
¼ tsp ground allspice
3½ oz/100 g arugula
2 oz/60 g watercress and mizuna, or mixed baby leaves
coarse sea salt and black pepper

1 Place the onion slices in a small bowl with the sumac, oil, vinegar, sugar, allspice, ½ teaspoon of salt, and a generous grind of pepper. Mix well and set aside for an hour, if possible, for the onion to soften.

2 Just before serving, place the arugula and watercress in a large bowl and pour over the onion and all the dressing. Mix together gently and serve.

MIXED CHINESE VEGETABLES

This works alongside so many main dishes. It is particularly good, however, with the Twice-Cooked Baby Chicken (page 167), Hanger Steak (page 188), Roasted Pork Belly (page 192), Gurnard (page 121), Tuna Skewers (page 138), and Five-Spiced Tofu (page 214). In the restaurant we use the store-bought crispy fried shallots you can find in Asian stores, but if you want to make your own, you can definitely do so. Just follow the instruction in the steamed haddock recipe (see page 110), omitting the Chinese five-spice. This will give you more shallots than you'll need here, but they will keep well for 2 to 3 days in an airtight container and can later be sprinkled on literally anything. Don't worry if you don't have them: the dish works well without.

Serves 4

3 tbsp peanut oil
1¼-inch/3-cm piece of ginger, peeled and julienned (1 oz/30 g)
4 cloves garlic, thinly sliced

2 large red chiles, seeded and julienned
14 oz/400 g bok choy, quartered lengthwise, or choi sum if unavailable
10½ oz/300 g broccolini

3 tbsp store-bought or home-made crispy fried shallots (½ oz/15 g) (optional)
1 lime, quartered, to serve
coarse sea salt

---

1 Put the peanut oil into a large frying pan or wok and place over high heat. When hot, add the ginger, garlic, and chile and fry for 2 minutes, stirring often, until fragrant. Add the bok choy and cook for 2 minutes, stirring often. Add the broccolini and 1 teaspoon of salt, toss well, and cook for another 4 minutes. Serve with the crispy shallots sprinkled on top and a wedge of lime alongside.

Paprika oven fries

Few meals don't benefit from the addition of slightly spicy, crunchy, oven-roasted potato "fries." Dishes that work particularly well, however, include the Lamb Fillet (page 149), Lamb Rump (page 155), Venison Fillet (page 161), Twice-Cooked Baby Chicken (page 167), Pepper-Crusted Beef Sirloin (page 186), Hanger Steak (page 188), Braised Pig's Cheeks (page 198), Bourbon-Glazed Spare Ribs (page 201), Steamed Haddock (page 110), Turbot (page 115), Soft-Shell Crab (page 141), and Corn Cakes (page 209).

Serves 4

6 large red-skinned potatoes (skin on), cut into ½-inch/1.5-cm wide batons (2 lb 10 oz/1.2 kg)

3 cloves garlic, crushed
½ tsp smoked paprika
1 tsp paprika
¼ cup/60 ml sunflower oil

2 tsp fine semolina
coarse sea salt and black pepper

1 Preheat the oven to 365°F/240°C (325°F/220°C convection).

2 Place a large saucepan with plenty of salted water over high heat. Bring to a boil, add the potatoes, and blanch for 5 minutes. Drain, then place in a bowl with the rest of the ingredients, 1½ teaspoons of salt, and plenty of pepper. Mix together well but gently—you don't want the potatoes to break apart—and then spread out on two large parchment-lined baking sheets: they need to be spaced well apart so that they color nicely. Roast for about 35 minutes, turning once halfway through, until the fries are cooked through, dark golden, and crisp.

Roasted carrots with coriander seeds and garlic

Honey, garlic, thyme, and coriander: all exceedingly good accompaniments to roasted carrots. This dish works particularly well alongside Smoked Lamb Cutlets (page 152), Lamb Sweetbreads (page 158), Chicken Supremes (page 163), Confit Duck Leg (page 177), Hanger Steak (page 188), Turbot (page 115), Spiced Buttermilk Cod (page 112), Octopus (page 132), and Pearl Barley Risotto (page 227).

Serves 4

2¼ lb/1 kg carrots, peeled and sliced into ½ by 3-inch/1.5 cm by 8-cm batons (1 lb 14 oz/850 g)

1 tbsp runny honey
1½ tbsp olive oil
1½ tsp coriander seeds, gently crushed

3 cloves garlic, crushed
5 thyme sprigs
coarse sea salt and black pepper

1 Preheat the oven to 425°F/220°C (390°F/200°C convection).

2 Place the carrots in a large bowl with the honey, oil, coriander seeds, garlic, 1½ teaspoon of salt, and plenty of pepper. Mix well, then transfer to two large parchment-lined baking sheets: you don't want the carrots to be overcrowded. Roast for 30 minutes, mixing in the thyme just 3 minutes before the end of cooking, until the carrots are cooked through and caramelized but still retain their bright color.

Potato and celery root gratin

We have deliberately kept the focus on the vegetable stock here, rather than the cream, to prevent the gratin from becoming too heavy to go alongside a hefty main course. However, a sprinkling of grated Cheddar on top will do no harm to anyone, if that's how you like your gratin. Lamb Fillet (page 149), Lamb Rump (page 155), Chicken Livers (page 169), Confit Duck Leg (page 177), Turbot (page 115), Scallops (page 129), and Corn Cakes (page 209) all make for great pairings. Use a mandoline, if you have one, for the celery root and potatoes.

Serves 6 to 8

1³⁄4 oz/50 g unsalted butter
3 cloves garlic, thinly sliced
1⁄3 oz/10 g sage leaves, thinly
  shredded

1 small celery root, peeled,
  cut in half, then each half cut
  widthwise into 1⁄16-inch/
  2 to 3-mm slices (1 lb 1 oz/500 g)

4 large potatoes, peeled and
  cut widthwise into 1⁄16-inch/
  2 to 3-mm slices (2¹⁄4 lb/1 kg)
3 cups/700 ml vegetable stock
3⁄4 cup/200 ml heavy cream
coarse sea salt and black pepper

1 Preheat the oven to 425°F/220°C (390°F/200°C convection).

2 Place the butter in a large saucepan over medium-high heat. Once melted, add the garlic and fry for 1 to 2 minutes, stirring continuously, until light golden brown. Add the sage and fry for a few more seconds before adding the remaining ingredients, 2 teaspoons of salt, and plenty of pepper. Bring to a boil, then reduce the heat to medium and simmer gently for 8 minutes, until the celery root and potatoes are just cooked but still retain a bite. Drain the vegetables—retaining the liquid—then spread them out in a high-sided ovenproof dish measuring about 11 by 8 inches/28 cm by 20 cm. Return the liquid to the pan and place over medium-high heat for 12 to 14 minutes, stirring a few times, until the liquid has reduced by half. Pour this over the vegetables and bake for 40 to 45 minutes, until the potatoes and celery root are cooked through and golden brown on top. Remove from the oven and set aside for 10 minutes before serving.

WILTED KALE WITH FRIED CHILE AND GARLIC

Wilted greens are the perfect accompaniment to a number of fish and meat dishes, but they are also what a veggie main can be looking for. Five-Spiced Tofu (page 214), Urad Dal Purée (page 221), and Spiced Chickpea Patties (page 223) all benefit from a green side.

Serves 6

1 lb 5 oz/600 g curly kale (3 medium bunches), thick stems discarded and leaves cut widthwise into 1½-inch/ 4 cm slices (13 oz/370 g)

2 tbsp olive oil
2 mild red chiles (seeded if you don't want the heat), sliced into ⅛-inch/3-mm rounds

3 cloves garlic, thinly sliced
coarse sea salt

1 Place a large saucepan over high heat with plenty of salted water. Bring to a boil, add the kale, and blanch for 1 minute. Drain well, pat dry with a clean kitchen towel, and set aside until ready to use.

2 Wipe the pan clean and return it to medium-high heat with the oil, chiles, and garlic. Fry for 1 to 2 minutes, until the garlic starts to turn golden and the chile crisp. Remove the pan from the heat, use a slotted spoon to lift out the chile and garlic, and set them aside. Return the pan to the heat—with the oil—and add the kale and ¾ teaspoon of salt. Stir for 2 minutes, then serve, with the chile and garlic sprinkled on top.

WHOLE ROASTED CELERY ROOT

This looks like a creature from outer space when it comes out of the oven. With its crunchy, salty skin and soft, buttery middle, though, a slice is the perfect accompaniment to a number of hearty dishes and a good alternative to fried potatoes: Hanger Steak (page 188), Beef Sirloin (page 186), Braised Pig's Cheeks (page 198), Quail (page 204), and Turbot (page 115), for example. We like to serve this with the skin on because it looks so great, but it can be slightly bitter, so you might instead just want a little bit of skin remaining on each slice, or avoid most of the skin when eating. We've suggested this as a simple side, but the dish can also be a stand-alone starter or snack to have before drinks, cut into wedges and served with a bowl of crème fraîche to dip them in and a wedge of lemon to squeeze over.

Serves 6

1 large celery root (2 lb 10 oz/ 1.2 kg), trimmed, hairy roots discarded, rinsed clean

1 tbsp olive oil, plus 2 tsp extra to serve

2 tsp coarse sea salt, plus a pinch to serve

1 Preheat the oven to 375°F/190°C (340°F/170°C convection).

2 Place the celery root on a small parchment-lined baking sheet, rub all over with the oil and salt, and roast for 3 hours, until a knife inserted into the flesh goes in very easily. Slice into 12 wedges and serve with a final pinch of salt and a drizzle of oil.

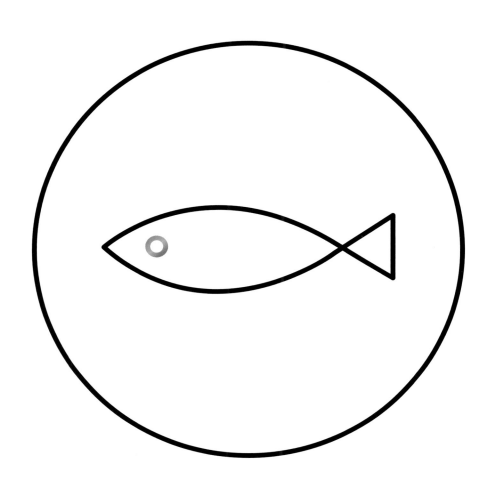

FISH

King prawns with Pernod, tarragon, and feta

The combination of prawns and feta is a classic Greek combination— prawns *saganaki*—which we've been playing with since the first Ottolenghi book. It's a lovely dish to make, as everything can be prepared in advance and just cooked before serving. If we were to enter any NOPI recipe for a 15-minute-supper competition, this would be it. Get prawns as fresh as you can: it means you can leave the heads on and their bright red bodies look just wonderful when they are cooked. It's almost a must to serve this with some crusty white bread, to mop up the juices.

Serves 4

16 tiger or king prawns (about 1 lb 5 oz/600 g), shells removed and deveined, heads and tails left on
1 tbsp thyme leaves
1 large clove garlic, crushed
finely grated zest of 1 large lemon

1/2 cup/120 ml olive oil
4 1/4 oz/120 g feta, broken into 1/2-inch/1.5-cm chunks
1/2 tsp dried chile flakes
1 tsp dried oregano
4 baby fennel bulbs or 1 large bulb, trimmed and cut lengthwise into 1/5-inch/5-mm slices (10 1/2 oz/300 g)

3/4 cup/180 ml Pernod
2/3 cup/150 ml vegetable stock
5 tbsp/70 g unsalted butter
3/4 oz/20 g tarragon, coarsely chopped
1/2 tsp sumac, to serve

1 Place the prawns in a bowl with the thyme, garlic, lemon zest, and 5 tablespoons/70 ml of the olive oil. Mix to coat, cover, and leave in the fridge to marinate for at least an hour or, preferably, overnight.

2 Place the feta in a bowl with 1 tablespoon of the oil and sprinkle over the chile flakes and oregano. Stir gently, cover, and keep in the fridge until ready to use. This can also be done a day ahead.

3 Heat the remaining 2 tablespoons of oil in a large sauté pan over high heat. Add the prawns and sear them for 1 to 2 minutes, turning them once or twice, until they are no longer translucent. Remove them from the pan and set aside. Add the fennel to the pan and fry for 6 to 7 minutes, stirring from time to time, until it starts to soften and gain a good bit of color. Add the Pernod and cook for 1 minute, to reduce by half, then pour in the stock. Cook for another 2 to 3 minutes, until the liquid is reduced by two-thirds and you have about 1/2 cup/120 ml of liquid left in the pan. Reduce the heat to medium and add the butter, tarragon, and a scant 1/2 teaspoon of salt. Stir to melt the butter, add the prawns, then stir for 2 minutes, until you get a smooth and glossy sauce and the prawns are just cooked through.

4 Divide the prawns and fennel among four plates, bowls, or individual copper pans that have been warmed up. Top with the chunks of marinated feta. Serve at once, with a sprinkle of sumac.

LOBSTER, FENNEL, AND GRILLED GRAPE SALAD

This is a version of a salad Yotam first made in Sardinia for his television series, *Mediterranean Feasts*. Without the necessary patience of a seasoned fisherman, Yotam was close to desperation after many hours spent bobbing about in a boat trying to will a single lobster to waddle into his fishing net. With a whole scene and a precious day's filming at risk of being lost, the stakes were pretty high. When a lobster finally arrived on the boat, Yotam was ecstatic. His cool, city-kid credentials were lost forever in the eyes of the local fishermen as he jumped up and down with excitement.

The salad is also completely delicious without the lobster, if you like. Fresh crabmeat is a good alternative if you want to be beside the seaside without having to kill and cook your lunch yourself.

Dukkah is an aromatic Egyptian seed and nut mix that can be sprinkled over leafy salads, roasted vegetables, legume pastes such as hummus, or simply over cooked rice or lentils. You can buy ready-made *dukkah* from supermarkets, specialty shops, and online, but it won't taste as good as the batch you make yourself. See page 307 for the recipe.

Serves 4

2 medium Maine lobsters
  (2 lb 10 oz/1.2 kg, yielding
  9½ oz/270 g of meat) or
  1 lb/450 g fresh crabmeat
coarse sea salt and black pepper

Salad
5¼ oz/150 g green or red
  seedless grapes
1½ tbsp sunflower oil

1 medium fennel bulb, trimmed
  (reserving any soft fennel
  fronds), cut lengthwise into
  ⅛-inch/2- to 3-mm slices
  (7 oz/190 g), and stored in cold
  water with a squeeze of lemon
1 large or 2 small pale yellow
  or red Belgian endive, core
  trimmed and leaves cut
  lengthwise into ⅓-inch/
  1-cm strips (2¾ oz/80 g)
6 round red radishes, trimmed
  and very thinly sliced (2 oz/60 g)

½ oz/15 g basil leaves, torn
½ oz/15 g dill leaves
⅓ oz/10 g tarragon leaves
2 tbsp dukkah

Dressing
⅓ cup/80 ml orange juice
1½ tsp arak, or another aniseed
  liqueur, such as Pernod, raki,
  ouzo, or sambuca
1½ tsp lemon juice
2 tbsp olive oil

1 The most humane way to kill a lobster is to put it into the freezer for 2 hours, which will render it unconscious. Once it is no longer moving, push the tip of a large, sharp knife or skewer though the center of the cross on its head and this will kill it instantly. Bring a large pan of water to a boil over high heat, with 1 tablespoon of salt. Add one of the lobsters, return the water to a boil, and cook for 5 to 6 minutes. Lift out the lobster and run it under cold water to cool. Set aside to drain while you repeat with the remaining lobster.

2 Separate the claws from each lobster body and lightly crack the shell all over with a small pan or hammer. Remove the meat from the shell and set aside. Hold the head, then twist the body to remove it. Discard the head, then, using a sharp knife or scissors, cut the inside skin of the body and lift out the flesh. Cut in half, lengthwise, removing the vein, and set aside.

3 Mix the grapes with 1½ teaspoons of the sunflower oil and ¼ teaspoon of salt. Place a grill pan over high

heat and, when hot, add the grapes to the pan. Grill for 1 to 2 minutes, turning a few times, so that the grapes are smoky, beginning to split, and have nice char lines. Transfer them to a large mixing bowl. Drain the fennel and pat dry very well, then mix with the remaining oil and ½ teaspoon of salt. Place the fennel in the grill pan for 1 to 2 minutes, turning over halfway so they have nice char marks and have softened. Place in the bowl with the grapes and set aside.

4 To make the dressing, pour the orange juice into a small pan and place over high heat. Bring to a boil and reduce for 4 to 5 minutes, until you have about 1½ tablespoons left. Remove from the heat and set aside to cool before pouring into a small bowl with the arak, lemon juice, oil, ½ teaspoon of salt, and a good grind of black pepper. Whisk to combine, then pour over the grapes and fennel. Add any fennel fronds, the endive, radish, herbs, and *dukkah*. Toss well before adding the lobster meat and giving everything a final gentle stir. Divide the salad among four plates and serve.

LOBSTER, FENNEL, AND GRILLED GRAPE SALAD

SEA BASS AND TURMERIC POTATOES IN RASAM BROTH

———————————

Tamarind is one of our favorite ingredients. Its taste is hard to describe—it has a sweet-sour flavor that adds a completely distinct tartness to sauces, soups, marinades, pastes, and dressings. It's an ingredient we use lots throughout the book in a number of savory fish and vegetarian dishes, as well in the sweet dish of Roasted Pineapple (page 260).

Here, its tartness is a key part of the *rasam* soup, a dish often served in South Indian cooking to balance the heat of other dishes. *Rasam* translates as "essence." The soup can be made in many ways—with varying contributions from tomato, pepper, lemon, cumin, chile, and tamarind water—but the result will always be food that comforts and restores. As with the halibut and vichyssoise (see page 118), our version is a meal in itself, somewhere between a hearty soup and a fish dish with a sauce.

We use five different spices when making *rasam* at NOPI, instead of the garam masala mix here. If you want to reinstate the original, use 1 teaspoon each of ground black pepper, cumin, coriander, caraway, and yellow mustard seeds. Find fresh or frozen curry leaves at Indian or Asian markets.

Serves 6

Potatoes

1 lb 6 oz/620 g red-skinned
    potatoes, or another firm, waxy
    variety, peeled and cut into
    1-inch/2.5-cm cubes
1 tbsp/15 g ghee
8 stems fresh curry leaves
    (3/4 oz/20 g)
1 1/2 tbsp yellow mustard seeds
1 medium onion, finely diced
    (3 1/2 oz/100 g)

4 cloves garlic, finely diced
1 tsp ground turmeric
2 medium tomatoes (6 oz/170 g),
    halved, seeded, and coarsely
    chopped (3 1/2 oz/100 g)
2 tsp/10 g unsalted butter

Rasam

3 1/2 oz/100 g tamarind pulp
1 tbsp sunflower oil
2 medium onions, thinly
    sliced (7 oz/200 g)
8 cloves garlic, crushed
1 1/2 tbsp garam masala

12 stems fresh curry leaves
    (1 oz/25 g)
2 large dried red chiles
3 large tomatoes (10 1/2 oz/300 g),
    each cut into six 3/4-inch/2-cm
    wedges

2 tbsp/30 g ghee
6 sea bass fillets (1 lb 14 oz/840 g),
    skin lightly scored
1 tbsp lemon juice
1/3 oz/10 g cilantro leaves
    (optional)
coarse sea salt and black pepper

1 Place the potatoes in a medium saucepan and cover with salted water. Bring to a boil, then reduce the heat to medium and simmer for 10 minutes, until just cooked. Drain and set aside.

2 Wipe the pan dry and return it to medium heat with the 1 tablespoon/15 g of ghee. When melted, add the 8 stems of curry leaves and mustard seeds and fry for 2 minutes, until fragrant. Add the onion and garlic and fry for another 3 or 4 minutes, until starting to soften. Add the turmeric, tomatoes, and cooked potatoes, stir to coat the potatoes with the spices, 1 teaspoon of salt, and a good grind of black pepper. Cook for a final minute, then set aside and just warm up when you need it.

3 To make the rasam, pour 4 cups/900 ml of boiling water over the tamarind and set aside for 30 minutes, for the pulp to soften and disintegrate in the water. Use your hands to break up and dissolve the pulp, then strain through a fine-mesh sieve and discard the seeds. Pour the sunflower oil into a large pot and place over medium heat. Add the onions and garlic and fry for 4 to 5 minutes, stirring from time to time, until starting to soften. Add the garam masala, 12 stems of curry leaves, and chiles and fry for another minute before adding the tomatoes. Pour over the tamarind water, reduce the heat to medium-low, and simmer very gently for 15 minutes; take care

that the mixture does not come to a boil, as this will cause the tamarind pulp to split. Add 2 teaspoons of salt, stir, and set aside. You can leave this to infuse for a few hours and then, when you're ready to serve, there are two options. For a more formal look, strain the rasam for a clear broth; for a more rustic and informal look, you can skip the straining and keep the onion, garlic, curry leaves, and chiles in the pot. Either way, you'll need to return it to the stove and warm it through before serving.

4 To cook the fish, place a large frying pan over medium heat and add the ghee. Sprinkle 1 1/2 teaspoons of salt over the skin side of all six fillets, along with a grind each of black pepper. When the ghee has melted, add the fish to the pan skin side down: you might need to do this in two batches so as not to overcrowd the pan. Fry for 3 to 4 minutes, until crisp and golden brown. Sprinkle another 1 1/2 teaspoons of salt on the flesh side of the fish, along with some more black pepper, then flip the fish over and cook for a final minute. Remove from the heat and drizzle with the lemon juice.

5 To serve, divide the warm potatoes among six bowls. Place a fish fillet on top or alongside, skin side up, and ladle over the rasam. Finish with a sprinkle of cilantro and serve.

SEA BREAM WITH MANGO AND PAPAYA SALAD

This is a dish where the salad steals the show. The fish is a wonderful accompaniment, but it's the mango and papaya that demand the attention. To get the flavors properly going, make sure you marinate the ingredients together for at least 4 hours. Still better, leave the mixture in the fridge overnight, holding back on the basil, cilantro, peanuts, and dried anchovies, and adding these just before you are going to eat.

Thai basil, with its distinct taste of aniseed, is completely different from regular sweet basil. You can find it in larger supermarkets and at Asian grocers. But if you can't find any, use regular basil leaves mixed with 1/3 ounce/10 g of tarragon leaves. If you can't get to an Asian grocer or can't find the dried anchovies online, don't worry—the salad can do without them and still works very well.

Serves 6

Mango and papaya salad
about 3/4 cup/200 ml sunflower oil, for frying, plus 1 tbsp
1 1/2 oz/40 g dried anchovies
5 red (Thai) shallots, peeled and quartered (3 1/2 oz/50 g)
1 or 2 bird's-eye chiles, depending on heat
1/4 cup/60 ml rice vinegar

1/4 cup/60 ml lime juice
1 3/4 oz/50 g palm sugar, coarsely grated if starting from a block
2 tbsp fish sauce
2 medium green papayas, peeled, halved, seeds removed, and julienned (1 lb/440 g)
2 medium green mangos, peeled and julienned (13 1/2 oz/380 g)
1 1/4 oz/35 g Thai basil leaves, torn

1 oz/30 g cilantro leaves, or sprouting cilantro
3 1/2 oz/100 g roasted peanuts

2 tbsp sunflower oil
6 sea bream fillets (2 lb/900 g), skin lightly scored and pin bones removed
2 tbsp/30 g unsalted butter
1 lime, cut into 6 wedges
coarse sea salt and black pepper

1 First make the salad. Pour enough oil into a small saucepan so that it rises 3/4 inch/2 cm up the sides. Place over medium-high heat and, when hot, add the anchovies. Fry for 1 to 2 minutes, until golden brown, then remove with a slotted spoon and set aside on a paper towel–lined plate.

2 Place the shallots, chiles, vinegar, lime juice, palm sugar, fish sauce, and 1 tablespoon of oil in the small bowl of a food processor and blitz to form a fine paste. Transfer to a large bowl, add the papaya and mango, and stir gently to coat. Cover and leave in the fridge for at least 4 hours, preferably overnight. When ready to serve, bring the salad back to room temperature and add the basil, cilantro, peanuts, and dried anchovies. Mix well and set aside.

3 Place a large frying pan over medium-high heat with the 2 tablespoons of sunflower oil. Season the fish fillets on both sides, using a total of 1 1/2 teaspoons of salt and a good grind of black pepper, then add the fish to the pan skin side down. You may need to cook the fillets in two batches, depending on the size of your pan or fish, so just halve the oil and butter accordingly. Fry for 2 to 3 minutes, until the skin is crisp and light golden brown. Flip the fish over, and at the same time add the butter to the corner of the pan. Cook for 2 minutes, basting the fish with the butter once it is foaming. Remove from the heat and serve with the mango and papaya salad alongside, as well as with the lime wedges.

Steamed haddock with sesame bagna cauda and lacinato kale

Bagna cauda is a warm dip popular in Piedmont, Italy, that's made with butter, garlic, and anchovies. It's traditionally served like a fondue, placed in a bowl in the center of the table for sharing. It also works well as a sauce, spooned on top of cooked vegetables. The addition of sesame seeds is completely untraditional. Taking the dip some way from its roots and giving it an Asian accent, we transform it into a thicker sauce that works well alongside fish or white meat. The idea for it came from a conversation that Scully's mum, Mary, had with a Nepalese friend of hers. Scully's mother added the anchovies, Scully added his signature Valdespino sherry vinegar, Yotam came up with the entirely nontraditional new name, and the sauce was born.

Fried shallots can be bought from Asian grocery stores if you don't want to make your own. Alternatively, toast some extra sesame seeds (about 1 1/2 teaspoons) and sprinkle these on top of the fish instead.

Serves 6

Sesame bagna cauda
1 3/4 oz/50 g sesame seeds
1/4 cup/60 ml olive oil
4 cloves garlic, thinly sliced
5 red chiles, seeded and thinly sliced
4 medium tomatoes, skin on, cut into 3/4-inch/2-cm cubes (1 lb 1 oz/500 g)
1 tbsp light brown sugar
2 1/2 tbsp Valdespino sherry vinegar, or another good-quality sherry vinegar

10 brown (canned) anchovy fillets (1 oz/30 g), rinsed and patted dry
4 tsp/20 g unsalted butter

Fried shallots (optional, see headnote)
5 tbsp/40 g all-purpose flour
4 tsp cornstarch
1 1/2 tsp Chinese five-spice
1 1/2 tsp ground white pepper
2 large shallots, cut into 1/5-inch/5-mm rounds (5 oz/150 g), and each round separated into little rings
about 1 2/3 cups/400 ml sunflower oil, for frying

Lacinato kale
2 tbsp olive oil
2 cloves garlic, thinly sliced
1 red chile, seeded and thinly sliced
1 lb 1 oz/500 g lacinato kale, tough stalks removed and leaves finely shredded (10 1/2 oz/300 g)
7 tbsp/100 ml white wine
finely grated zest of 1/2 lemon

6 haddock fillets, or another firm white fish such as cod or halibut, skinless and boneless (2 lb/900 g)
1 tbsp olive oil
1 tbsp lemon juice
coarse sea salt and black pepper

1 Preheat the oven to 340°F/170°C (300°F/150°C convection).

2 Start with the bagna cauda. Place the sesame seeds on a small baking sheet and bake for about 25 minutes, until deep golden brown. Remove from the oven and set aside.

3 Pour the olive oil into a medium saucepan and place over medium-high heat. Add the garlic and chile and cook for 5 to 6 minutes, stirring often, until the garlic starts to turn golden. Add the rest of the ingredients for the bagna cauda, apart from the sesame seeds, and continue to cook for 8 to 9 minutes, stirring constantly, until thick. Remove from the heat and stir in the sesame seeds, along with 1/2 teaspoon of salt and a good grind of black pepper. Transfer to a blender and purée for a few minutes to form a completely smooth paste. Spoon into a medium bowl and set aside somewhere warm until ready to serve. If the sauce cools down, gently warm it up again before serving.

4 If you choose to fry your own shallots, combine the flour and cornstarch in a small bowl with the Chinese five-spice, white pepper, and 1 1/2 teaspoons of salt. Add the shallots and use your hands to toss everything together, so that the shallots are coated. Pour enough sunflower oil into a small saucepan so that it rises 1 1/2 inches/4 cm up the sides. Place over high heat and, once hot, add half the shallots and fry for 2 to 3 minutes, until crisp. Transfer to a paper towel–lined plate and set aside while you continue with the remaining batch.

5 To cook the kale, put the oil into a large saucepan and place over medium-high heat. Add the garlic and chile and cook for 2 to 3 minutes, until the garlic is light golden brown. Add the kale and cook for 2 minutes, stirring constantly, until wilted. Add the wine, 1/4 teaspoon of salt, and some pepper and cook for another minute. Remove from the heat, stir in the lemon zest, and set aside somewhere warm until ready to serve.

6 Just before serving, brush the fish with the olive oil and season with 1 1/2 teaspoons of salt (for all six fillets) and a grind of black pepper. Line the bottom of a steaming basket (or a colander that fits easily inside a lidded pot) with parchment paper. Pour boiling water into the bottom of your pot and place over medium heat to simmer gently. Place half the fish in the steaming basket or colander, place over the bubbling water (make sure the bottom doesn't touch the water), seal the pot with a lid, and simmer for about 5 minutes, until the fish is cooked through; the fillets should just start to flake apart when you press them. Keep somewhere warm while you repeat with the remaining fillets.

7 To serve, divide the warm sesame bagna cauda among six plates, with the kale on top or alongside. Place a haddock fillet on top, drizzle over the lemon juice, sprinkle with the shallots, and serve.

SPICED BUTTERMILK COD WITH URAD DAL

There are various levels of testing that a recipe has to go through before it is deemed a success. One of these is the CDP (or Cornelia Dinner Party) test, named for the trusted adviser, exacting critic, and general backbone of all things Ottolenghi and NOPI. If a recipe makes it into the repertoire of Cornelia's home cooking, we know it has arrived. This one became such a staple that weekly emails were involved as Cornelia made it once again, honing it to perfection.

It's a great dish to make for a dinner party as you can get everything ready in advance—the fish needs marinating for 4 to 6 hours, so you'll have to start early—up to the point just before the spinach goes into the dal. This can then be done when the fish is cooking, and your main course, needing no more than some plain steamed rice alongside, is ready.

When we make this at NOPI we use two different types of dal: creamy-white urad dal and pale yellow mung dal. The contrast of texture and color works well but, for the sake of simplicity, we've gone for just the urad dal (skinned split black lentils) here. If you want to use both, just use ¼ cup/60 g of each, adding them to the pan at the same time.

We also finish this off with olive oil that has been infused with the slightly bitter and distinctive taste of Italian bergamot oranges. If you want to reinstate this as well but can't get hold of any bergamot oil, you can easily replicate the flavor. Simply bring a little olive oil to a gentle simmer in a small pan with a couple of Earl Grey tea bags in it. Set aside to cool and infuse, then strain the oil, discarding the tea bags. Alternatively, and more simply, plain olive oil works well.

One last point: it's really important to toast the mustard seeds before they are added to the pan. Doing so removes a bitterness they will impart throughout the whole dish if you skip this step.

Serves 6

1/2 tsp cumin seeds

1/2 tsp coriander seeds

1/2 tsp fennel seeds

1/2 tsp dried chile flakes

1/2 tsp ground cardamom

2/3 cup/150 ml buttermilk

2 1/4 lb/1 kg cod fillet, skinless and boneless, cut into six (3 by 5-inch/8 by 12-cm) pieces

1 tbsp olive oil or bergamot oil (see headnote, page 112), to serve

1 lemon, cut into 6 wedges, to serve

coarse sea salt and black pepper

Urad dal

2 1/2 tbsp yellow mustard seeds

4 tbsp/60 g ghee

2/3 cup/120 g urad dal, rinsed

3 large onions, thinly sliced (1 lb 5 oz/600 g)

8 cloves garlic, crushed

1 tbsp tomato paste

3-inch/7-cm piece of ginger, peeled and finely chopped (2 oz/60 g)

4 red chiles, seeded and finely diced

5 stems fresh curry leaves (1/3 oz/10 g)

8 plum tomatoes, quartered (1 3/4 lb/800 g)

5 1/4 oz/150 g baby spinach

1 In a dry frying pan, lightly toast the cumin, corinder, and fennel seeds until their aroma is released and they start to pop. Transfer to a spice grinder or mortar and pestle, along with the chile flakes, cardamom, 1 1/2 teaspoons of salt, and a good grind of black pepper. Grind to a fine powder, then transfer to a large mixing bowl. Pour over the buttermilk, stir to combine, then add the pieces of cod, making sure that all the fish is submerged. Cover with plastic wrap and leave in the fridge to marinate for 4 to 6 hours. Don't leave it overnight, as the fish will break down.

2 To make the dal, place a small pan for which you have a lid over medium-high heat. Once hot, add the mustard seeds and cover with the lid. When you hear the popping begin, after about 1 minute, remove the pan from the heat and give it a little shake. Leave the lid on for another minute before transferring the seeds to a bowl and setting aside.

3 Place the ghee in a medium saucepan over medium heat. Add the urad dal and fry for 2 minutes, stirring often, until fragrant. Add the onions along with 1/4 teaspoon of salt, and cook over medium heat for 8 minutes, until they are soft but have not taken on any color. Add the garlic, tomato paste, ginger, chiles, and curry leaves and cook for another 5 minutes, stirring from time to time, adding a tablespoon or so

of water to the pan if the mixture starts to stick to the bottom. Add the tomatoes and cook for about 15 minutes, stirring from time to time, until they have broken down and started to caramelize. Add the toasted mustard seeds, pour over 1/3 cup/80 ml of water, and cook for another 5 minutes, stirring once or twice, until the tomatoes have completely softened. Transfer the mixture to the large bowl of a food processor with 2 teaspoons of salt and a good grind of black pepper. Pulse a few times—you want the mixture to retain some texture—then return to the pan and set aside somewhere warm until ready to use.

4 Preheat the oven to 425°F/220°C (390°F/200°C convection).

5 Lift the cod out of the marinade and lay the pieces on a foil-lined baking sheet. Place in the oven and roast for 8 to 10 minutes, then broil for a final 2 minutes, until the fish is cooked through.

6 Return the dal to the heat just before serving, and add the spinach. Stir for 30 seconds, just to wilt the spinach, then spoon onto individual plates. Top with the cod, finish with a drizzle of oil, and serve with the lemon wedges.

TURBOT WITH OYSTER MAYONNAISE AND CUCUMBER SALSA

Of all the radishes available—white, purple, black, yellow—it's the white-tipped, pink, and torpedo-shaped breakfast radishes that we often choose to cook with at NOPI. They're slightly milder than other varieties, so they don't tend to dominate a dish in the same way that the more fiery globe-shaped varieties can. Their name comes from the French tradition of smearing radishes with butter and dipping them into a bowl of flaky sea salt before eating them as a snack before lunch. Don't forget to eat the leaves as well: they're not only useful to hold on to when eating the radish, they also—like watercress or arugula—provide a peppery kick.

Once you've prepared the mayonnaise and salsa, which aren't difficult to make and can be kept in the fridge until you're happy to allow feasting to commence, it is only a matter of minutes to put the dish together. It is therefore ideal for (relatively) simple, yet grandly delicious entertaining. All you'll need with it is a slice of good bread or some simply roasted potatoes.

Making your own mayonnaise only takes a moment. If you're looking for a shortcut, start with 1/4 cup/60 g of good-quality store-bought mayo. This can just be blitzed up with the mustard, cayenne, and oysters, and the teaspoon of oyster juice. Either way, the combination of oyster and fish will definitely transport you to the sea. The mayonnaise won't keep, so enjoy the view while you are there.

With thanks to Craig Tregonning, evening chef at Islington, for this.

Serves 6

Oyster mayonnaise
1 egg yolk
1 tbsp white wine vinegar
1 tbsp Dijon mustard
a pinch of cayenne pepper
2/3 cup/150 ml sunflower oil
3 large oysters, shucked
  (1½ oz/40 g), along with
  1 tsp of the oyster juice

Salsa
1 tsp superfine sugar
2 tbsp rice vinegar
1 tsp olive oil
2 small (or 1 large) cucumbers,
  peeled, quartered lengthwise,
  seeded, and cut into ⅓-inch/
  1-cm dice (5¼ oz/150 g)
20 breakfast radishes, or 12 round
  red radishes, cut into ⅓-inch/
  1-cm dice (3½ oz/100 g)

½ medium red onion, finely diced
  (2¾ oz/80 g)
⅓ oz/10 g dill, finely chopped

2 tbsp olive oil, plus extra to serve
6 turbot fillets, skin on, fins
  trimmed (1¾ lb/800 g)
2 tsp/10 g unsalted butter
2 tsp lemon juice
coarse sea salt and black pepper

1 First make the mayonnaise. Place the egg yolk, vinegar, mustard, and cayenne in the small bowl of a food processor, along with ¼ teaspoon of salt. Turn on the machine, then slowly and steadily pour in the sunflower oil, followed by the oysters, oyster juice, and 1 tablespoon of water. Continue to mix until everything is combined and the consistency is thick. Set aside in the fridge until ready to use, but for no longer than 7 hours.

2 Place the sugar and vinegar for the salsa in a small bowl and whisk until the sugar dissolves. Add all the remaining salsa ingredients, along with ½ teaspoon of salt, mix well, and keep in the fridge. Bring the salsa back to room temperature before serving.

3 Place a large frying pan over medium heat and add the olive oil. Season the fish on both sides, using 1 teaspoon of salt (for all six fillets) and a good grind of black pepper, and place half the fish in the pan, skin side up. Fry for 3 minutes, until golden brown, then turn the fillets over, at the same time adding half the butter to the corner of the pan. Cook for 1 or 2 more minutes, basting the fish with the butter once it has foamed up, until cooked through. Remove from the heat, pour over half of the lemon juice, and keep somewhere warm while you repeat with the remaining fish, butter, and lemon juice.

4 To serve, spoon 1½ tablespoons of mayonnaise onto the center of each of six shallow bowls or plates and spread it out to form a circle. Lay the fish on top and serve, with a spoonful of salsa alongside and a final drizzle of olive oil around the dish.

Pistachio and pine nut–crusted halibut with wild arugula and parsley vichyssoise

In the restaurant, we serve this with vichyssoise made from nettles and lovage, rather than the wild arugula and parsley we've suggested here. Lovage is widely available all over Europe, but it's not always easy to get hold of in the U.K., sadly (or in the U.S.). The flavor is a bit like parsley and celery combined with a hint of aniseed. Again, with nettles, unless you are picking your own, the leaves are not as easy to get hold of as they could be, given their natural abundance. If you can find lovage and nettles, though, do try the NOPI-style vichyssoise. Follow the recipe but, instead of the parsley and arugula, use 2¾ ounces/80 g of lovage leaves and 4¼ ounces/120 g of nettle leaves.

We pass all soups that we want completely smooth through a fine-mesh sieve at NOPI, but, if you're not too fussed by a little bit of texture, you can let the restaurant standards slip with this detail. As with all things green and blended, Scully also plunges his container of vichyssoise straight into a big bowl of ice-cold water. Halting the cooking in this way helps preserve the vibrant green color. Your guests will probably forgive you if you also bypass this stage.

The vichyssoise can be a stand-alone soup here, if you like. As with the sea bass in *rasam* (see page 105), we love these sorts of dishes, which are somewhere between a hearty fish soup and a fish dish with a sauce. Whichever way you look at them, they're a meal in themselves, to be served with little more than some crusty white bread to mop up the juices. The soup and the nut crust can be made up to a day ahead of time if you like, and left in the fridge.

Serves 6

6 halibut fillets, skinless and
    boneless (1 lb 14 oz/950 g)
2 tbsp olive oil
2 tbsp lemon juice
12 breakfast radishes, leaves
    and tips left on, sliced in half
    lengthwise (or 6 round red
    radishes, halved)
coarse sea salt and black pepper

*Wild arugula and parsley
vichyssoise*
3 1/2 oz/100 g parsley stems
    and leaves
5 1/4 oz/150 g wild arugula
1 tbsp olive oil
3 tbsp/40 g unsalted butter
2 medium shallots, coarsely
    chopped (3 1/2 oz/100 g)
3 cloves garlic, crushed
1 medium leek, green and white
    parts thinly sliced (7 oz/200 g)
2 large all-purpose potatoes,
    peeled and cut into roughly
    3/4-inch/2-cm pieces (13 oz/370 g)

4 1/2 cups/1 liter chicken stock
1 oz/30 g spinach leaves

Pistachio and pine nut crust
10 tbsp/150 g unsalted butter,
    cut into 1/3-inch/1-cm dice
2 oz/60 g shelled pistachios,
    lightly toasted and coarsely
    chopped
2 oz/60 g pine nuts, lightly
    toasted and coarsely chopped
1/4 tsp superfine sugar
2 tbsp lemon juice

1 Place the butter for the nut crust in a medium saucepan over medium-high heat. Cook for 4 minutes, until the butter is nutty smelling and golden brown. Remove from the heat and strain the butter through a fine-mesh sieve to remove any black bits. Add the pistachios, pine nuts, sugar, lemon juice, and 1/4 teaspoon of salt. Mix well, then spread out on a parchment-lined baking sheet that measures about 6 by 8 inches/16 by 21 cm. Chill in the fridge for 2 to 3 hours, until the butter has set firmly, then cut the mixture into six equal rectangles. Return the rectangles to the fridge until ready to use.

2 To make the vichyssoise, bring a medium saucepan of salted water to a boil and add the parsley and arugula. Blanch for 30 seconds, then refresh under cold water. Strain, squeeze out the excess water, set aside to dry, then coarsely chop.

3 Place the oil and butter in a medium saucepan over medium heat. Add the shallots and sauté for 4 to 5 minutes, stirring once or twice, until soft but not colored. Add the garlic and leek and cook for another 2 to 3 minutes. Add the potatoes and cook for 5 to 6 minutes, stirring frequently, until shiny and glossy. Pour over the chicken stock and bring to a boil over medium-high heat, then simmer for 8 to 10 minutes, until cooked but still retaining a bite. Add the blanched parsley and arugula and cook for a final minute, then remove from the heat and add the spinach, along with 1 1/2 teaspoons of salt and a good grind of black pepper. Transfer to a blender, blitz well until completely smooth, and set aside until ready to use.

4 Preheat the broiler to its highest setting. Spread out the halibut fillets on a large foil-lined baking sheet and brush them with the 2 tablespoons of olive oil. Season with 1 1/2 teaspoons of salt in total and a good grind of black pepper and broil for 6 to 7 minutes, until the halibut is almost cooked. Remove the baking sheet from under the broiler and lay a rectangle of nut butter on top of each fillet. Return to the broiler and cook for a final 2 to 3 minutes, until the crust is golden brown. Remove from the broiler and squeeze over the lemon juice.

5 Warm the vichyssoise and ladle it into shallow, wide bowls. Lay a halibut fillet on top, place the radish pieces alongside, and serve at once.

GURNARD BAKED IN BANANA LEAF WITH PINEAPPLE AND CHILE SAMBAL

This is one of Scully's creations, inspired by the banana tree in his childhood backyard and travels in Thailand in the late 1990s. For all the signs of Scully's pantry in this recipe—the banana leaves, the fish sauce, the shrimp paste, the kaffir lime leaves—there's one thing hiding away that shows our constant interplay in the kitchen: those poppy seeds! Just one teaspoon can go a long way and in many different directions, as anyone who follows Yotam's recipes closely will spot.

If you don't want to make your own red curry paste, there are plenty of good ready-made options available: the Maesri Prik Khing brand is a NOPI favorite and is available online. Just steer clear of anything with preservatives, artificial flavors, and MSG and you'll be okay. You'll need 1/3 cup/80 g for the gurnard. If you do make your own, the recipe on the next page makes 1 1/3 cups/300 g, so you'll have plenty left over for a good few more fish, meat, or vegetable curries. It keeps for up to a month when covered or kept in a sealed container in the fridge. It also freezes well.

Gurnard, until recently dismissed as a trash fish, is enjoying a culinary moment. It's local to British waters, though, so cod, haddock, and hake can be used as an alternative when gurnard's not available. They're all robust enough to be marinated overnight without collapsing. The fish can be baked in parchment paper if you can't get hold of banana leaves. You'll still be transported to Thailand, even if the mode of transportation is not so exotic. If you do use parchment, you won't need to soften it in the oven.

If you want to prepare the recipe in advance, you can take the fish up to the point where it is wrapped in the banana leaf and placed on the baking sheet. You can then keep everything in the fridge, ready to go straight into the oven. Serve with simple sticky rice (see page 83) or steamed jasmine rice.

Serves 4

Red curry paste (if not using store-bought)
1 tsp shrimp paste
4 small shallots, peeled and quartered (2 oz/60 g)
3 large cloves garlic, crushed
1½-inch/4-cm piece of ginger, peeled and coarsely chopped (1¼ oz/35 g)
7 bird's-eye chiles, seeded and coarsely chopped
5 lemongrass stalks, trimmed, lightly bruised with a rolling pin, and finely chopped
18 fresh kaffir lime leaves
1 tsp ground turmeric, or ¾ oz/ 20 g fresh turmeric, peeled and coarsely chopped

1 tbsp coriander seeds, toasted
¾ tsp ground cumin
1 tsp ground cardamom
3 tbsp sunflower oil
⅓ cup/80 ml coconut milk

⅓ cup/80 g coconut cream
long shaved zest of 1 lime
17 oz/500 g gurnard, or another firm white fish, skinless and boneless, cut into four 2 by 4-inch/5 by 10-cm pieces
4 banana leaves, cut into 8 by 6-inch/21 by 16-cm rectangles, or use parchment paper
⅓ oz/10 g baby cress, for garnish (optional)
2 limes, halved, cut side charred in a hot pan if you like
coarse sea salt

Pineapple sambal
1 small pineapple, peeled, tough inner core removed, and flesh cut into ⅓-inch/1-cm dice (10½ oz/300 g)
½ large cucumber, peeled, seeded, and cut into ⅓-inch/ 1-cm dice (5 oz/140 g)
2 red chiles, finely diced
2 small shallots, thinly sliced (1 oz/30 g)
3 tbsp lime juice
1½ tbsp fish sauce
¾ tsp superfine sugar
½ oz/15 g cilantro leaves, coarsely chopped
1 tsp poppy seeds

1 If making your own, start with the curry paste. Preheat the oven to 425°F/220°C (390°F/200°C convection). Wrap the shrimp paste in a small parcel of foil, place in a baking pan, and roast for 8 minutes, until there is a strong fishy aroma. Remove from the oven and transfer to a food processor with all the remaining curry paste ingredients, apart from the coconut milk. Blitz well to form a coarse but uniform paste. Add the coconut milk and blend again until smooth. Store in the fridge until ready to use.

2 Place ⅓ cup/80 g of the curry paste in a large mixing bowl with the coconut cream, lime zest, and ½ teaspoon of salt. Stir to combine, then add the fish. Mix gently but thoroughly so that all the fish gets coated. Cover and leave in the fridge to marinate for 2 hours or up to overnight.

3 Place all the ingredients for the *sambal* in a large bowl, apart from the cilantro and poppy seeds. Mix well and set aside for half an hour, stirring once or twice.

4 Preheat the oven to 425°F/220°C (390°F/200°C convection) (if it is not already on).

5 Place the banana leaves in the oven for a minute: this will help to soften them so they don't split when rolling. Place the leaves on a work surface, shiny side down. Divide the fish among the banana leaves, laying it along the long length of the leaf, then gently but tightly roll each banana leaf to encase the fish, keeping the ends open but making sure the fish doesn't fall out. Place on a baking sheet, seam side down.

6 When ready to serve, place the fish parcels in the oven and cook for 7 to 8 minutes, until the fish is just cooked. Transfer to serving plates and gently open the top of each banana leaf to expose the fish.

7 Stir the cilantro and poppy seeds into the *sambal* just before serving and spoon this alongside or over the fish. Serve with the baby cress, if using, and the lime wedges.

LEMON SOLE WITH BURNT BUTTER, NORI, AND FRIED CAPERS

When Scully worked at Bathers' Pavilion on Balmoral Beach in Sydney, he learned many things about life in the kitchen. The Australian restaurant rating system gives out hats (rather than stars) for outstanding places to eat and Bathers' was a three-hat joint. Scully had worked in many kitchens elsewhere, but this, with its solid tile-top work surface and homemade butter, was in a different league. The hours were long, the head chef tough, the cooking traditional French, and the learning curve steep. It was here that Scully made his first ever tomato concassé (in the kitchens he'd worked in before, it was called passata and it came from a jar) and shucked his first oyster. Getting to the restaurant each day required a long walk up a steep hill overlooking the sea, which also taught Scully that fish never tastes better than when you're eating it while looking out at the sea. For those not privy to a view of the waves, we've ground up some nori seaweed instead, so that you can at least close your eyes and pretend.

Serves 4

about 1/2 cup/130 ml sunflower oil, for frying
2 oz/60 g capers, rinsed and patted dry with paper towels
4 whole cleaned lemon soles (3 1/2 lb/1.6 kg), skin removed, patted dry

2 tbsp olive oil
7 tbsp/100 g unsalted butter, roughly cut into 1 1/4-inch/ 3-cm cubes
2 1/2-inch/6-cm piece of ginger, peeled and finely grated (1 3/4 oz/50 g)

3 tbsp lemon juice
1 sheet nori seaweed, ground in a spice grinder to form 1 tbsp fine powder
1/3 oz/10 g parsley, finely chopped
1 lemon, quartered, to serve
coarse sea salt and black pepper

1 Pour enough sunflower oil into a small saucepan so that it rises 3/4 inch/2 cm up the side of the pan. Place over high heat and, when hot, carefully (the oil will spit!) add the capers and fry for 1 minute, until crisp and starting to brown. Use a slotted spoon to transfer them to a paper towel–lined plate and set aside until ready to use.

2 Preheat the broiler to its highest setting. Lay out the fish on a large foil-lined baking sheet, head side down, and sprinkle with 1 teaspoon of salt. Turn them over, brush with the olive oil, and evenly sprinkle over another 1 teaspoon of salt and a good grind of black pepper. Broil for 8 to 10 minutes, until cooked, then keep somewhere warm until ready to serve.

3 While the fish is boiling, place the butter in a medium saucepan over medium heat. Cook for 5 to 6 minutes, until it starts to foam, turns a light brown color, and begins to smell nutty. Remove from the heat and stir in the ginger, lemon juice, seaweed, and parsley.

4 To serve, spoon 1 1/2 teaspoons of the butter sauce onto each plate and dot with a few fried capers. Place the fish on top, followed by the remaining sauce and capers, spread out along the fish. Serve at once, with the lemon wedges.

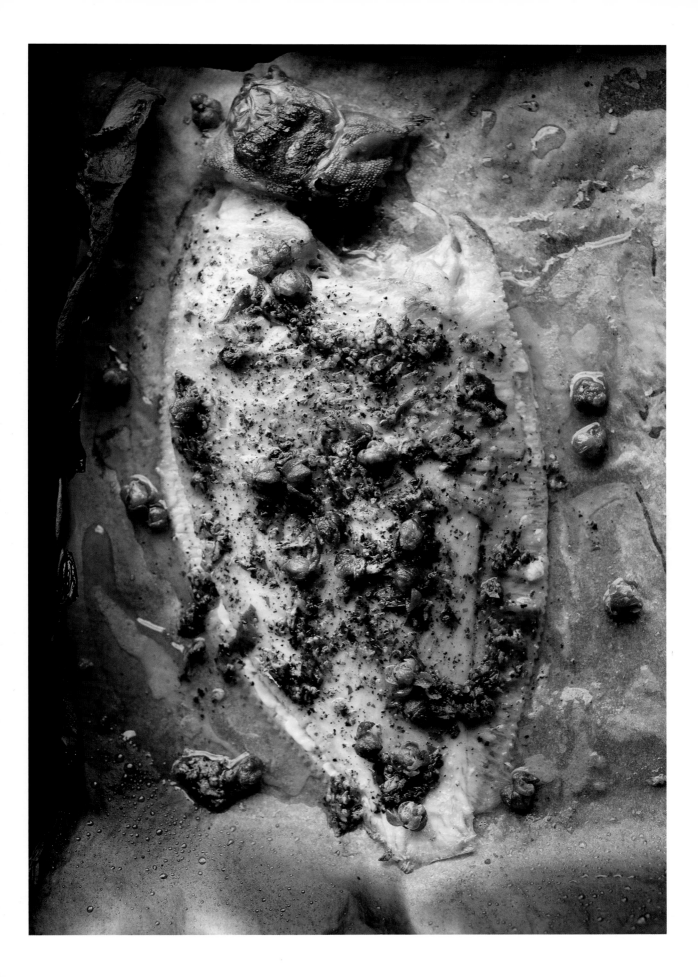

Basil Spätzle in Saffron Broth with Red Mullet, Clams, and Mussels

---

Spätzle are a type of soft egg noodle or dumpling popular in southern Germany and Austria. They're one of Yotam's deserted island meals. The seafood would be there for the catching, and the gnocchi-like dumplings would (with their ability to comfort and nurture) remind him of home.

Cooking the spätzle takes a little bit of practice, and you need to work quite fast when pushing the ribbons of batter off the chopping board into the pot. You'll quickly get the knack, though, and once you do it's a satisfying and fun way to produce an extremely sustaining bowl of food. There are different ways to produce the spätzle ribbons—some pass the batter through a large slotted spoon or metal colander into the water, others drip it in with two teaspoons, some make ribbons with a piping bag. Our chopping board method is, we think, the most straightforward. Experiment each time you make it, though: the colander-pushers are pretty firm in their belief that their method is the fail-safe one.

If you want an alternative here, just the spätzle by themselves—without the seafood broth—are delicious. Once you've made them, give them a final fry in a pan before serving them with some burnt butter drizzled on top. To make the burnt butter, melt about 7 tablespoons/100 g of butter on medium heat for 5 to 6 minutes, until it starts to foam, turns a light brown color, and begins to smell nutty.

Serves 6

Spätzle
4¼ oz/130 g baby spinach
1½ oz/40 g basil leaves
1⅔ cups/200 g all-purpose flour, sifted
2 eggs
¼ tsp grated nutmeg
a scant ¾ cup/200 ml whole milk
coarse sea salt and black pepper

Gremolata
1 oz/30 g parsley, finely chopped
finely grated zest of 1 large lemon
⅓ cup/80 ml olive oil
½ tsp dried chile flakes

Seafood broth
3 tbsp olive oil
2 large shallots, finely diced (5 oz/140 g)
3 cloves garlic, crushed
2 celery stalks, finely diced (3½ oz/100 g)
2 cups/500 ml dry vermouth
1¼ cups/300 ml dry white wine

10½ oz/300 g clams, rinsed well under cold running water
8 oz/250 g cockles, rinsed well under cold running water
10½ oz/300 g mussels, beards removed, shells scrubbed, and rinsed well under cold running water
¼ tsp saffron threads
4 medium tomatoes, quartered, seeds removed and flesh cut into ¾-inch/2-cm cubes (10½ oz/300 g)
1 cup/250 ml chicken stock
6 small red mullet fillets, skin lightly scored (10½ oz/300 g)

1 Bring a medium pan of water to a boil and add the spinach and basil. Blanch for 30 seconds, then drain in a colander. Refresh under cold water and squeeze well to remove excess water. Finely chop and set aside.

2 Place the flour in a large mixing bowl. Add the eggs and nutmeg, along with 2 teaspoons of salt and a good grind of black pepper. Slowly whisk the ingredients together as you pour in the milk, continuously whisking to form a smooth batter. Stir in the basil and spinach and leave in the fridge for 1 hour to thicken.

3 Place all the ingredients for the gremolata in a small bowl, with ¼ teaspoon of salt and a grind of black pepper. Mix well and set aside.

4 To cook the spätzle, fill a large bowl with ice water and bring a large saucepan of salted water to a boil. Using a spatula, spread enough of the batter on a chopping board—a smooth wooden board is perfect—to form a 6-inch/15-cm square, ⅕ inch/5 mm thick. Perch the chopping board on the edge of the saucepan, lifting it up at a 45 degree angle. Using the spatula or a long knife, quickly push the batter in small ribbons, about 1½ inches/4 cm long by ⅓ inch/1 cm wide, into the softly boiling water, cutting them with the spatula as you do. Make sure the water is not boiling too rapidly, as this will cause the spätzle to break up. You will need to do this in two or three batches so that you do not overcrowd the pan. Cook for 1 minute, until the spätzle float to the surface of the water. Use a slotted spoon to lift them out

of the boiling water and plunge them straight into the ice water. Repeat with the remaining batter before draining the spätzle and setting them all aside on a clean kitchen towel to absorb any excess water.

5 For the broth, put the oil into a large saucepan for which you have a lid and place over medium heat. Add the shallots and garlic and cook for 3 to 4 minutes, stirring once or twice, until starting to soften. Add the celery and cook for another minute. Increase the heat, pour over the vermouth and wine, and cook for 5 minutes, until the liquid has reduced by half. Add the clams, cockles, and mussels, cover the pan, and cook for 2 to 4 minutes, until the shells open (throw away any that fail to do so). Use a slotted spoon to scoop out the shellfish into a colander. Set aside and, when cool enough to handle, remove two-thirds of the shellfish from the shells, keeping the remaining third intact.

6 Reduce the heat to medium and add the saffron, tomatoes, stock, and mullet, along with ½ teaspoon of salt and a good grind of black pepper to the saucepan. Cover and cook for 3 minutes, then carefully remove the cooked fillets, skin side up, keeping them somewhere warm while you add the spätzle to half the gremolata. Stir gently, and simmer for 2 more minutes.

7 Divide the broth, shellfish, and spätzle among six shallow bowls and place the fillets on top. Serve at once, with the remaining gremolata spooned on top.

BASIL SPÄTZLE IN SAFFRON BROTH WITH RED MULLET, CLAMS, AND MUSSELS

Scallops with corn and merguez salsa and sorrel sauce

We always serve this with the sorrel sauce at NOPI, but the astringent leaf is not easy to get hold of, even when it's in season during the summer months. You can substitute tender young arugula or mustard leaves plus a squeeze of lemon. Alternatively, serve the dish without the sorrel sauce altogether; with just the salsa and sumac cream, it still works very well.

Shaving the kernels off a fresh ear of corn takes just a minute and, if the corn is super fresh, yields fantastically sweet, little golden gems that can easily be thrown—as is or lightly grilled—into vegetable or legume-based salads. If you can't get fresh corn, a bag of frozen (which is free of the water that makes canned corn soggy, slimy, and completely out of the question in our books) is your next best bet. Don't worry if the fresh kernels clump together; they will break up once they are fried. To make 8 ounces/250 g of kernels, you'll need to start with two ears. In the U.S. it can be difficult to source scallops with their corals still attached, so don't worry if you can't find them. They'll still be stunning without.

Serves 6

Sorrel sauce
2¹/2 oz/70 g sorrel leaves
1 tbsp rice vinegar
2 tbsp olive oil

Sumac cream
2/3 cup/160 g sour cream
2 tsp sumac
1 tbsp olive oil

Scallops and corn salsa
6 tbsp/85 ml olive oil
8 oz/250 g fresh or frozen
corn kernels
1/2 small red onion, finely diced
(2 oz/60 g)
2³/4 oz/80 g piquillo peppers, or
any jarred roasted red peppers,
cut into ¹/3-inch/1-cm dice
2 large celery stalks, cut into
¹/5-inch/5-mm dice (3¹/2 oz/100 g)
1/3 oz/10 g tarragon, finely
chopped

³/4 oz/20 g cilantro leaves,
finely chopped
finely grated zest of 2 limes,
plus 1¹/2 tbsp lime juice
1 red chile, seeded and finely
chopped
10¹/2 oz/300 g uncooked lamb
or beef merguez sausages
30 sea scallops, corals attached
if available (1³/4 lb/800 g)
1 tbsp lemon juice
coarse sea salt and black pepper

1 Start with the sauces. Place the sorrel, rice vinegar, and olive oil in the small bowl of a food processor along with ¹/4 teaspoon of salt and 1 tablespoon of water. Blitz until smooth and set aside in the fridge.

2 Place the sour cream in a small bowl with the sumac, olive oil, and ¹/4 teaspoon of salt. Mix to combine and keep in the fridge.

3 To make the scallops and salsa, place a large frying pan over high heat with 1 teaspoon of the olive oil. When hot, add the corn and fry for 4 to 5 minutes until golden brown, stirring occasionally. Don't worry if a few of the kernels turn black: they will give the salsa a nice smoky flavor. Remove from the heat, transfer to a medium bowl, and set aside to cool. Add the onion, piquillo peppers, celery, tarragon, cilantro, lime zest and juice, chile, 3 tablespoons of the olive oil, 1¹/4 teaspoons of salt, and a good grind of black pepper. Set aside.

4 When ready to eat, wipe out the frying pan and place it over medium-high heat with 1 teaspoon of the olive oil. When the oil is smoking, add the sausages and cook for between 8 and 12 minutes, depending on their thickness, until they are cooked through and golden brown. Remove from the heat and transfer the sausages to a paper towel–lined plate to cool. Cut crosswise into ³/4-inch/2-cm pieces and mix through the corn salsa.

5 Wipe the pan clean again, leaving about 1 tablespoon of fat in the pan, and place over medium-high heat. Toss the scallops with the remaining 2 tablespoons of olive oil and sprinkle over 1 tablespoon of salt and a good crack of black pepper. Use your hands to coat the scallops with the oil, then, when the pan is hot, press half of the scallops firmly down in the pan. Cook for about 4 minutes—the timing will depend on the scallops' size—turning once halfway through, until they are just cooked and golden brown. Remove from the heat, repeat with the remaining scallops, and squeeze over the lemon juice.

6 To serve, spoon the sorrel sauce into the bottoms of six serving plates. Top with the corn salsa and arrange the scallops on top. Serve at once, with the sumac cream alongside.

OCTOPUS AND STIR-FRIED KALE WITH BLACK OLIVE AND GOLDEN RAISIN SALSA

Don't be put off by having to prepare the octopus. They can look pretty beast-like, we know, but just roll up your sleeves and embrace the challenge offered by the tentacled cephalopod!

It's best to buy frozen octopus for this and defrost it before cooking. Freezing helps tenderize the meat and prevents it from becoming chewy. If you start with fresh octopus, however, there are other ways to tenderize. Banging the octopus against a stone wall or step is a method advocated by some, as is using a rolling pin to bash the tentacles. Brining also works, as does popping a wine cork into the cooking pot and blanching the tentacles three or four times in boiling water.

If the octopus challenge is not for you, though, don't turn the page: the salsa and kale both work very well alongside some panfried mackerel fillets.

With thanks to David Bravo for this.

Serves 6

1 large octopus, with head and tentacles (3½ lb/1.8 kg, or 3¼ lb/1.5 kg after it has been cleaned)
1 small celery stalk, chopped into ¾-inch/2-cm pieces (3½ oz/50 g)
1 small fennel bulb, trimmed, chopped into ¾-inch/2-cm pieces (2¾ oz/80 g)
1 small leek, trimmed and sliced
2 thyme sprigs
2 bay leaves
1 tsp black peppercorns
1 tsp coriander seeds

2 cups/500 ml white wine
3 tbsp olive oil
1 tbsp rose harissa, or 1 tbsp regular harissa mixed with ½ tsp rose water
1½ tbsp lemon juice
coarse sea salt

Salsa
1¾ oz/50 g golden raisins
1 small red onion, finely diced (3¾ oz/110 g)
3½ oz/100 g pitted Kalamata olives, sliced into thin circles
1½ tbsp Valdespino sherry vinegar, or another good-quality sherry vinegar

1 tbsp olive oil
⅓ oz/10 g mint leaves

Kale
2 tbsp olive oil
2 tsp/10 g unsalted butter
1 clove garlic, thinly sliced
10½ oz/300 g curly kale, stalks removed and discarded, coarsely chopped (6⅓ oz/180 g)
⅓ cup/80 ml vegetable stock
⅓ cup/80 ml white wine

1 If you need to clean the octopus, cut the head from the body, just below the eyes, and discard the head. Remove the beak from the top of the tentacles by turning the tentacles inside out and pushing the beak through. Peel away and discard any excess skin, leaving the tentacles intact and all still held together at top, with the suckers still on.

2 Put the celery, fennel, leek, thyme, bay leaves, peppercorns, coriander seeds, and white wine into a large, deep pot with 1 teaspoon of salt. Pour over 5 cups/1.2 liters of water, bring to a boil, then reduce the heat to medium-low. Using a pair of tongs to hold the octopus, dip the whole thing into the hot water for about 5 seconds. Lift out, then repeat this process twice more, so that the tentacles curl up. This technique is called "scaring" and will prevent the octopus's skin from peeling during cooking. Return the octopus to the water, so that it is fully submerged. Cover with a cartouche—a round of parchment paper the same diameter as the pan—and place a large plate on top to hold the octopus down. Simmer over medium heat for 40 to 50 minutes, until the octopus is cooked through. You want the texture to be tender, but still retain a bite. The cooking time will vary according to the size of the octopus, so if yours is a smaller one, it might take as little as 35 minutes.

3 Remove the octopus from the pot and set aside to cool before transferring it to the fridge for an hour, until chilled. You should now have about 1 1/2 pounds/650 g of cooked octopus. The stock and vegetables can be discarded.

4 Slice the octopus 3/4 inch/2 cm thick on the diagonal, leaving the tips of the tentacles uncut so that they are about 1 1/2 inches/4 cm long. Place everything in a bowl with 1 tablespoon of the olive oil and the harissa. Mix well to coat, then set aside in the fridge for 2 hours or up to overnight.

5 To make the salsa, place the raisins in a small pan with 1/3 cup/80 ml of water. Bring to a boil, then remove from the heat and set aside for 1 hour, until the raisins are plump and soft. Drain away any remaining liquid and place the raisins in a small bowl with the rest of the salsa ingredients, apart from the mint, along with a good grind of black pepper. Mix well and set aside until ready to serve.

6 To cook the kale, place the olive oil and butter in a medium pan over medium-high heat. When hot, add the garlic and cook for 1 minute, stirring constantly, then add the kale. Keep the stirring constant while you pour in the stock and wine. Add 1/2 teaspoon of salt and a little bit of black pepper and cook for 3 to 4 minutes, until the kale has wilted. Drain the kale, shaking it in the colander to dry, then keep warm until ready to serve.

7 Just before serving, place a grill pan or large frying pan over high heat. Toss the octopus in the remaining 2 tablespoons olive oil and, once the pan is smoking hot, add the octopus and grill or fry for 1 to 2 minutes, turning over or stirring it once or twice, until it is warmed through and charred. You don't want the pan to be overcrowded, so do this in two or three batches if you need to. Transfer to a medium bowl and toss at once with the lemon juice.

8 Divide the warm kale among six plates and scatter the octopus on top. Shred the mint and stir it into the salsa. Sprinkle this over the octopus and serve.

Panfried mackerel with fresh coconut and peanut salad

There are various ways to open a coconut: holding it over a bowl and bashing it until it cracks open, for example. Or draining it by pricking one of the three eyes with a screwdriver and then hitting it with a hammer on a hard floor. Cleavers, heavy chisels, rolling pins—they all work. Some people swear by putting a drained coconut in a hot oven for 15 minutes to get the whole thing to crack. There are lots of options, including, of course, buying the already prepared flesh in the supermarket. However you get to the sweet, white flesh, the resulting coconut in this fresh herb salad is the perfect match for the oily fish here. It also pairs well with any other oily fish, or with Caribbean-style chicken thighs marinated in jerk sauce and grilled. We also love eating the salad on its own, as a light snack.

When making this for four customers in the restaurant, we'll always have two large frying pans on the go so that all the fish can be cooked and plated up at the same time. If you don't have the space for two large pans on your stovetop, or don't fancy the washing up, just cook half the fish and keep them in a low oven while you continue with the remaining fish. Alternatively, dispense with the pans altogether and cook the fish all at the same time under a hot broiler, turning once so that both sides are cooked. You won't have the seared lime halves if you do this, but you can serve the fish with a squeeze of fresh lime instead.

Serves 4

2 limes, halved
8 mackerel fillets (about
    1¹/2 lb/640 g), pin bones
    removed, skin lightly scored
2 tbsp olive oil
coarse sea salt and black pepper

Dressing
1¹/4 oz/35 g palm sugar, coarsely
    grated if starting from a block

5 tsp/25 ml rice vinegar
2 tbsp/30 ml lime juice
1 tsp fish sauce

Coconut salad
7 tsp mirin
7 tsp rice vinegar
2 tsp superfine sugar
1¹/2-inch/4-cm piece of
    ginger, peeled and julienned
    (1¹/2 oz/40 g)

5¹/4 oz/150 g fresh coconut flesh,
    coarsely grated (flesh from
    1 medium coconut)
1 long red chile, seeded and
    julienned
2 green onions, julienned
    (2¹/4 oz/65 g)
4 oz/120 g roasted salted peanuts,
    coarsely chopped
¹/2 oz/15 g cilantro leaves
¹/3 oz/10 g mint leaves, torn

1 Start with the ginger for the coconut salad. Pour the mirin and rice vinegar into a small saucepan with the superfine sugar and a pinch of salt. Place over medium heat, bring to a simmer, and cook, stirring often, until the sugar dissolves. Remove from the heat, add the ginger, and set aside for 10 to 15 minutes, until cool.

2 Next, make the dressing. Place the palm sugar in a small saucepan with 1¹/2 tablespoons of water. Place over medium heat and cook for a couple of minutes, stirring, until the sugar dissolves. Set aside to cool for a few minutes before whisking in the rice vinegar, lime juice, and fish sauce. Set aside.

3 To make the salad, place the coconut, chile, green onions, peanuts, cilantro, and mint in a large bowl. Drain the ginger and add to the salad, discarding the marinade. Pour over the dressing, stir gently and set aside.

4 When you are ready to serve, heat a large frying pan over medium-high heat. Place the lime halves in the pan, flesh side down, and sear for 2 to 3 minutes, until caramelized. Remove from the pan and set aside.

5 Brush the fillets with the oil and season with 1 teaspoon of salt (total for the eight fillets) and a good grind of black pepper. Place half the fish in the pan, skin side down, and cook for 2 to 3 minutes, until golden brown and crisp. Turn the fish over and cook for a final minute. Keep somewhere warm while you continue with the second batch. Transfer the fish to plates and serve each with a seared lime half and salad alongside.

Tuna skewers with coconut mochi cakes and carrot and yuzu salad

───────────────

Yuzu is an East Asian citrus fruit that tastes somewhere between a lime and a mandarin. You can get yuzu juice in some large supermarkets (as well as in specialty stores) but, as an alternative, lime juice also works.

Glutinous rice flour—also known as sweet rice flour—has a very high starch content, which gives it a sticky feel. You can get it in Asian markets as well as in many health food stores. Despite its name, it doesn't contain any gluten—in fact, it is often used in gluten-free baking to bind and bring moisture to all sorts of muffins and pastries. It's the main ingredient in the Japanese dessert mochi, which we give a savory spin here.

If you want to get ahead with your preparation, the mochi cake can be made in advance up to the point where it has been baked and cut, then it can be wrapped in foil. It just needs reheating for a few minutes before serving. The glaze for the tuna can also be made in advance, as can the salad; just keep the dressing separate so the salad doesn't go soggy. All you'll be left to do is cook the tuna and serve.

We serve this as a main dish, but for a smaller, starter-size portion serve only half a piece of mochi, with the tuna off the skewer and alongside the salad.

Serves 6 as a main, 12 as a starter

Tuna and glaze
2/3 cup/150 ml sake
6 tbsp/90 ml mirin
6 tbsp/90 ml light soy sauce
3 tbsp superfine sugar
1 cup/250 ml chicken stock
6 medium tuna steaks, 1 inch/
  2.5 cm thick, cut into 1-inch/
  2.5-cm cubes (2 1/4 lb/1 kg)
2 tbsp sunflower oil
coarse sea salt and black pepper

Coconut mochi cake
2 cups/500 ml coconut cream

2 large lemongrass stalks, gently
  bruised with a rolling pin
8 kaffir lime leaves (fresh or
  frozen)
4 pandan leaves, or 1 vanilla bean,
  split lenghtwise
1 1/3 cups/220 g glutinous rice
  flour
1 1/2 tbsp baking powder
3 tbsp/50 g unsalted butter,
  melted
2 eggs, lightly beaten
1 tsp superfine sugar

Carrot and yuzu salad
2 medium carrots, peeled and
  julienned (5 oz/140 g)

3 1/2 oz/100 g sugar snap peas,
  thinly sliced on the diagonal
7 green onions, thinly sliced
  (3 1/4 oz/90 g)
4 medium red chiles, seeded and
  julienned
5 oz/140 g shiitake mushrooms,
  stems discarded, and thinly
  sliced (3 3/4 oz/110 g)
4 tsp toasted sesame seeds
2 tbsp yuzu juice, or lime juice
3 tbsp rice vinegar
3 tbsp mirin
3/4-inch/2-cm piece of ginger,
  peeled and finely grated
  (1/3 oz/10 g)
2 tsp sunflower oil

1 First make the mochi cake. Place the coconut cream, lemongrass, and kaffir lime and pandan leaves in a medium saucepan and place over medium heat. Bring to a boil, then remove from the heat right away. Set aside for at least half an hour for the flavors to infuse, then strain. Discard the aromatics and set the coconut cream aside.

2 Preheat the oven to 390°F/200°C (360°F/180°C convection).

3 Place the rice flour and baking powder in a large mixing bowl and make a well in the middle. Add the butter, eggs, and infused coconut cream, along with the sugar and 1 teaspoon of salt. Whisk to form a smooth batter, then pour the batter into a parchment-lined 8 by 12-inch/20 by 30-cm baking pan—the size of the pan is important here, as the batter needs to rise 3/4 inch/2 cm up the sides—and bake in the oven for 45 minutes. The batter will double in height and sink again while in the oven. Remove from the oven and set aside to cool. Once cool, flip the mochi cake onto a chopping board, peel off the parchment, trim the edges, and cut into twelve small rectangles, each measuring 1 1/2 by 4 inches/4 by 10 cm. Return the mochi rectangles to the baking pan and set aside. Keep the oven on until ready to serve: the mochi cakes need warming through for 3 to 4 minutes just before they are served.

4 To make the glaze for the tuna, place the sake, mirin, soy sauce, sugar, and chicken stock in a medium saucepan over medium heat. Bring to a boil, then simmer for 35 to 40 minutes, stirring from time to time, until the sauce is shiny and thick. Remove from the heat, transfer to a bowl, and set aside. Cover twelve wooden skewers with water; set aside.

5 Next make the salad. Place the carrots, peas, green onions, chiles, mushrooms, and sesame seeds in a medium bowl and mix well. Whisk together the yuzu juice, rice vinegar, mirin, ginger, oil, and 1/2 teaspoon of salt. Keep the dressing and salad separate until ready to serve.

6 Mix the tuna in a medium bowl with the 2 tablespoons of oil, 2 teaspoons of salt, and a good grind of black pepper. Place about six cubes of tuna on each skewer and set aside. Place a grill pan over high heat and ventilate your kitchen well. When the pan is hot, add the skewers and grill for 3 minutes, turning frequently so that all sides get charred. Remove from the heat and brush the tuna all over with half the glaze.

7 Place two pieces of warmed mochi cake on each plate, the tan side facing upwards. Place two skewers on top of each portion and drizzle the remaining glaze on top. Pour the dressing over the salad, mix to combine, spoon alongside the tuna, and serve.

TUNA SKEWERS WITH COCONUT MOCHI CAKES AND CARROT AND YUZU SALAD

SOFT-SHELL CRAB WITH SWEET BLACK PEPPER SAUCE, OKRA, AND CINNAMON PICKLED CUCUMBER

Okraphobes, don't be put off: you can leave it out if you don't like it! We love okra but the dish still works very well without.

Some chefs make a point of cleaning and trimming soft-shell crabs, but we like to eat them whole. If you use frozen ones, take care when defrosting and handling them, though, so that their small legs don't get broken.

The pepper sauce and pickled cucumber can both be prepared in advance here, but don't be tempted to fry the crab or okra long before you are serving them: they need to be eaten fresh out of the pan. The sauce is a traditional Malaysian one, with the addition of some completely un-traditional pancetta. Both the sauce and the pickle work well alongside lots of things—a fresh tuna or tofu steak, for example, fresh out of the pan. They both keep well in the fridge, so double the recipe, if you like, to save for the next meal.

Serves 6

Pickled cucumber
1 large cucumber, peeled
 (14 oz/400 g)
1/2 cup/120 ml rice vinegar
1 1/2 tbsp mirin
1 1/2 tbsp sake
3 tbsp superfine sugar
3 whole star anise
2 small cinnamon sticks
1 long red chile, seeded
 and thinly sliced
1/3 oz/10 g cilantro, leaves
 and stems coarsely chopped
coarse sea salt

Black pepper sauce
1 1/2 tsp sunflower oil
2 3/4 oz/80 g smoked pancetta,
 cut into 1/5-inch/5-mm batons
4 tbsp/60 g unsalted butter
2 small shallots, thinly sliced
3 cloves garlic, finely chopped
2 stems fresh curry leaves,
 stems removed (1/5 oz/5 g)
2 long red chiles, seeded
 and finely chopped
1 oz/30 g dried shrimp, well rinsed
 and patted dry, then ground
 in a spice grinder or a mortar
 and pestle until flosslike
1 1/2 tbsp superfine sugar
1 1/2 tsp white miso paste
3 tbsp light soy sauce
2 tbsp dark soy sauce
2 tbsp oyster sauce

1/2 cup/120 ml chicken stock
1 tbsp black peppercorns, ground
 in a spice grinder or a mortar
 and pestle until fine

Okra (optional)
about 12 okra pods (4 1/2 oz/130
 g), cut in half lengthwise, seeds
 removed with a small teaspoon

12 soft-shell crabs, defrosted if
 frozen, patted dry carefully
 and thoroughly (20 oz/560 g)
1 1/2 cups/200 g cornstarch
1 tbsp coarse sea salt, coarsely
 ground in a mortar and pestle
 or spice grinder
1 tsp coarse black pepper
about 4 1/2 cups/1 liter sunflower
 oil, for frying

1 First pickle the cucumber. Use a vegetable peeler to shave long ribbons off the cucumber, moving around it as you go and stopping when you get to the seeds. These can be discarded. Put all the ingredients for the pickle into a small saucepan, apart from the red chile, cilantro, and cucumber, along with 3½ tablespoons/50 ml of water and 1 teaspoon of salt. Bring to a boil, then simmer over medium heat for 7 to 8 minutes, until the liquid has reduced by a third and you have about ⅔ cup/150 ml left in the pan. Remove from the heat and set aside for 20 minutes, until the temperature is lukewarm. Place the cucumber ribbons in a small bowl, pour over the pickling liquid, mix to coat, and set aside to cool.

2 To make the black pepper sauce, put the oil in a small saucepan and place over high heat. Once it starts to smoke, add the pancetta and fry for 3 minutes, stirring constantly, until crisp. Drain the pancetta, discarding the fat, and set aside.

3 Return the saucepan to medium heat. Add the butter and once it starts to foam, add the shallots and garlic. Cook for 6 to 7 minutes, until soft and transparent, then add the curry leaves, chiles, and dried shrimp. Cook for 2 to 3 minutes, until fragrant, then add the sugar. Cook for another 1 to 2 minutes, stirring constantly, until the sugar starts to caramelize and darken. Add the miso and stir for a minute before pouring in the light soy sauce, dark soy sauce, oyster sauce, chicken stock, and ⅓ cup/80 ml of water. Return the cooked pancetta to the pan, increase the heat to medium-high, and simmer for 6 minutes. Remove from the heat, stir in the pepper, and set aside to cool. The sauce can be stored in the fridge for up to a week; you just need to warm it through before serving.

4 Place the cornstarch in a medium bowl with the crushed salt and black pepper. Mix well and set aside.

5 When you are ready to serve, add the frying oil to a large saucepan and place over high heat. Add the okra to the cornstarch mix and stir well until thoroughly coated. When the oil is hot (it should be between 340°F and 360°F/170°C and 180°C, if you have a thermometer), add half the okra and fry for 2 to 3 minutes, until crisp. Use a slotted spoon to transfer the okra to a paper towel–lined plate and sprinkle with a pinch of salt. Set aside while you continue with the remaining batches and keep somewhere warm.

6 Dip the crabs in the cornstarch mixture, two at a time, and toss gently to coat. Lower the crabs into the oil and fry for 3 to 4 minutes, turning once, until they are golden brown and crisp. Use a slotted spoon to transfer them to a paper towel–lined plate, sprinkle with a pinch of salt, and continue with the remaining crabs.

7 Stir the chile and cilantro into the pickled cucumber and arrange on serving plates, with the crab and okra alongside. Serve at once, with the sauce in a small bowl alongside.

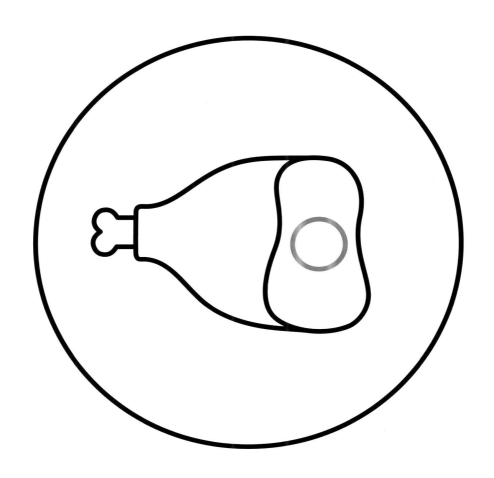

MEAT

LAMB MEATBALLS WITH WARM YOGURT AND SWISS CHARD

Yotam was writing *Jerusalem* at the same time NOPI was opening, so there was a degree of interaction in some of the recipes and ingredients. Recipes like this one were the result. It is an easy dish to make and can be made in full the day before. In fact, we think it tastes even better, reheated, the next day.

Using yogurt in a warm sauce yields a wonderful result—creamy but not cloying—and is an ideal complement to the rich lamb here. Don't worry if the sauce separates: just lift out the meatballs, add a spoonful of stock or yogurt, and whisk it in before returning the meatballs to the pan and continuing.

Don't discard the white stalks of the Swiss chard—they are lovely shaved raw into a salad or blanched and tossed with olive oil, lemon zest, garlic, and chile flakes. If you prefer, use spinach instead of Swiss chard.

Serves 6

2¼ lb/1 kg ground lamb
5¼ oz/150 g fresh bread crumbs
2½ oz/70 g pine nuts, toasted
1 tsp ground cinnamon
2 tsp ground coriander
½ tsp dried mint
4 tsp ground allspice
4 cloves garlic, crushed

¼ cup/60 ml olive oil
1 medium onion, finely chopped
  (4½ oz/120 g)
1 red chile, seeded and finely
  diced
10½ oz/300 g Swiss chard,
  white stalks removed and
  green leaves coarsely
  shredded (4½ oz/120 g)
1¼ cups/300 ml chicken stock

2½ tbsp lemon juice
2¼ cups/500 g Greek yogurt
1 tbsp cornstarch, mixed to
  a paste with 2 tsp water
1 egg, lightly beaten
seeds of 1 medium pomegranate
  (5¼ oz/150 g) (optional)
¾ oz/20 g cilantro leaves,
  coarsely chopped
coarse sea salt and black pepper

1 Place the first six ingredients in a large bowl with half of the allspice, half of the garlic, 2 teaspoons of salt, and ½ teaspoon of black pepper. Mix well, then shape into 2-inch/5-cm meatballs, weighing 3½ ounces/50 g each. You should make about 24 balls.

2 Heat 2 tablespoons of the olive oil in a medium saucepan with the onion and the remaining garlic. Fry over medium heat for 8 to 10 minutes, stirring from time to time, until the onions have softened but not taken on any color. Add the chile and chard and cook for 2 to 3 minutes, until the chard has wilted. Stir in the remaining allspice, along with the chicken stock and lemon juice. Bring to a boil, then remove from the heat.

3 Place the yogurt, cornstarch paste, and egg in a large mixing bowl with ⅔ cup/150 ml of water. Whisk well to form a smooth paste. Gradually spoon the hot chard mixture into the yogurt, stirring well after each addition, until the two mixtures are combined. Add 2 teaspoons of salt, along with a good crack of black pepper, stir, and set aside.

4 Pour the remaining oil into a large, high-sided sauté pan and place over medium-high heat. Add half the meatballs and fry for 4 minutes, turning a few times so that all sides get browned. Remove from the pan and repeat with the remaining batch, adding a little bit more oil if you need to.

5 Wipe out the pan and pour in the yogurt sauce. Bring to a very gentle simmer over medium-low heat—it should barely be bubbling—stirring continuously in one direction to prevent the yogurt from curdling. Return the meatballs to the pan—they should just be covered with sauce—and cook over low heat, covered, for 20 to 25 minutes, until the meatballs are cooked through. Serve at once, with the pomegranate seeds and cilantro sprinkled on top.

Lamb loin with peanuts, coconut milk, and red onion salsa

―――――――――

Both the peanut sauce and the salsa in this recipe are very versatile and work well with other dishes. Large chunks of tofu, for example, marinated in soy sauce, ginger, and lemon juice before being baked or fried, work nicely with the peanut sauce spooned over some rice.

"Fusion cooking" is not a term we often use. Singling out dishes that bring together ingredients from separate cuisines suggests that they should, normally, be kept separate. That being said, the combination of anchovies and coconut milk really *is* fairly unusual and sounds as though it just might not work. Trust us on this one, and in return, we won't mind if you describe it as fusion.

The eye of the loin with all the fat removed is the most tender part of the animal. It's a really versatile cut; it can be panfried, roasted, or grilled. The lamb needs marinating for at least 4 hours, preferably overnight, so we'd start this a day ahead.

Thanks to David Bravo, head chef in the evening at Ottolenghi Spitalfields, for this recipe.

Serves 4

1 lb 7 oz/650 g trimmed lamb loin

5 rosemary sprigs, stems
  discarded and leaves coarsely
  chopped

6 cloves garlic, skin on, crushed
  with the flat side of a large knife

3 tbsp olive oil

4 or 8 caper berries, halved
  lengthwise, to serve

coarse sea salt and black pepper

Peanut sauce

$3^1/2$ oz/100 g roasted salted
  skinless peanuts

5 tsp sesame seeds, toasted

1 medium red chile, coarsely
  chopped

3 anchovies in oil, drained and
  coarsely chopped ($1/3$ oz/10 g)

2 tbsp olive oil

$1^1/2$ tbsp lemon juice

$1/3$ oz/10 g cilantro, leaves and
  stalks coarsely chopped

3 tbsp coconut milk

Pickled onion salsa

$1/2$ small red onion, sliced
  into $1/32$-inch/1-mm rounds
  ($3^1/2$ oz/50 g)

$1/2$ tsp sumac

$1/4$ tsp superfine sugar

1 tbsp cider vinegar

$2^1/2$ oz/70 g jarred piquillo
  peppers, sliced into
  $1/32$-inch/1-mm rounds

$1/3$ oz/10 g parsley, finely chopped

1 Place the lamb loin in a nonmetallic container with the rosemary, garlic, olive oil, 1 tablespoon of salt, and $1/2$ tablespoon of black pepper. Mix well and leave to marinate in the fridge for at least 4 hours or, preferably, overnight. Take the lamb out of the fridge half an hour before you are going to cook it, to bring it to room temperature.

2 Place all the ingredients for the peanut sauce in a food processor. Blitz to form a smooth paste and set aside until ready to use.

3 To make the salsa, place the onion slices in a bowl and add the sumac, sugar, and $1/4$ teaspoon of salt. Rub in the seasonings before pouring over the vinegar. Add the peppers and parsley, mix gently, and set aside.

4 Place a grill pan over high heat. Remove the lamb from the marinade and discard the marinade. Season all sides of the lamb with $1/2$ teaspoon of salt and some black pepper, then sear for 2 to 3 minutes, turning so that all sides get browned. Reduce the heat to medium and cook for another 6 to 8 minutes, until pink in the middle, or a minute or two longer if you want it well done. Let the lamb rest for 2 minutes before cutting it crosswise into $1/3$-inch/1-cm slices. Divide the slices among four plates and spoon the peanut sauce and salsa on top or alongside. Garnish each plate with a caper berry or two and serve.

LAMB LOIN WITH PEANUTS, COCONUT MILK, AND RED ONION SALSA

Smoked lamb chops with eggplant purée, jalapeño sauce, and kohlrabi pickle

The equipment needed for home smoking is not complicated, and it's a great way of infusing a load of flavor into whatever is being smoked. All you need here is lots of foil, a high-sided baking pan (the older the better!), and a cooling rack that fits inside the baking pan. Timing for the smoking are important, so a timer is also useful. You'll need to start this a day ahead, to get the lamb marinating.

Those looking for a shortcut can do without the kohlrabi pickle: there's enough going on for the dish to work without this element. It does all work together very well, though, so the alternative is to double the quantity for the kohlrabi and make a spare batch to have around for future use. Being pickled, its shelf life is long.

The eggplant, jalapeño sauce, and pickle are also great served with other meat: spooned into a pulled pork sandwich, for example, or served alongside a slow-roasted shoulder of lamb.

With thanks to Tom Catley, whose dish this was when he was head chef at Ottolenghi Upper Street.

Serves 4

1³/4 oz/50 g cilantro, leaves
  and stems coarsely chopped
3 cloves garlic, crushed
1¹/4-inch/3-cm piece of ginger,
  coarsely chopped (³/4 oz/20 g)
1 medium red onion, coarsely
  chopped (7 oz/140 g)
2¹/2 tbsp sunflower oil
2 racks of lamb (6 ribs each),
  trimmed, all fat removed apart
  from a thin layer about
  ¹/16 inch/2 mm thick, lightly
  scored (2 lb 10 oz/1.2 kg)

1¹/4 cups/200 g basmati rice
coarse sea salt and black pepper

Kohlrabi pickle
²/3 cup/150 ml rice vinegar
7 tbsp/100 ml mirin
1 tbsp superfine sugar
¹/4 tsp black peppercorns
¹/4 tsp whole cloves
2 whole star anise
1 medium kohlrabi, peeled,
  cut in half and then each half
  thinly sliced into ¹/5-inch/5-mm
  wedges (7 oz/200 g)

Eggplant purée
2 large eggplants (2 lb 2 oz/950 g)
¹/4 cup/60 ml olive oil
3 cloves garlic, thinly sliced
2 tbsp lemon juice
2 tbsp tahini
1 tsp ground cumin

Jalapeño sauce
4 green jalapeño chiles
  (3³/4 oz/110 g)
¹/3 oz/10 g capers
³/4 oz/20 g cilantro leaves
1 tbsp rice vinegar
1 tbsp sunflower oil

1 First marinate the lamb. Place the cilantro, garlic, ginger, red onion, and 1½ tablespoons of the sunflower oil in a food processor. Blitz until fine, then transfer to a large nonmetallic container. Add the lamb racks and then use your hands to coat the meat evenly with the marinade. Cover and leave in the fridge overnight.

2 Place the rice vinegar for the pickle in a small saucepan with the mirin, sugar, peppercorns, cloves, star anise, and 1 teaspoon of salt. Bring to a boil, then simmer for 3 to 4 minutes over medium-low heat, stirring once or twice, until the sugar dissolves. Remove from the heat and set aside for 10 minutes. Place the kohlrabi in a nonmetallic container and pour over the pickling liquid. Seal, then set aside in the fridge until ready to use—it can be used right away, but the flavors will improve if left overnight. It will keep in the fridge for up to a month.

3 Preheat the oven to 425°F/220°C (390°F/200°C convection).

4 To make the eggplant pureé, trim the stems off the eggplants and slice them in half lengthwise. Use a small knife to score the flesh of the eggplant five or six times, then lay them skin side down on a parchment-lined baking sheet. Brush the scored side with 2 tablespoons of the olive oil, press the sliced garlic into the slits, and sprinkle with 1 teaspoon of salt. Place in the oven and roast for 40 minutes, until the flesh is cooked and golden brown. Remove from the oven and scoop out the hot flesh and roasted garlic slices with a spoon into a medium bowl. Add the lemon juice, tahini, cumin, the remaining 2 tablespoons oil, 1¼ teaspoons of salt, and a good grind of black pepper. Mix well and set aside somewhere warm until ready to serve.

5 To make the jalapeño sauce, seed two of the jalapeños and coarsely chop the remaining two. Place all of them in a blender and purée with the capers, cilantro, rice vinegar, sunflower oil, and 1 teaspoon of salt. Blitz well to form a fine purée—add a splash or two of water if the sauce is too thick—and keep in the fridge until ready to serve.

6 Remove the lamb from the fridge half an hour before smoking; it needs to be at room temperature.

7 Line an old, large, high-sided, flameproof baking pan (9 by 12 inches/24 by 30 cm) with two layers of foil. Spread the rice out in the bottom of the pan and add ¼ cup/60 ml of water. Use your hands to rub off the marinade from the lamb, then sit the two racks together on top of a small wire rack above the rice, leaning them together like a crown. Tightly cover the pan with foil—it needs to be fully sealed so that will no smoke will leak out, so you'll need quite a lot of foil to do this. Place the pan across two burners at medium-high heat. It should take 2 to 3 minutes to start smoking and needs another 7 minutes after that. Remove from the heat and set the pan aside, still covered, for 5 more minutes. Uncover the pan and transfer the lamb to a chopping board, discarding the rice. Cut into single lamb cutlets and set aside until ready to serve.

8 Just before serving, preheat a grill pan over high heat. Place the cutlets in a bowl with the remaining 1 tablespoon of sunflower oil, 2 teaspoons of salt, and plenty of pepper. Mix together, and then, when the pan is hot, grill the cutlets for 3 minutes, turning once halfway through, so that both sides are seared. To serve, smear 2 teaspoons of jalapeño sauce on each plate and spoon the warm eggplant purée on top. Lean the cutlets up against the eggplant and serve, with the kohlrabi pickle (drained of its liquid) alongside.

Lamb rump with vanilla-braised endive and sorrel pesto

The use of vanilla in a savory dish is not something we normally go crazy for. Its common pairing with prawns, salmon, or lobster has never fully worked in our minds, but the sweet vanilla really does make sense here alongside the bitter Belgian endive.

Lamb rump—also called lamb chump or chump end in the U.K.—is where the leg and loin meet. It's a very tender and tasty cut of meat, usually served off the bone. The meat needs marinating overnight, so you need to start a day ahead.

If you can't get sorrel—it's only in season during the summer months—an alternative pesto can be made by using ¾ ounce/20 g of parsley and 1½ ounces/40 g of spinach instead, puréed in a blender with 1 teaspoon of lemon juice, 1 teaspoon of red wine vinegar, and all the remaining pesto ingredients, including the mint.

Serves 4

1 oz/30 g rosemary sprigs, stems
　discarded and leaves picked
1/2 oz/15 g thyme sprigs, stems
　discarded and leaves picked,
　plus 2 thyme sprigs
3 cloves garlic
1/3 cup/80 ml olive oil
2 1/4 lb/1 kg lamb rump,
　fat trimmed and scored

2 tbsp/30 g unsalted butter
1 vanilla bean, halved lengthwise
　and seeds scraped
2 large white Belgian endives,
　quartered lengthwise
　(12 oz/350 g)
1 tbsp superfine sugar
1 tsp coriander seeds
3 1/2 tbsp chicken stock
3 1/2 tbsp dry white wine
coarse sea salt and black pepper

Sorrel pesto
1 1/2 oz/40 g sorrel leaves
1/2 oz/15 g mint leaves
finely grated zest of 1/2 lemon
1/2 oz/15 g capers, rinsed
7 anchovies, excess oil removed,
　rinsed if salty (3/4 oz/20 g)
1 clove garlic, crushed
1 medium red chile, seeded
　and diced
1 tbsp olive oil

1 Place the rosemary and thyme leaves and garlic in the small bowl of a food processor with 2 tablespoons of the oil. Blitz to form a rough, dry paste. Rub all over the lamb and leave in the fridge to marinate overnight. Remove it from the fridge half an hour before cooking, so that the meat can return to room temperature.

2 Place all the ingredients for the pesto in a food processor with 1/2 teaspoon of salt and a good grind of black pepper. Blend to form a smooth paste and set aside.

3 Place a large sauté pan over medium-high heat and add half the butter. Once it starts to foam, add 1 1/2 teaspoons of the olive oil, along with the vanilla pod and seeds. Sprinkle the cut sides of the endives, evenly with the sugar and 1/2 teaspoon of salt, and place them in the pan, cut side down. Cook for about 4 minutes, turning once halfway through, until the endive has caramelized and turned golden brown. Lower the heat to medium and add the thyme sprigs, coriander seeds, chicken stock, wine, and a good grind of black pepper. Bring to a simmer and cook gently for 2 minutes, until the endive is tender; it is ready when a small knife inserted near the core

goes in smoothly. Remove the endive from the liquid (which can now be discarded) and set aside somewhere warm until ready to serve. The vanilla bean can be washed and dried and used to make vanilla sugar.

4 Preheat the oven to 425°F/220°C (390°F/200°C convection). Use your hands or some paper towels to wipe off the marinade, then evenly sprinkle 1 tablespoon of salt and plenty of freshly ground black pepper all over the meat. Place a medium ovenproof frying pan over medium-high heat with 1 tablespoon of the oil and, when the pan is hot, add the lamb rump. Cook for 4 to 5 minutes, until golden brown, then turn over. Add the remaining 1 tablespoon/15 g of butter to the pan and cook for another minute, until the butter starts to foam. Transfer the pan to the oven and cook for a final 5 to 6 minutes for medium-rare, or longer if you want it well done. Remove from the oven and set aside to rest for 2 to 3 minutes before slicing 1/3 inch/1 cm thick.

5 To serve, spread 1 tablespoon of pesto on each plate. Lay two pieces of endive on top and lean the lamb slices alongside. Drizzle with the remaining olive oil and serve.

WHITE PEPPER–CRUSTED LAMB SWEETBREADS WITH PEA PURÉE AND MISO

The thought of eating sweetbreads—the juicy little thymus and pancreas glands from young sheep, calves, or lambs—is off-putting to some. They are the most delicate of delicacies, though, so we urge you to put aside any preconceptions you may have. They have an incredibly soft texture that, when the sweetbreads are coated in flour and fried, provides the perfect melt-in-the-mouth contrast to a panfried and crispy crust. Their creaminess also welcomes a range of piquant sauces: garlic butter studded with capers, for example, or a punchy salsa verde.

Lamb sweetbreads are best during the spring, when they are small and incredibly tender. You'll be able to get them from your butcher and they should, ideally, be eaten within a day of purchase. They need to be incredibly fresh, so don't buy them unless they are firm to the touch, nice and plump, and white in color. Veal sweetbreads, if you prefer, can also be used.

For a quick little starter or snack, and as an alternative to guacamole, the pea purée makes a lovely dipping sauce. Serve it with a little bit of feta crumbled on top and a final drizzle of olive oil. The sweetbreads are perfect for a light supper, but if you want to make a more substantial meal, serve them with the Potato and Celery Root Gratin (page 94).

Serves 4

1³/₄ lb/800 g lamb sweetbreads
(between 12 and 16, depending
on size), rinsed gently but well
about 1²/₃ cups/400 ml whole milk
¹/₄ cup/30 g cornstarch
¹/₄ cup/30 g all-purpose flour
1 tbsp ground white pepper
²/₃ cup/150 ml sunflower oil

3 tbsp/40 g unsalted butter
³/₄ oz/20 g pea shoots or mâche,
to garnish
1 lemon, cut into 6 wedges,
to serve
coarse sea salt and black pepper

Pea purée
14 oz/400 g frozen or fresh
shelled peas

1 oz/30 g mint leaves
finely grated zest of 1 lemon
2 tbsp olive oil

Dressing
3 tbsp white miso paste
1¹/₂ tbsp rice vinegar
1 tbsp mirin
¹/₈ tsp sesame oil

1 Place the sweetbreads in a bowl and pour the milk over them. The sweetbreads need to be covered, so add more milk if you need to. Cover and leave in the fridge for 2 hours. Drain, discard the milk, and rinse under fresh water.

2 Bring a large pot of salted water to a boil. Add the sweetbreads and blanch for 5 minutes, until starting to firm up. Drain, then rinse well but gently under cold water before peeling off their outer membrane. Pat dry with a clean kitchen towel and set aside.

3 For the purée, bring a medium pan of salted water to a boil and add the peas. Blanch for 2 minutes, then drain and refresh under cold water. Drain and set aside to dry before placing in a food processor along with the mint, lemon zest, olive oil, and 1 teaspoon of salt. Pulse a few times to form a rough purée, then set aside to come to room temperature until ready to use.

4 For the dressing, place the miso, vinegar, mirin, sesame oil, and 1 tablespoon of water in a small bowl. Whisk to combine, then set aside.

5 Place the cornstarch, all-purpose flour, and ground white pepper in a large bowl along with 1 tablespoon of salt and 1¹/₂ teaspoons of ground black pepper. Roll the sweetbreads in the flour mixture.

6 Place a large frying pan over high heat. Add the sunflower oil and, when hot, add half the sweetbreads. Fry for 10 minutes, turning occasionally so that all sides turn golden brown. Remove from the pan with a slotted spoon and set aside while you fry the remaining sweetbreads. Once browned, return the first batch to the pan, add the butter, and continue to fry for another 2 minutes, basting a few times with the butter, until the crust is crunchy and the sweetbreads are soft and cooked through. Strain in a colander, discarding the fat, and sprinkle with a pinch of salt.

7 To serve, divide the pea purée among four plates and place the sweetbreads on top. Drizzle with the miso dressing, sprinkle the pea shoots on top, place a lemon wedge alongside, and serve.

Venison fillet with date labneh, blackberries, and peanut crumble

There are a number of components to this dish, we know, but don't be put off: all the elements can be prepared the day before, ready for the dish to be put together once the venison is cooked. It's a real show-stealer.

At NOPI, we lay out our trimmed venison fillets on a clean viscose kitchen cloth in the fridge, and leave them for about 16 hours, turning once halfway through, so that both sides can dry out. Getting the meat to this stage before it's seared in the pan results in a sealed crust that rewards all patience. Even if you don't have the time to leave the fillets for the full 16 hours, it's worth employing the same technique, even if only for a couple of hours on each side.

In the restaurant, this is served with caramelized yogurt that has been whipped up, vacuum-packed, and steamed at 185°F/85°C for about 12 hours. In the test kitchen, we experimented with converting this method into one that could be recreated at home: mason jars were filled with yogurt and boiled on the stove for hours and hours, as you would a can of condensed milk to make dulce de leche. The risks were too high, though—glass jars on stoves for hours on end were making everyone nervous—so we returned to the drawing board and simplified the method. The resulting labneh—a thick, strained yogurt—is so very good that doubts were whispered as to why we bothered with the 12-hour steaming at the restaurant in the first place! You'll need to get going with the yogurt a day ahead but, if you don't have the time, you can reduce the number of hours needed to about 6, squeezing the muslin throughout the hanging process to help ease out the liquid.

Use fresh blackberries, if you can, to serve alongside the venison, though the blackberry sauce can be made with either fresh or frozen fruit. The result will be the same: you'll just need to simmer the fresh blackberries for a bit longer in the pan when their liquid is being evaporated. If you can't find stem ginger in syrup—used in the peanut crumble—you can make your own (see page 48) or use crystallized ginger as a substitute.

Serves 4

Labneh
1 generous cup/320 g
   Greek yogurt
1¹/₂ tbsp date syrup
1¹/₂ tbsp pomegranate molasses
coarse sea salt

Blackberry sauce
³/₄ cup/200 ml red wine
²/₃ cup/150 ml port
²/₃ cup/150 ml red wine vinegar
¹/₂ cup/100 g superfine sugar
8 oz/250 g blackberries
   (fresh or frozen)

Juniper salt
2 tbsp juniper berries
3 tbsp coarse sea salt
1¹/₂ tsp cracked black pepper

Peanut crumble
1 oz/30 g cacao nibs
1 oz/30 g unsalted skinless
   peanuts, roasted and finely
   chopped
1¹/₂ oz/40 g stem ginger in syrup
   (see page 48), finely diced

Venison
2 medium venison fillets (2¹/₄ lb/
   1 kg), fat trimmed, then each
   fillet cut in half widthwise, so
   that you have 2 bigger top fillets
   and 2 thinner tail fillets
3 tbsp sunflower oil
5 tbsp/70 g unsalted butter
5 thyme sprigs
5 rosemary sprigs
4 cloves garlic, lightly crushed

To serve
15 fresh blackberries (2³/₄ oz/
   80 g), halved lengthwise
¹/₅ oz/5 g baby basil leaves, or
   regular basil leaves, shredded

1 To make the labneh, place the yogurt, date syrup, and pomegranate molasses in a medium bowl with ¹/₈ teaspoon of salt. Whisk until smooth, then transfer to a muslin-lined sieve. Draw together the edges of the muslin and tie together so that you have a ball of yogurt. Keep it in the sieve, placed over a jug to collect the liquid that drains out. Store in the fridge overnight and remove it 1 hour before serving.

2 To make the blackberry sauce, put the red wine, port, red wine vinegar, and sugar into a medium saucepan. Bring to a boil, then simmer over medium-high heat for 18 to 20 minutes, stirring from time to time, until the sauce is glossy and thick and there is about ³/₄ cup/ 200 ml left in the pan. Add the blackberries, return to a boil, and cook over high heat, stirring gently, for 2 minutes if starting with frozen and 6 minutes if starting with fresh. Transfer to a small bowl and set aside in the fridge to chill. If you make this in advance, you may need to add 2 tablespoons of water to the sauce to thin it down. The consistency should be that of a pourable jam.

3 To make the juniper salt, place the juniper berries and salt in a spice grinder and grind to a fine, sandy texture. Stir in the black pepper. Set aside.

4 Preheat the oven to 360°F/180°C (320°F/160°C convection).

5 Spread the cacao nibs out on a baking sheet and roast in the oven for 5 to 7 minutes. Transfer to a small bowl, add the peanuts and stem ginger, and mix well.

6 Increase the oven temperature to 465°F/240°C (425°F/220°C convection).

7 Pat the fillets dry with a clean kitchen towel, then place on a tray and season with all but 1 teaspoon of the juniper salt. Place two ovenproof frying pans over high heat with 1¹/₂ tablespoons of oil in each pan. When hot, add the larger top fillets to one pan and the smaller tail fillets to the other. Sear the larger fillets for 2 to 3 minutes, until a dark brown crust forms, then turn the fillets over. Cook for another 2 minutes, then add half the butter to the side of the pan, along with half the thyme, rosemary, and garlic. The smaller fillets in the second pan are cooked in just the same way, with the remaining butter and herbs, but for a minute less. Let the butter foam and smell nutty, then cook both sets of fillets for another minute, basting the venison throughout. Transfer the two pans to the oven and roast for 3 minutes. Return to the stovetop and continue to baste for a final minute with the foaming butter. Transfer the fillets to a small baking sheet and pour over the burnt butter, herbs, and garlic. Set aside for 6 to 8 minutes, uncovered, before slicing ¹/₃ inch/1 cm thick and sprinkling the remaining teaspoon of juniper salt evenly over the meat.

8 To serve, spread the labneh out in the middle of each plate and scatter 1 teaspoon of the peanut crumble over each one. Lay the venison slices on top and spoon over the blackberry sauce. Sprinkle over the remaining crumble and serve at once, with the basil leaves and fresh berries dotted alongside.

CHICKEN SUPREMES WITH ROASTED GARLIC AND TARRAGON BRIOCHE PUDDING

Twice Yotam made a bread pudding for his column in the weekend magazine of the *Guardian* and both times he recommended that it would be perfect served alongside a roast chicken. So it's about time for a recipe that builds the bird into the list of ingredients and for there to be no call to serve this with anything at all. Except, perhaps, a simple green salad with a sharp, lemony dressing.

We serve this at NOPI using pheasant breasts, rather than chicken breasts. With pheasant being seasonal—from the beginning of October to the beginning of February—here we've gone for the more available chicken supremes (the breast with first wing joint attached), but if you want to reinstate the original, you'll need six pheasant breasts, weighing 2¼ pounds/ 1 kg, trimmed of excess fat, with their feathers plucked and skin on. The only difference from the recipe below is that the pheasant will need slightly less cooking time than the chicken: just 2 minutes in the pan, then 3 to 4 minutes in the oven, or a minute or two longer if you don't want it pink inside.

Serves 6

Tarragon brioche pudding
2 heads garlic
¼ cup/60 ml olive oil
4 eggs
1¼ cups/300 ml heavy cream
½ tsp freshly grated nutmeg
¼ tsp ground cinnamon
½ oz/15 g tarragon, finely chopped
2 tsp/10 g unsalted butter, melted

14 oz/400 g crustless brioche loaf, trimmed and cut lengthwise into three 9 by 4-inch/22 by 9-cm slices
coarse sea salt and black pepper

Pea and tarragon jus
2 cups/500 ml chicken stock
5 tbsp/70 g cold unsalted butter, cut into ¾-inch/2-cm dice

6½ oz/180 g fresh or frozen shelled peas, blanched for a minute in boiling water and drained
½ oz/15 g tarragon leaves

Chicken
2 tbsp olive oil
6 chicken supremes (3¼ lb/1.5 kg)
⅓ oz/10 g sprigs thyme
7 tbsp/100 g unsalted butter, cut into ¾-inch/2-cm dice
1 tbsp lemon juice

1 Preheat the oven to 425°F/220°C (390°F/200°C convection).

2 First make the pudding. Slice off and discard the top quarter of each garlic head, so that the cloves are exposed, and place the heads on an 8-inch/20-cm square of foil, cut side up. Drizzle with 2 tablespoons of the olive oil, sprinkle with salt, wrap in a tight bundle, and roast for 35 minutes, until the garlic is soft and caramelized. Remove from the oven, set aside for 10 minutes, then squeeze the garlic cloves out of their skins, along with the oil. Use the back of a fork to crush them to a fine paste.

3 Place the eggs in a medium bowl and whisk. Add the cream, nutmeg, cinnamon, and tarragon, along with 1 teaspoon of salt and a good grind of black pepper. Whisk well and set aside.

4 Lightly grease a 9 by 4-inch/24 by 10-cm loaf pan with butter and line it with parchment paper. Brush a bit more butter on top of the parchment once it's inside the pan, then layer the bottom with one long slice of brioche. Spread half the roasted garlic purée on top and pour over a third of the cream mixture. Lay another slice of brioche on top and push this down so that it gets soaked in the liquid. Spread the remaining garlic purée on top, pour over another third of the cream mixture and top with the last slice of brioche. Finish with the remainder of the cream mixture and lightly press down the brioche so that it is fully submerged. Set aside for 30 minutes to let all the liquid to soak into the brioche.

5 Transfer the pudding to the oven and bake for 25 to 30 minutes, until the pudding is cooked through and the brioche is golden brown on top. Check that it is ready by inserting a knife through the middle: it should come out clean. Remove from the oven and set aside to rest for 15 minutes before removing it

from the pan, with the paper still attached. Transfer to a baking rack to cool, then remove and discard the paper. Trim the ends and cut the pudding widthwise into six 1½-inch/3.5-cm slices. Set aside until required.

6 While the pudding is baking, make the jus, then cook the chicken. For the jus, place the chicken stock in a small saucepan and bring to a boil. Cook for about 12 minutes, until reduced by half. Remove from the heat and whisk in the butter, along with ½ teaspoon of salt. Stir in the peas and tarragon and set aside. Warm up slightly before using.

7 To cook the chicken, pour the oil into a large sauté pan and place over high heat. Evenly sprinkle 1 tablespoon of salt over both sides of all the breasts, along with a good grind of black pepper. Once the oil is smoking, lay the breasts in the pan skin side down; you might need to do this in two batches so as not to overcrowd the pan. Fry for 2 to 3 minutes, turning halfway through, until golden brown. Add the thyme and butter to the pan and cook for another minute, basting the chicken with the foaming butter. Transfer to the oven (either in the pan, if it's ovenproof and it will fit, or after first transferring the breasts to a roasting pan) and cook for 12 to 15 minutes, until cooked through. Remove from the oven, drizzle with the lemon juice, and baste with the juices from the pan. Set aside to rest for 1 minute, then slice the breasts in half on the diagonal, or leave whole.

8 A few minutes before the chicken is ready, place the remaining 2 tablespoons of olive oil for the bread pudding in a frying pan over medium-high heat. Add the bread pudding slices and fry for 2 to 3 minutes, turning once so that both sides are golden brown. Divide the bread pudding among six plates and place the chicken breasts on top or alongside. Spoon the warm pea and tarragon jus on top and serve.

Twice-cooked Baby Chicken with Chile Sauce and Kaffir Lime Leaf Salt

----

This is to NOPI what grilled broccoli is to Ottolenghi: a signature dish that our customers will not let us take off the menu. The process of marinating and then cooking the chicken in the master stock makes this a genuine surprise to people who tend to think of the bird as a bland meat and who would not normally order it in a restaurant.

The dish needs a bit of advance planning—the stock needs to be ready so that the chicken can be marinated in it overnight. Most of the work is done in advance, though, so it's a very easy dish to cook for friends. The chicken can be marinated for longer than just a night, if you like: the longer the better, for up to 3 days. At NOPI, we make this with the very young chickens called poussins, which weigh about 1 pound/450 g each. Spring chickens and cornish hens, found in the U.S., are usually larger, though you could use them if you couldn't find poussins—or just use regular chicken supremes (the breast with the first wing joint attached).

Scully was based in the Motcomb Street branch of Ottolenghi, in Belgravia, when he was developing this dish for NOPI. The close proximity of Harvey Nichols to the deli meant that he was often found wandering the aisles of the food hall, looking for inspiration for new and wonderful ingredients. It was here that he discovered lemon myrtle salt. It was the perfect accompaniment to the chicken—until Cornelia costed up the dish for the menu and put a swift ban on the ingredient (as well as any future recon trips to the dangerously fascinating food hall). Nowadays, we source pure myrtle flakes from Queensland and mix them at NOPI with flaky sea salt. If neither the flakes nor the ready-made salt are available to you, our suggested alternative of dried kaffir lime leaf salt (given here) works very well.

The Asian Master Stock used here (page 304) is like liquid gold. Once you've made and cooked with it, it can be kept and used again: the more you use it the more intense and rich the flavors become. We love to poach whole fish in it, but the possibilities are endless. Simply strain the stock, discard the solids, and return the liquid to a boil. Reduce the heat to low and simmer for 5 minutes, skimming any impurities from the surface. Remove from the heat and leave to cool before transferring it to a plastic container. It will keep in the freezer for up to 3 months.

Serves 4

5 cups/1.2 liters Asian Master Stock (page 304)

4 poussins, wing tips clipped, backbones removed, and sliced in half lengthwise, or normal chicken supremes, skin on (4 lb/1.8 kg)

1 lime, quartered, to serve

Chile sauce

1 tbsp peanut oil

7 cloves garlic, finely chopped (3/4 oz/20 g)

1 1/2 oz/40 g ginger, peeled and finely grated (1 oz/30 g)

8 red chiles, seeded and finely diced

4 tsp superfine sugar

3 tbsp ml rice vinegar

Kaffir lime leaf salt

8 medium dried (that's important—fresh won't grind easily) kaffir lime leaves, stems discarded

coarse sea salt

1 Pour the stock into a large saucepan and place over medium-high heat. Bring to a boil, skim any impurities off the surface, then carefully lower the chicken halves into the pot, skin side up. Lay a sheet of parchment paper on top of the stock and place a plate on top of that, to hold the chicken down and keep it submerged in the liquid. Reduce the heat to medium and poach gently for 20 to 25 minutes, until an incision between the chicken's breast and thigh shows a light pink flesh. Remove the chicken from the stock and set aside until both stock and chicken have cooled. Return the chicken to the stock, cover, and leave in the fridge to marinate overnight.

2 To make the chile sauce, heat the peanut oil in a small saucepan and place over medium-low heat. Add the garlic and ginger and sauté for about 6 minutes, stirring occasionally, until fragrant. Add the chiles and cook for a further 12 minutes. Add the sugar and cook for another 2 minutes, stirring the whole time, until caramelized. Add the rice vinegar and cook for 4 more minutes, before adding about 1/4 cup/50 ml of water. Cook for a final 15 minutes, stirring from time to time, until the sauce has the consistency of thick jam. Add 1/8 teaspoon of salt, mix well, and remove from the heat.

3 To make the kaffir lime leaf salt, place the leaves in a spice grinder with 1 teaspoon of salt. Grind to a powder, and then pass the powder through a fine-mesh sieve. If you don't have a spice grinder (or

dedicated coffee grinder) then break up the lime leaf with your hands and chop as finely as you can before mixing with the salt and passing through the sieve.

4 Preheat the oven to 425°F/220°C (390°F/200°C convection).

5 Remove the chicken from the stock and leave at room temperature for 30 minutes. Line a 9 by 12-inch/22 by 33-cm roasting pan with enough foil so that it rises up the sides of the pan. Spoon 1 cup/250 ml of stock into the pan (reserving the rest to cool and freeze), then place the chicken on top, turning once so that it is coated in the marinade. Roast for 15 minutes, basting a few times during cooking. Turn the broiler to high and cook for a further 5 minutes, until the chicken is cooked and the skin is golden brown and crisp. Watch carefully when broiling, as the chicken can burn very quickly. Remove the chicken from the pan and keep somewhere warm.

6 Pour the juices from the pan into a small saucepan. Place over high heat and reduce for 6 to 8 minutes, until you are left with about 1/2 cup/100 ml of rich, sticky sauce.

7 Divide the chicken among four plates, drizzle the reduced marinade on top, and serve at once, with the kaffir lime salt, chile sauce, and lime wedges in mini ramekins or alongside.

CHICKEN LIVERS WITH RED WINE, SMOKY BACON, AND CHERRIES

This started off as a dinner dish at Ottolenghi Upper Street, where the chicken livers were served on toasted brioche, with mushrooms and baby pearl onions. It's probably the most traditional recipe in the book, in the classical French sense. No miso or molasses, no star anise or sumac, no pandan or pomegranate. The thing we love about it, though, is the traditional reliability of flavor—the hard herbs, the red wine reduction—and the fact that there is no twist. Serve with a chunk of good bread, that's all.

Make double the red wine jus, if you want, and freeze half for future use. It's a rich and delicious alternative to gravy when you are next roasting some chicken, game, or beef.

Serves 4

Chicken livers
1 lb 5 oz/600 g chicken livers,
  fat trimmed and sinew
  removed (1 lb/450 g)
2/3 cup/150 ml whole milk
14 oz/400 g smoked bacon,
  cut into 3/4-inch/2-cm cubes
4 tsp/20 g unsalted butter
3/4 oz/20 g parsley, finely chopped
coarse sea salt and black pepper

Red wine jus
3 tbsp olive oil
2 medium red onions, thinly
  sliced (9 oz/250 g)
6 thyme sprigs
1 large clove garlic, peeled and
  left whole but lightly crushed
  with the flat side of a knife
1 bay leaf
5 black peppercorns
1 1/2 tbsp superfine sugar
1 1/4 cups/300 ml red wine
2 cups/500 ml beef stock

Cherries
3/4 cup/200 ml red wine
7 tbsp/100 ml red wine vinegar
6 tbsp/80 g superfine sugar
1 lb 1 oz/500 g fresh cherries,
  pitted (15 oz/420 g) or frozen
  pitted cherries

Radicchio
1 large red radicchio (1 lb/460 g),
  sliced lengthwise into 6 long
  wedges, 2 inches/5 cm thick
1 tbsp olive oil

1 Place the chicken livers in a bowl and pour over the milk. Cover and leave in the fridge overnight. The next day, rinse well, pat dry, and set aside on a paper towel–lined plate.

2 Place a large frying pan over medium-high heat. Once hot, add the bacon cubes and sear for 10 to 12 minutes, stirring from time to time, until golden brown and crisp all over. Pour any bacon fat that is released into a small bowl: you should have about a tablespoon. Transfer the bacon to a paper towel-lined plate and set aside.

3 Place the olive oil for the red wine jus in a medium sauté pan over medium-high heat. Add the onions, along with 1/4 teaspoon of salt, and cook for 5 to 6 minutes, stirring often, until soft. Add the thyme, garlic, bay leaf, peppercorns, and sugar and sauté for 2 to 3 minutes, until the sugar has caramelized. Add the red wine and cook for 5 to 6 minutes, until reduced by half; you should have about 3/4 cup/170 ml of liquid left in the pan. Pour in the beef stock, bring to a boil, then reduce the heat to medium–high. Simmer for 15 to 20 minutes, until the liquid has reduced to just a quarter of its original volume—you should have about 3/4 cup/200 ml left in the pan—and is shiny, with the consistency of light cream. Remove from the heat, strain through a fine-mesh sieve—discarding the aromatics—and set aside.

4 While you are reducing the jus, prepare the glazed cherries. Place the red wine, red wine vinegar, and sugar in a medium saucepan over high heat. Bring to a boil, then reduce the heat to medium-high and cook for about 15 minutes, until the liquid has formed into a sticky glaze and you have about 1/4 cup/100 ml left in the pan. Reduce the heat to low, fold in the cherries and simmer for 2 minutes. Remove from the heat and tip the cherries out on to a parchment-lined pan to cool: they should have a sticky, rich, and shiny coating.

5 Place a grill pan over high heat. Mix the radicchio in a medium bowl with the olive oil, 1/4 teaspoon salt, and some black pepper. When the pan is hot, add the radicchio and grill for 2 to 3 minutes, turning halfway through, until blackened and soft on both sides. Remove from the pan and set aside somewhere warm.

6 When you are ready to serve, put any bacon fat you've set aside into a large sauté pan and place over high heat: you want 2 tablespoons, so top up with olive oil, if you need to. Season the livers evenly with 1 1/2 teaspoons of salt and some black pepper. Once the pan is hot, add the livers. You don't want the pan to be overcrowded, so you might need to do this in two batches. Sear for about 3 minutes, turning once, so that both sides are browned. Add the cooked bacon, the cherries, and the red wine jus to the livers, along with the butter. Cook for a final 2 to 3 minutes, stirring gently, then stir in half the parsley. Serve at once, with the radicchio alongside and the remaining parsley sprinkled on top.

CHICKEN PASTILLA

Time and effort are needed for this dish, but it's well worth it. The result is a delicious, highly exotic feast with which to feed a huge table of friends.

This was first served at NOPI as a rabbit pastilla, which we then changed to pheasant over the Christmas season. We've changed it to chicken here, for the sake of ease of preparation, but switch back to the rabbit or pheasant if you like. Your butcher can help you prepare the rabbit for cooking if you're not keen to do it. Those sticking with chicken must not worry about missing out on a gamey quality, though: the depth of flavor in the sauce—heavy in chocolate, smoky chiles, stock, and wine—imparts such an unusual richness that people are often surprised that they are eating chicken rather than pheasant in the first place.

If you want to get ahead in terms of preparation, you can bring the dish up to the point where the cooked chicken meat has been pulled off the bones and returned to the sauce. Leave the meat in the sauce overnight in the fridge and bring it back to room temperature before continuing the next day.

This recipe was a team effort at NOPI. It started with Scully's need to use up some excess dried chiles that were hanging at the NOPI reception for a while, like garlands to welcome guests as they entered the restaurant. Thanks to Andreu Altamirano, whose recipe for the Catalan spinach came from his father.

Serves 12

3¼ lb/1.5 kg chicken, divided into 6 pieces (or 2 breasts, 2 drumsticks and 2 thighs, all skin on and bone in)
2 tbsp sunflower oil
2 medium onions, thinly sliced (8 oz/250 g)
12 cloves garlic, thinly sliced
4 large plum tomatoes, cut lengthwise into 8 long wedges (12 oz/350 g)
4 long cinnamon sticks

1 tsp pink peppercorns
2 whole dried chipotle chiles, or 1 urfa and 2 dried red chiles, seeds removed
7 tbsp/100 ml brandy
2 cups/500 ml white wine
2 cups/500 ml chicken stock
1½ oz/40 g dark chocolate (70 percent cocoa solids), coarsely chopped
7 tbsp/100 g ghee, melted
8 oz/250 g filo pastry (18 to 20 sheets)
2½ tbsp confectioners' sugar
coarse sea salt and black pepper

Catalan spinach
7 tbsp/100 ml Valdespino sherry vinegar or another good-quality vinegar
7 tbsp/100 ml brandy
3½ oz/100 g currants
5 oz/150 g pine nuts, toasted
1½ tbsp olive oil
1 tsp smoked paprika
3 small shallots, thinly sliced (3½ oz/100 g)
2 cloves garlic, thinly sliced
¾ cup/200 ml heavy cream
10½ oz/300 g baby spinach leaves

1 Season the chicken pieces with 1½ teaspoons of salt and a good grind of black pepper. Heat the sunflower oil in a large sauté pan and place over high heat. Add half the chicken pieces and sear for 7 to 8 minutes, turning once halfway through, until deep golden brown on both sides. Remove from the pan and set aside to cool while you continue with the remaining batch.

2 Keep the pan on the heat and add the onions and garlic. Cook over medium-high heat for 15 to 18 minutes, until the onions are soft, dark, and caramelized like jam. Keep a close eye on it toward the end and stir constantly to make sure it does not catch on the bottom of the pan. Add the tomatoes, cinnamon, peppercorns, and dried chiles, along with ½ teaspoon of salt. Continue to cook for another 4 to 5 minutes, stirring from time to time, then slowly pour over the brandy. Cook for a further 2 minutes, then return the chicken pieces to the pan. Pour over the wine and stock, reduce the heat to low and simmer, covered, for 1 hour. Remove the chicken pieces, increase the heat, and let the sauce bubble away for 30 to 35 minutes, until it has reduced by a quarter and has the consistency of caramel. Remove and discard the cinnamon stick and chiles, add the chocolate and cook for 2 minutes, stirring often. Remove from the heat and set aside to cool; you should have about 2 cups/500 ml in the pan.

3 Once the chicken is cool enough to handle, use your hands to pick all the meat off the bones. Discard the skin. Return the meat to the sauce, stir gently and set aside.

4 To make the Catalan spinach, pour the sherry vinegar and brandy into a small saucepan and place over medium-low heat. Warm through for 5 minutes, then remove from the heat. Stir in the currants and set aside to cool. Mix the pine nuts with 1 teaspoon of the olive oil and the paprika and set aside. Pour the remaining olive oil into a very large sauté pan, place over medium-low heat and add the shallots. Cook for about 8 minutes, until soft and lightly colored.

Add the garlic, along with 1 teaspoon of salt, and cook for a further 2 minutes. Add the currant and brandy mixture along with the pine nuts, and cook for 2 more minutes. Pour in the cream, increase the heat, and cook for 3 minutes, to reduce the sauce by a quarter. Stir in the spinach and cook for 3 to 4 minutes, uncovered, until the leaves wilt and the liquid reduces to about 2 tablespoons.

5 Preheat the oven to 390°F/200°C (360°F/180°C convection).

6 Brush the bottom and sides of a large, deep ovenproof sauté pan—about 10 inches/25 cm wide and 3 inches/8 cm deep—with about a tablespoon of the melted ghee. Brush the first sheet of filo pastry with ghee and line the bottom of the pan with it. Continue with the next sheet, generously overlapping as you go, and leaving about a 3-inch/8-cm overhang over the edge of the pan with each sheet. Work quite quickly here, so that the pastry does not dry out, brushing each sheet liberally with melted ghee. Continue until you have used two-thirds of the pastry sheets, then spoon the spinach mixture into the pan. Spread the chicken mixture on top, then continue with the remaining pastry sheets, tucking the edges into the pan, as though making a bed with fitted sheets. Continue until all the filo has been used before drawing in the overhanging pastry sheets and sealing them on top of the pie with a final brush of the melted ghee.

7 Place in the oven and cook for 1 hour, uncovered. Cover with foil and cook for a final 10 minutes, so that the bottom gets golden brown without the top burning. Remove from the oven and set aside for 10 minutes before inverting the pastilla onto a platter. Sift over the confectioners' sugar using a fine-mesh sieve, and serve warm as is. You can also make a mesh pattern on top of the pastilla by heating up a metal skewer with a blow-torch until red hot. Create parallel lines by burning the sugar in straight lines, spaced ¾ inch/2 cm apart, and then repeating at a 90° angle.

CONFIT DUCK LEG WITH CHERRY MUSTARD AND KOHLRABI SLAW

In the restaurant, we soak our dried sour cherries in Earl Grey tea instead of the plain water suggested here. Once the cherries have been strained, we keep the cherry-flavored Earl Grey liquid so that it can be added to the reduction for the cherry mustard. If you want to do this—the bergamot in the Earl Grey brings a nice twist to the reduction—you'll need to soak the dried cherries in 1 to 1 1/4 cups/250 to 300 ml of Earl Grey tea. Pour the liquid in when you add the red wine, sugar, and red wine vinegar to the saucepan—and you'll then need to simmer it for about 25 minutes, rather than 17, to get the thick glaze consistency required.

It might seem crazy to buy 1 3/4 pounds/800 g of duck fat when the legs that you cook will, themselves, release a lot of fat. Once you have it, though, it lasts for more than 12 months, so you won't need to buy any fat the next time you cook this or are looking for a way to make your roast potatoes rather special.

You'll make more cherry mustard than you need here, but it keeps well in the fridge. It's delicious to have at the ready to serve with cheese, as you would quince paste, or to spoon over mackerel, salmon, or slices of roast beef.

Curing salt
1/2 oz/15 g thyme sprigs, tough stalks removed and leaves coarsely chopped
1/2 oz/15 g rosemary sprigs, tough stalks removed and leaves coarsely chopped
1/3 cup/100 g coarse sea salt
1/2 tsp whole cloves
1 tbsp coriander seeds
1 small cinnamon stick
1 tsp black peppercorns

Duck
3/4 oz/20 g thyme sprigs
1/3 oz/10 g rosemary sprigs
1 tsp black peppercorns
1 head garlic, skin on and cut in half horizontally
4 large duck legs (2 1/4 lb/1 kg)
1 3/4 pounds/800 g duck fat, melted

Cherry mustard
3/4 cup/200 ml red wine
6 tbsp/80 g superfine sugar
7 tbsp/100 ml red wine vinegar
4 1/2 oz/130 g dried sour cherries, soaked in hot water for 30 minutes
7 oz/200 g pitted frozen cherries, defrosted and drained (or 4 1/2 oz/130 g fresh pitted)
1 tbsp Dijon mustard
1 tbsp English mustard powder

Kohlrabi salad
1 medium kohlrabi, peeled, julienned, and stored in ice water until ready to use (8 oz/250 g)
1 Granny Smith apple, cored, julienned, and stored in ice water until ready to use (3 1/2 oz/100 g)
8 large breakfast (or 12 regular round) radishes, thinly sliced and stored in ice water until ready to use (2 3/4 oz/80 g)
1 oz/30 g parsley, finely shredded
2 1/2 tbsp lemon juice
1 1/2 tbsp olive oil
coarse sea salt and black pepper

1 Place all the ingredients for the curing salt in a food processor and blitz well to form a rough paste. Transfer to a large plastic mixing bowl, add the duck legs, and use your hands to rub the salt in evenly and well. Cover the bowl and store in the fridge for 2 hours. Rinse the legs well under water, then pat them dry with a clean kitchen towel. Set the duck legs aside and discard the curing salt.

2 Preheat the oven to 320°F/160°C (280°F/140°C convection).

3 Spread half the thyme, rosemary, and peppercorns for the duck in the bottom of a casserole dish measuring 10 inches/24 cm in diameter by 4 1/2 inches/12 cm deep; for which you have a lid. Add one half of the garlic head, place the duck legs on top, skin side up, and spread the remaining herbs and garlic on top. Pour over the duck fat, cover, and place in the oven. Cook for 3 hours, until the duck meat is very tender and almost falling off the bone. Remove and set aside to cool completely. Strain the duck fat—the herbs can be discarded but the fat should be reserved and saved for future use—then place the duck legs on a wire rack set in a baking sheet and set aside until ready to serve.

4 To make the cherry mustard, pour the red wine, sugar, and red wine vinegar into a small saucepan and place over medium-high heat. Bring to a boil and simmer for 15 to 17 minutes, until the liquid has reduced to 6 to 7 tbsp/80 to 100 ml and has a thick glaze consistency—it should be able to coat the back of a spoon—then set aside.

5 Drain the soaking dried sour cherries and place them in a food processor with the frozen cherries, Dijon mustard, English mustard powder, and 1 1/2 teaspoons of salt. Blitz for 2 minutes to form a smooth paste, then transfer to a small mixing bowl. Fold in the red wine reduction and store in the fridge until needed.

6 Drain the kohlrabi, apple, and radishes for the salad, thoroughly pat them dry with a clean kitchen towel, and place in a small mixing bowl. Add the parsley, lemon juice, olive oil, 1/8 teaspoon of salt, and a good grind of black pepper and mix well.

7 Set the oven to its hottest setting and return the duck to the oven for 4 minutes, to warm through and crisp the skin. Serve at once, with the salad alongside and spoonfuls of cherry mustard on top.

Roasted duck breast with hazelnut beer butter, red quinoa, and mushrooms

For a book where butter has, there's no denying it, a certain presence, it's ironic that this recipe—which has no butter in its list of ingredients—has the word in its title instead!

Serves 6

Hazelnut beer butter
2¹/2 oz/70 g hazelnuts, skin on and lightly toasted
¹/3 cup/80 ml dark beer, ale, or stout
¹/2 tsp Dijon mustard
¹/2 tsp date syrup
5 tbsp/75 ml sunflower oil

Quinoa and mixed mushrooms
²/3 cup/110 g red quinoa
1¹/2 tbsp olive oil
1 medium shallot, finely diced (3¹/2 oz/50 g)
1 large clove garlic, crushed
4¹/4 oz/120 g brown shimeji mushrooms, cut into ¹/3-inch/1-cm slices
4¹/4 oz/120 g oyster mushrooms, cut into ¹/3-inch/1-cm slices

2 tsp rice vinegar
2 tsp mirin
2¹/2 tsp light soy sauce
¹/2 oz/15 g chives, finely chopped

Duck
6 medium duck breasts, skin on (2 lb/900 g)
2 tsp muscovado sugar
1 large lime, cut into 6 wedges
coarse sea salt

1 Place the hazelnuts, beer, mustard, and date syrup in the small bowl of a food processor along with ¹/4 teaspoon of salt. Blitz to form a fine paste, and then, with the machine still running, slowly pour in the sunflower oil until combined. Set aside until ready to use.

2 Bring a small pan of lightly salted water to a boil, add the quinoa, and simmer for 11 minutes, until cooked but still retaining a bite. Drain, refresh under cold water, and set aside to dry.

3 Pour the olive oil into a large sauté pan and place over medium heat. Add the shallot and garlic and sauté for 2 minutes, until starting to soften. Add the shimeji and oyster mushrooms, along with ¹/2 teaspoon of salt, and cook for another 2 minutes, shaking the pan once or twice, until the mushrooms have softened but not gained any color. Add the cooked quinoa, along with the rice vinegar, mirin, soy sauce, and chives. Cook for a final 2 minutes, stirring gently, for the liquid to evaporate, then set aside.

4 Score the skin of each duck breast six times: the scores should be ³/4 inch/2 cm apart and ¹/8 inch/3 mm deep. Mix the sugar with 2 teaspoons of salt and use your hands to rub this very well over the skin of the breasts. Lay half of them in a large cold frying pan, skin side down. (Starting out with a cold pan like this, rather than hot as you might expect is a good way of rendering the fat from the meat as it cooks.) Place the pan over medium heat and cook for 8 to 12 minutes for medium-rare, depending on size. Sprinkle the meat with ¹/2 teaspoon of salt, then turn the breasts over. Cook for another 2 to 3 minutes, basting a few times with the released fat. Remove the duck from the heat and set aside to rest for 2 minutes before slicing it on the diagonal ¹/3 inch/1 cm thick. Keep somewhere warm while you continue with the second batch.

5 To serve, spread a tablespoon of hazelnut butter on each plate. Place the mushroom and quinoa mix on top, lean the duck slices alongside, and serve at once with the lime wedges.

Beef brisket croquettes with Asian coleslaw

These were on the menu from day one at NOPI and we had to bypass the customer union, as it were, when they were eventually moved off to make way for new dishes. They were *the* reason some of our regulars came to the restaurant.

This is another recipe—like Chicken Pastilla (page 172) and the Venison Fillet (page 161)—that we would have filed under "epic" had there been such a chapter. Don't be put off, though. You need to be organized—the stock needs to be ready and the brisket needs to have been cooked—but there is nothing complicated or overtechnical here. Moreover, much of the work can be done in advance, taking the croquettes up to the point where they are ready to be fried. You can freeze them at this stage and fry them from frozen, so when the time for eating comes, it's all actually very relaxed.

Brisket is from the breast or lower chest of the cow. It has a generous fattiness and open-grained texture that make it incredibly suitable for slow roasting. Ask your butcher for the thick end, if you can, and make sure the fat doesn't get trimmed: this is where all the flavor will be.

Make more of the slaw if you wish. Use a mandoline if you have one, or delight in the improvement in your knife skills that will result from all the chopping! The resulting salad is delicious either by itself or piled into a pulled pork or roast beef sandwich.

Serves 8

2¼ lb/1.3 kg beef brisket

3 tbsp sunflower oil, plus about 3½ cups/800 ml for frying

5 cups/1.2 liters Asian Master Stock (page 304); if you don't have the full 5 cups/1.2 liters, add water to bring it up to this amount

1 large carrot, peeled and cut into ⅕-inch/5-mm dice (3¾ oz/110 g)

3 shallots, cut into ⅕-inch/5-mm dice (4 oz/120 g)

1 medium celery stalk, cut into ⅕-inch/5-mm dice (2⅔ oz/75 g)

3 eggs, lightly whisked

2 tbsp whole milk

1½ cups/150 g panko bread crumbs

6 tbsp/50 g all-purpose flour

coarse sea salt and black pepper

Asian coleslaw

1½ oz/40 g palm sugar, coarsely grated if starting from a block

2½ tbsp rice vinegar

3½ tbsp lime juice

3 tbsp olive oil

½ small red cabbage, shredded (10½ oz/300 g)

2 large carrots, peeled and julienned (6 oz/170 g)

7 oz/200 g snap peas, finely shredded

2 red chiles, seeded and thinly sliced

1 oz/30 g cilantro leaves, chopped

1 oz/30 g mint leaves, chopped

2 limes, quartered, to serve

1 Preheat the oven to 360°F/180°C (320°F/160°C convection).

2 Rub 1 teaspoon of salt and ½ teaspoon of pepper all over the beef, making sure that both sides get covered. Put 2 tablespoons of the sunflower oil into a medium Dutch oven and place over medium-high heat. Add the beef fat side down and cook for about 10 minutes, turning so that all sides are sealed and golden brown. Remove from the pan and set aside.

3 Wipe the pot clean and pour in the stock. Bring to a boil, skim off any impurities from the surface, then gently lower the beef, fat side up, into the stock. Place a sheet of parchment paper on top, then a plate to weigh down the brisket. Cover the pan with a lid and cook in the oven for 3½ to 4 hours, until the meat is tender and falling apart. Remove from the oven (you can turn it off now), take off the lid, and leave the brisket to cool in the stock for at least an hour before lifting it out of the liquid and setting it aside. Strain the stock, wipe the pot clean, and then return the strained stock to a boil over medium-high heat. Boil for 8 to 10 minutes, until about half the liquid—around ¾ to 1 cup/200 to 250 ml—is left in the pan and it has the consistency of thick syrup. Take care not to thicken it too much, as it will become bitter. Set aside.

4 Heat the remaining 1 tablespoon of sunflower oil in a medium frying pan. Add the carrots, shallots, and celery and sauté over medium-high heat for 10 to 12 minutes, until soft. Remove from the heat and set aside to cool.

5 Meanwhile, use your hands to pull off and discard the fat from the brisket, and then use your hands or a knife to finely shred the meat. Place it in a large mixing bowl along with the cooked vegetables and 6 or 7 tablespoons/100 ml of the master stock reduction. Mix well and use your hands to shape the mixture into small, flat round croquettes weighing

1½ oz/40 g each: you should make about 24. Place them on a parchment-lined baking sheet in the fridge for at least an hour to firm up—any less and they won't hold together as much as they need to before being fried.

6 Mix together the beaten eggs and milk and place the mixture in a bowl. Pour the bread crumbs and flour into separate bowls, then coat the croquettes—flour first, egg next, followed by the crumbs, pressing these into the croquettes—and set aside until ready to cook.

7 To make the coleslaw, place the palm sugar in a small saucepan along with 2 tablespoons of water. Heat, stirring constantly, until the sugar dissolves, then remove from the heat and stir in the rice vinegar, lime juice, and olive oil along with 1½ teaspoons of salt and some black pepper. Place all the remaining ingredients for the salad in a large bowl and pour over the dressing. Stir gently and set aside.

8 Preheat the oven to 390°F/200°C (360°F/180°C convection).

9 Pour enough sunflower oil into a large sauté pan so that it rises ¾ inch/2 cm up the sides. Place over medium-high heat and, when hot, add a batch of croquettes (don't crowd them together) and cook for 3 to 4 minutes, turning once so that both sides are golden brown. Transfer to a baking sheet and continue with the remaining batches, adding more oil if needed. Once all the croquettes are on the baking sheet, place in the oven for 8 minutes, or until the centers are heated through. While they are in the oven, place the remaining master stock reduction in a small pan over medium heat and warm through. Place three croquettes on each of six plates and drizzle with the reduction. Serve with the slaw alongside, with the lime wedges.

Roasted beef tenderloin with cucumber kimchi and fresh plum

There are some ingredients that will always show the hand of either Scully or Yotam at work in a dish. When thinking about names for this book, Pandan and Pomegranate was thought of, to highlight our two pantries at play. Sumac and Star Anise was another, as was Miso and Molasses. There's one thing, though, that's so much a part and parcel of *both* our cooking styles that you won't be able to guess where a recipe originated: a shared love of anything fermented. Miso paste, fish sauce, shrimp paste, oyster sauce, Parmesan cheese, the Iranian *kashk* that Yotam loves so much: the list is a long one. There was, therefore, a whole of lot of team excitement for this dish when it appeared.

Kimchi—fermented vegetables—is Korea's national dish and is eaten with every meal. Family recipes are a closely guarded secret but the one universal ingredient is time: the longer you can leave your raw vegetables to mature and ferment in the spices, the more pungent and dramatic the result will be. Don't be put off by the smell: it's all part of the experience. One of Scully's first jobs was working for Novitel aboard the Sydney showboats, knocking out meals for four hundred Korean tourists at a time. The combination of ten kilos of kimchi plus the heat of a boat's hull is a memory of Scully's that we should be grateful to not have too many details on.

A quick alternative to making your own kimchi is to buy it (or some sauerkraut) ready-made and stir in some peaches or plums just before serving.

Gochujang is the Korean fermented red chile paste that Scully loves to pile up on the open shelves in the basement of NOPI. Its taste is distinct— it's got the sweet kick from the chiles with a savory, almost Marmite-like (or Vegemite-like, as Scully would feel compelled to correct) element, brought into the equation by the fermented soybeans and glutinous rice powder from which it's made. We urge you to seek it out in Asian stores or online, but, if you can't find it, an adequate alternative can be made by mixing 1/4 cup/60 ml of dark soy sauce with 1/4 cup/60 ml of fish sauce and 1 teaspoon of sugar. Finely chop four red bird's-eye chiles and mix these in before leaving it to sit for a couple of hours.

Nanami togarashi (also called *shichimi togarashi*) is a common Japanese seven-spice mixture. See the headnote to the French Beans with Freekeh and Miso (page 56) for more information.

Serves 6

Kimchi

2 large cucumbers, peeled and then shaved with a vegetable peeler into long thin strips, stopping when the seeds are reached (1 lb 5 oz/600 g)

2 tbsp superfine sugar

3 carrots, peeled and shaved with a vegetable peeler into long, thin strips (8 oz/220 g)

1 1/2 tbsp fish sauce

1 1/2 tbsp light soy sauce

2 tbsp rice vinegar

8 green onions, trimmed and julienned (3 1/2 oz/100 g)

6 cloves garlic, thinly sliced

2-inch/5-cm piece of ginger, peeled and julienned (1 3/4 oz/50 g)

3/4 oz/20 g cilantro, coarsely chopped

3 plums or small peaches, halved, stones removed, cut into 1/5-inch/5-mm wedges (7 oz/200 g)

1/2 cup/140 g Korean gochujang red pepper paste

1 tbsp sunflower oil

1 tbsp light soy sauce

1 tbsp mirin

4 cloves garlic, crushed

1 1/2-inch/4-cm piece of ginger, peeled and finely grated (1 1/4 oz/35 g)

3 1/4 lb/1.5 kg beef tenderloin, fat removed, cut into two pieces, each about 2 1/2 by 4 1/2 by 6 inches/6 by 12 by 16 cm (2 lb 10 oz/1.2 kg)

coarse sea salt

To serve

1 tsp nanami togarashi, or a good pinch of regular dried chile flakes

---

1 Place all the ingredients for the kimchi, except for the cilantro and the plums, in a large bowl. Cover and leave in the fridge for at least 24 hours—the longer the better.

2 To marinate the beef, place the red pepper paste, sunflower oil, soy sauce, and mirin in a large bowl. Mix to form a smooth paste before adding the garlic and ginger. Mix again, then place the beef in the bowl and use your hands to rub the paste all over the meat. Refrigerate for 24 hours.

3 Preheat the oven to 425°F/220°C (390°F/200°C convection).

4 Remove the meat from the fridge at least an hour before cooking it: you want it to be room temperature. Rub off the marinade and keep this aside for later. Place a grill pan over high heat and, when smoking hot, add the beef. Cook for 3 to 4 minutes, turning so that all sides get charred. Transfer to a parchment-lined baking sheet, brush all sides with the reserved marinade, and roast in the oven for 9 to 12 minutes for medium-rare, another 2 to 3 if you want it medium. Remove, cover with foil, and set aside to rest for 10 minutes before slicing the beef 1/5 inch/5 mm thick and dividing among six plates.

5 Stir the cilantro and plums into the kimchi just before serving and spoon alongside the beef. Sprinkle over the *nanami togarashi* and serve.

ROASTED BEEF TENDERLOIN WITH CUCUMBER KIMCHI AND FRESH PLUM

Pepper-crusted beef tenderloin and fennel salad with pecorino and truffle

In the weird world of NOPI dishes, this is pretty much a 15-minute supper in terms of prep time required, despite (you'll have to forgive us) the 4-hour (or overnight) interval for the meat to marinate.

Truffle oil is one of NOPI's must-have pantry ingredients, but it's not to everyone's liking. If you find the taste overpowering, just replace it in the dressing with a little more olive oil.

Serves 4

1/2 oz/15 g thyme sprigs, leaves finely chopped
1/3 oz/10 g rosemary sprigs, leaves finely chopped
1 1/2 tbsp black peppercorns, finely crushed with a mortar and pestle
1 1/2 tbsp pink peppercorns, finely crushed with a mortar and pestle

2 1/4 lb/1 kg tenderloin beef, fat removed, cut into two pieces, each about 3 by 4 inch/ 8 by 10 cm (2 lb/900 g)
2 tbsp Dijon mustard
coarse sea salt

Truffle dressing
1 tbsp Dijon mustard
2 tbsp lemon juice
1/4 cup/60 ml olive oil
2 tbsp truffle oil (optional)

Salad
2 large celery stalks, sliced widthwise into 1/8-inch/3-mm pieces (5 oz/140 g)
6 baby or 1 regular fennel bulbs, tops and bottoms trimmed, sliced lengthwise into 1/8-inch/ 3-mm strips (5 oz/140 g)
1 oz/30 g parsley leaves
3 1/2 oz/100 g pecorino, thinly shaved

1 Place the thyme, rosemary, and black and pink peppercorns in a small bowl with 2 1/2 teaspoons of salt. Place a sheet of plastic wrap underneath each piece of beef—large enough to wrap it up—then brush the mustard all over the meat. Scatter the herb and salt mixture evenly over both sides of the meat, making sure they are well coated. Draw up the plastic wrap to wrap each piece tightly, twisting the ends to make it very secure, and place in the fridge for at least 4 hours, preferably overnight.

2 To make the dressing, place the mustard and lemon juice in small bowl. Slowly pour in both oils while whisking continuously until well combined. Whisk in 1 tablespoon of water, along with 1/3 teaspoon of salt, and set aside.

3 Preheat the oven to 500°F/260°C (480°F/250°C convection) or the highest setting. Place a large baking sheet in the oven to heat up.

4 Remove and discard the plastic wrap from the meat and place both pieces of meat on the hot baking sheet. Roast for 8 minutes, then reduce the oven temperature to 425°F/220°C (390°F/200°C convection) and continue to cook for another 12 or 14 minutes for medium, or longer if you want the beef well done. Remove from the oven, cover the meat with foil, and leave to rest for 5 minutes.

5 Place all the salad ingredients in a bowl and pour the dressing over it just before serving. Mix gently and divide among four plates. Slice the beef against the grain 1/5 inch/5 mm thick. Arrange these alongside the salad and serve.

HANGER STEAK WITH CARAMELIZED SHIITAKE KETCHUP AND PICKLED RED ONION

Make more of the ketchup than you need here. This is brown sauce, NOPI-style. It's a rich and addictive addition to any cold meat sandwich, and is also great with baked tofu and brown rice. Making your own dashi for the ketchup is simple and delicious—and you'll have the shiitake stems to use up—but don't worry if you don't have the ingredients or the time. Dashi powder is readily available as an alternative; just put 1 tablespoon into a bowl and pour in 1²/₃ cups/400 ml of water.

Hanger steak is a large, sausagelike strip of meat from the center of the animal. It runs next to the diaphragm and is dark red. The depth of flavor is what we love here: it's well marbled, with an almost chewy texture, but if you allow the meat to rest properly after cooking this is not a problem. The crucial thing with cuts like this is to slice them against the grain. The difference in texture depending on how you cut the meat is huge: slicing with the grain will result in something tough and chewy. Bavette steak (also called flap steak), from the other end of the inner flank, has a texture similar to hanger steak and is another favorite cut.

Serves 6

6 tbsp/100 g barley miso or brown rice miso

6 cloves garlic, crushed

3 tbsp mirin

3 tbsp sake

3 tbsp sunflower oil, plus 1 tbsp for frying

4 pieces hanger steak, trimmed of sinew, but some fat left on (2¼ lb/1 kg)

Shiitake ketchup

8 oz/250 g shiitake mushrooms, stems and cups separated, both thinly sliced but kept separate

3 small sheets kombu, broken in half if they don't fit into the saucepan (½ oz/15 g)

¼ cup/50 g superfine sugar

2½ tbsp light soy sauce

1 tbsp/15 g unsalted butter

1½ tsp Valdespino sherry vinegar, or another good-quality sherry vinegar

coarse sea salt and black pepper

Pickled red onion with grilled cucumber

3 small Lebanese cucumbers (9 oz/260 g) or 1 regular cucumber, trimmed, unpeeled, and cut lengthwise into ⅓-inch/1-cm slices

3½ tbsp olive oil

3 medium red onions, root ends trimmed, cut into 1¼-inch/3-cm wedges, and then separated into individual petals (13 oz/ 375 g)

3 tbsp Valdespino sherry vinegar, or another good-quality sherry vinegar

¾ oz/21 g chopped tarragon leaves

1 Place the miso in a small mixing bowl along with the garlic, mirin, sake, sunflower oil, and a grind of black pepper. Mix well to form a paste, then transfer to a nonmetallic container. Add the steaks and use your hands to rub the marinade into the meat so that it is evenly coated. Cover and set aside in the fridge for 4 hours or, preferably, overnight. The steaks need to be brought back to room temperature before they get cooked, so take them out of the fridge half an hour beforehand.

2 To make the shiitake ketchup, place the shiitake stems and kombu in a small saucepan. Add 2 cups/450 ml of water and set aside to soak for 15 minutes. Place over medium heat and cook for about 8 minutes, until the water is nearly boiling. Strain and set aside. The kombu and stems can be discarded.

3 Place a medium saucepan over medium-low heat and spread the sugar evenly over the bottom of the pan. Cook for 7 to 8 minutes, resisting the urge to stir, until the sugar is a light caramel color. Carefully add the soy sauce—it will sizzle rapidly, so take care here—stir to get rid of any lumps, then add 2 tablespoons of water. Continue to stir, then add the mushroom caps. Stir to combine, so that they are evenly coated, then increase the heat to medium-high. Keep cooking for 3 to 4 minutes, until the moisture has evaporated and the mushrooms have caramelized. Add the strained mushroom and seaweed stock, mix well, bring to a boil, and cook for about 8 minutes, until the sauce has reduced by half. Remove from the heat, transfer to a food processor, and blitz to form a smooth, thick sauce. With the machine still running, add the butter and sherry vinegar, along with a pinch of salt and a grind of black pepper. Continue to blitz to form a fine purée: the texture should be nice and smooth, so add a splash of water if you need to. Set aside in the fridge until ready to use—it will keep for at least 2 weeks. Remove it from the fridge an hour before serving; it should be room temperature, rather than fridge-cold.

4 To grill the cucumbers, mix the cucumber slices in a small bowl with 1 1/2 tablespoons of the olive oil, 1/4 teaspoon of salt, and a crack of black pepper. Preheat a grill pan over high heat and, once hot, add the cucumber slices—you might need to do this in two batches. Cook for 4 minutes, turning once halfway through, so that both sides are charred. Remove from the heat and set aside to cool before cutting the cucumber into 3/4-inch/2-cm squares. Transfer to a mixing bowl and set aside.

5 To make the pickled red onion, bring a medium saucepan of salted water to a boil over high heat. Add the onion petals and blanch for 4 to 5 minutes, until soft but still retaining a bite. Drain, then add to the cucumber with the sherry vinegar, the remaining 2 tablespoons of olive oil, 1/4 teaspoon of salt, and a grind of black pepper. Mix well and set aside. Mix in the tarragon when you are ready to serve (it discolors if you leave it too long).

6 Preheat the oven to 425°F/220°C (390°F/200°C convection).

7 Remove the steaks from their marinade and keep the marinade aside. Place a grill pan over high heat and add 1 tablespoon of sunflower oil. When hot, add the meat—you might need to do this in two batches—and grill for 6 to 8 minutes, turning once halfway through so that both sides are grilled.

8 Transfer the steaks to a wire rack and place the rack in a parchment-lined baking sheet. Brush half the marinade evenly over both sides of the steaks; the remainder can be discarded. Transfer the steaks to the oven and cook for 3 to 4 minutes for medium-rare: cooking any longer will make the meat very tough. Remove from the oven and let them rest for 3 to 4 minutes before slicing 1/5 inch/5 mm thick against the grain. Spread about 1 1/2 tablespoons of ketchup on each plate and place the beef on top. Serve at once, with the pickled red onion alongside.

GRAPE LEAF BEEF PIE

You can easily do without the bone marrow here, but it is packed with flavor and adds a creamy richness, so we would urge you to try to get hold of some. Extracting the paste-like fatty marrow from the bone is very easy. Help it along by soaking the marrow pieces in salted water for an hour or so, and then, once softened, just stick your thumb in and pop out the marrow.

Serves 8

3 tbsp olive oil
1 medium celery root (1 lb 3 oz/ 550 g), peeled, trimmed, and cut into 1/3-inch/1-cm dice (1 lb/460 g)
1 medium onion, cut into 1/3-inch/1-cm dice (5 1/4 oz/150 g)
2 cloves garlic, crushed

14 oz/400 g ground beef
1 tsp ground cinnamon
1 tsp ground allspice
4 1/2 oz/130 g Arborio rice
1 tomato, finely diced (3 1/2 oz/100 g)
1 oz/30 g pine nuts, toasted
1 oz/30 g barberries (see page 198)
1 tsp dried mint
1/5 oz/5 g mint leaves, shredded

7 oz/200 g jarred grape leaves (about 36), rinsed well and patted dry
1 3/4 oz/50 g beef bone marrow (optional; see headnote)
2 cups/500 ml beef stock
1 cup/250 g Greek yogurt
1 lemon, cut lengthwise into 8 wedges, to serve
coarse sea salt and black pepper

1 Pour the oil into a medium high-sided ovenproof sauté pan, about 10 inches/25 cm wide, and place over medium-high heat. Add the celery root and cook for 5 to 6 minutes, stirring from time to time, until it starts to turn a very light brown. Add the onion and garlic, along with 1 teaspoon of salt, and cook for another 2 minutes, stirring once or twice, to soften. Set aside to cool, then transfer to a bowl and wipe the pan clean.

2 Place the beef, cinnamon, allspice, rice, tomato, pine nuts, barberries, and dried and fresh mint in a large mixing bowl, along with 1 teaspoon of salt and a good grind of black pepper. Use your hands to mix well, then add the celery root mixture. Stir and set aside.

3 Line the bottom of the same sauté pan with a circle of parchment paper and, one by one, lay two-thirds of the grape leaves in the pan, shiny side down and slightly overlapping, to cover the bottom and rise up slightly over the sides of the pan. Place the beef mixture inside and press down evenly. Make five or six teaspoon-sized dents in the beef mixture and spoon in the marrow. Draw the edges of the leaves over the filling and lay the remaining grape leaves on top, shiny side up, so that the beef is well sealed and the leaves are tucked in nicely.

4 Preheat the oven to 390°F/200°C (360°F/180°C convection).

5 Pour the stock over the pie and place an ovenproof plate or pan lid on top, to keep the pie immersed in liquid and gently pressed down. Place over medium-high heat and bring to a boil before reducing the heat to low and simmering gently for 15 minutes. Transfer to the oven, still covered with the plate, and cook for 45 minutes, until the beef is cooked through and most of the stock has been absorbed. Remove from the oven and set aside, uncovered, for 10 minutes for the last of the stock to be soaked up. Carefully invert onto a clean plate, remove the parchment paper and serve at once, with large spoonfuls of the yogurt and the lemon wedges.

ROASTED PORK BELLY WITH CRUSHED BUTTERNUT SQUASH AND APPLE AND WALNUT SALSA

Scully thought he knew all there was to know about getting a good crackling on his pork belly until, at a food show in Sydney in 2009, he learned the real secret. It was passed on to him by a woman in her late seventies. Scully didn't get her name, but he did get her secret of rubbing half a lemon all over the pork skin, squeezing out the juice as you go, before sprinkling the salt over. It paves the way to crackled glory.

Both the squash and the salsa are great as sides to other dishes: the squash goes with any roasted bird or wine-braised shallots and the salsa is wonderfully happy spooned on top of any grilled oily fish.

Serves 4, generously

3/4 oz/20 g thyme sprigs
12 large cloves garlic, skin left on but bruised with the flat side of a large knife
4 lemongrass stalks, lightly bruised with a rolling pin
4-inch/10-cm chunk of ginger (3 1/2 oz/100 g), unpeeled and cut into 1/3-inch/1-cm slices
3 1/4 lb/1.5 kg pork belly, ribs intact and skin on
1 lemon, halved

3 tbsp coarse sea salt
2 cups/500 ml dry white wine

Butternut squash
1 large butternut squash (3 1/4 lb/ 1.5 kg), peeled, seeded, and cut into 3/4-inch/2-cm chunks
2 tbsp olive oil
2 tbsp/30 g unsalted butter
1 tbsp rice vinegar
3 tbsp white miso paste

Salsa
1 Granny Smith apple, unpeeled, quartered, cored and cut into 1/3-inch/1-cm dice
2 1/2 oz/70 g walnuts, toasted and lightly crushed
1 3/4 oz/50 g pickled walnuts, rinsed and cut into 1/3-inch/1-cm dice
1 tbsp rice vinegar
2 tbsp yuzu juice (or lime juice, if unavailable)
1 tbsp mirin
1/3 oz/10 g tarragon, finely chopped
3 tbsp olive oil
coarse sea salt and black pepper

1 Preheat the oven to 465°F/240°C (425°F/220°C convection).

2 Spread the thyme, garlic cloves, lemongrass, and ginger over the bottom of a high-sided 10 by 13-inch/24 by 32-cm roasting pan. Lay the pork belly on top of the herbs, skin side up, and use paper towels to thoroughly pat the meat dry. Rub the lemon all over the pork skin, squeezing the juice out as you rub. Set aside to dry for 10 minutes before sprinkling half the salt evenly all over the skin. Place in the oven and roast for 1 hour, until the crackling is semi-hard and the salt has turned gray: the aromatics will be very crisp and charred at this point, but don't worry: this is normal.

3 Remove from the oven and scrape off and discard the salt. Spread the remaining half of the salt evenly all over the skin, then return it to the oven. Cook for another half an hour, until the crackling is solid and hard. Remove the tray from the oven and reduce the oven temperature to 375°F/190°C (340°F/170°C convection). If a bubble has formed on the skin, insert a small knife and gently push it down to let out the air. Pour the wine into the roasting pan, taking care not to touch or wet the sides or skin of the pork belly, followed by 1²/₃ cups/400 ml of water. Return the pan to the oven and cook for another hour. Reduce the heat to 230°F/120°C (210°F/100°C convection) and cook for a final hour. Remove from the oven and set aside to rest for 30 minutes.

4 While the pork is roasting for the last hour, prepare all the ingredients for the butternut squash

and the salsa, and as soon as the pork is out of the oven increase the oven temperature to 425°F/220°C (390°F/200°C convection).

5 Mix the squash with the olive oil and spread it out on a large baking sheet. Roast in the oven for 30 to 40 minutes, until cooked through and golden brown. Transfer to a large bowl, add the butter, and use a potato masher to crush the squash—don't overmash it, as you want some texture to remain—before stirring in the rice vinegar, miso, 1 teaspoon of salt, and a grind of black pepper. Keep warm.

6 Mix together all the ingredients for the salsa in a medium bowl, along with ¹/₂ teaspoon of salt and a grind of black pepper.

7 Transfer the rested pork to a chopping board. The liquid left in the roasting pan can either be discarded—it's done its work on the pork—or used as a base for a soup or a stew. Discard the herbs from the pork and use a metal spoon or pastry brush to scrape or brush off any excess salt from the skin, then use a large serrated knife to slice the meat into evenly sized rectangles, 1¹/₄ to 1¹/₂-inch/3 to 4-cm thick. If you want to remove the ribs before you slice the meat, you can pull and twist them out, but otherwise you can slice between them and serve the meat on the ribs.

8 To serve, divide the warm crushed squash among four plates and place a slice of pork on top. Spoon the salsa alongside or on the side and serve.

Spiced pork roast with physalis relish

We always try to suggest alternatives for ingredients you have to work a bit to find. Some things are so distinct, though, that their taste really is hard to replicate. Annatto seeds, available in Asian or Latin grocers, natural food shops, and online, are one of these. Also known as achiote, the taste of these yellow-orange seeds is not strong but it is unique—slightly peppery with a hint of nutmeg. They're what gives Red Leicester cheese its color, and they are often used in Mexican and Caribbean cooking as food coloring. They're a key part of the marinade for the pork here, but if you can't get hold of any, don't pass this recipe by! The relish alone is well worth making and works well served with any simply grilled meat.

If you can't get hold of physalis (cape gooseberries), try making the relish with either regular gooseberries or tomatillos, which have a longer growing season than either gooseberries or cape gooseberries, and peak in June and July.

You'll need to get started a day ahead here, for the meat to marinate overnight.

Serves 6, generously

1 oz/30 g annatto seeds

2 dried chipotle chiles, seeded and ground fine in a spice grinder

1¹/2 tsp dried oregano

2 tsp ground allspice

¹/2 small onion, coarsely chopped (2¹/2 oz/75 g)

3 cloves garlic, crushed

¹/2 cup/120 ml orange juice

¹/3 cup/80 ml cider vinegar

finely grated zest of 1 lime, plus 1 tbsp lime juice

2¹/4–2¹/2 lb/1 kg boneless pork butt, large areas of fat cut to about ¹/4 inch/.24 cm, cut in half and tied to form two small roasts

coarse sea salt and black pepper

Chile paste

1 tbsp sunflower oil

1 small shallot, finely diced (1¹/2 oz/40 g)

1 large clove garlic, crushed

2 dried chipotle chiles, seeded, soaked in warm water for 15 minutes until soft, and drained

1¹/2 tsp cider vinegar

Relish

1¹/4-inch/3-cm piece of ginger, peeled and finely grated (1 oz/30 g)

2 tbsp sake

2 tbsp mirin

2 small green jalapeño chiles, seeded and finely diced

1 medium red chile, seeded and finely diced

2 tbsp olive oil

7 oz/200 g physalis, halved; or 11 oz/320 g fresh gooseberries, kept whole; or 5 tomatillos, husks removed, cut into ¹/5-inch/5-mm wide wedges

¹/3 oz/10 g cilantro, leaves and stalks finely chopped

1 Place 1 cup/250 ml of water in a small saucepan and bring to a boil over medium heat. Add the annatto seeds and simmer for 15 minutes, until they have softened enough to crush between your fingers and the water is vibrant red. Remove from the heat and set the pan aside, covered, for 1 hour, for the seeds' bitterness to be released. Drain the seeds, discard the liquid, then transfer the seeds to a blender or food processor with the chipotle powder, oregano, allspice, onion, garlic, orange juice, cider vinegar, lime zest, lime juice, 2 teaspoons of salt, and 1 teaspoon of freshly cracked pepper. Blitz to form a smooth purée, then transfer to a large nonmetallic container. Add the pork and use your hands to coat thoroughly. Cover and set aside in the fridge overnight. The meat needs to be room temperature before it goes in the oven, so take it out of the fridge 1 hour before cooking.

2 To make the chile paste for the relish, put the sunflower oil in a small saucepan and place over medium-high heat. Add the shallot and sauté for 2 minutes, until soft and transparent. Add the garlic and chipotle chile and sauté for another minute before adding the vinegar and a pinch of salt. Remove from the heat and transfer to the small bowl of a food processor. Blitz to form a fine paste and set aside.

3 To make the relish, place the ginger in a medium bowl with the sake, mirin, jalapeño, red chile, olive oil, 1 teaspoon of salt, and all the chile paste. Mix well, then add the physalis, crushing gently with a fork but leaving some whole. Mix together and set aside: the cilantro should be stirred in just before serving.

4 Preheat the oven to 425°F/220°C (390°F/200°C convection).

5 Lift the pork out of the marinade and set the marinade aside. Put the pork on a roasting rack, and place in a foil-lined baking pan. Roast for 20 minutes, then brush half the marinade over the pork. Reduce the oven temperature to 320°F/160°C and roast for another 30 minutes. Turn the pork over, brush the remaining marinade over the pork, and roast for 1 hour to 1 hour and 15 minutes. The pork should be light pink in the middle but cooked through and tender. If you have a meat thermometer the temperature should be 162°F to 167°F/72°C to 75°C. Remove from the oven and set aside to rest for 10 minutes before cutting the pork widthwise into ¹/3-inch/1-cm slices. Serve warm, with some relish spooned alongside.

Braised pig's cheeks with celery root and barberry salad

Barberries are a staple of the Ottolenghi and NOPI kitchens. It's amazing to think that Scully had never heard of them before Yotam raved about the dark red dried Iranian berries he loves so much. They have a sweet-sour sharpness that raisins lack and they bring a welcome burst of astringency to a dish. They work equally well cutting through a rich and sticky meat such as pig's cheeks as they do in lighter dishes like roasted vegetables or frittatas. You can get barberries in Middle Eastern grocers or online, but if you don't have any, chopped up dried sour cherries or dried currants soaked in lemon juice can be used instead.

You will have about 2 1/2 cups/600 ml of braising liquid left over here, which, like Asian Master Stock (page 304), should be treated like liquid gold. It's gelatinous, rich, and packed full of flavor, so keep it in the fridge or freeze it to use as a stock for your next soup or stew. If you want to prepare the celery root in advance, keep it covered with ice-cold water to prevent discoloration, then drain and pat it dry before the salad is put together.

Use a mandoline if you have one for the celery root: being eaten raw, it needs to be cut very fine indeed. The pig's cheeks can be prepared well in advance—a day or two before you want to serve. You can take the recipe up to the point just before the salad is made.

Please excuse us for using three (!) types of wine here. Once you've seen and tasted the rich, complex, and glossy sauce coating the melting cheeks, this extravagance will suddenly make total sense.

Serves 8 as a starter,
4 as a main

20 pig's cheeks, trimmed of all
    hard fat and sinew (3 lb/1.4 kg)
3 tbsp coarse sea salt,
    plus extra for seasoning
3 tbsp sunflower oil
2 tbsp/30 g unsalted butter
2 large carrots, peeled and cut
    into ¾-inch/2-cm chunks
    (8 oz/250 g)
1 large onion, peeled and cut
    into 1¼-inch/3-cm wedges
    (7 oz/190 g)

1 small leek, cut into ¾-inch/
    2-cm chunks (5 oz/150 g)
3 medium celery stalks,
    cut into ¾-inch/2-cm chunks
    (4½ oz/130 g)
7 cloves garlic, peeled and
    lightly crushed
¾ cup/200 ml Madeira,
    or a rich red wine
1 tsp black peppercorns
½ oz/15 g thyme sprigs
⅓ oz/10 g rosemary sprigs
2 bay leaves
4½ cups/1 liter beef or
    chicken stock

Celery root and barberry salad
1 tsp superfine sugar
¼ cup/40 g dried barberries
1 small celery root, peeled
    and julienned (14 oz/400 g)
1½ oz/45 g parsley,
    finely chopped
¼ cup/60 ml olive oil
2½ tbsp lemon juice
black pepper

Madeira jus
3 tbsp superfine sugar
⅔ cup/150 ml Madeira
⅔ cup/150 ml port
¾ cup/200 ml red wine

1 Place the pig's cheeks in a bowl with the salt. Rub the salt evenly over the meat. Cover and refrigerate for at least 2 hours or overnight.

2 Preheat the oven to 265°F/130°C (230°F/110°C convection). Wash the salt off the cheeks and pat dry. Put half of the sunflower oil into a large heavy-bottomed ovenproof sauté pan for which you have a lid, and place over high heat. When hot, add half the cheeks and sear for 6 to 7 minutes, turning once, until both sides are golden brown. Remove from the pan and set aside while you add the remaining sunflower oil and continue with the second batch.

3 Remove any excess oil from the pan—don't worry about wiping it clean—then reduce the heat to medium-high and add 4 teaspoons/20 g of the butter. When it starts to foam, add the carrots, onion, leek, celery, and garlic. Sauté for about 10 minutes, stirring occasionally, until golden brown. Add the Madeira and simmer for 1 minute. Add the peppercorns, herbs, and stock and bring back to a simmer. Return the cheeks to the pan, making sure they are submerged. Cover with a round of parchment, place a plate on top to keep the pig's cheeks submerged in the liquid, and then place the lid on the pan. Put the pan in the oven and cook for about 2½ hours, until the meat is soft and tender but not falling apart. Lift out the pig's cheeks and set aside. Strain the braising liquid, discarding the vegetables but preserving the liquid. Allow the cheeks and the liquid to cool, then put both into the fridge until ready to use.

4 Make the salad 45 minutes before you're ready to serve. Place 7 tbsp/100 ml of water in a small saucepan and bring to a boil. Add the sugar, stir to dissolve, then add the barberries. Remove from the heat and allow to cool before straining and discarding the liquid and setting aside. Place the celery root and parsley in a large bowl. Mix together the olive oil and lemon juice in a small bowl with 1 teaspoon of salt and a good grind of black pepper. Pour this over the celery root, along with the barberries, stir gently, and set aside for about half an hour, for the celery root to soften.

5 Next make the Madeira jus. Place a large sauté pan over medium heat, add the sugar, and cook for 4 to 5 minutes, stirring, until the sugar caramelizes and is dark golden brown. Very carefully add the Madeira, port, and red wine. Simmer over medium-high heat for about 15 minutes, until you have about ¾ cup/ 200 ml of liquid left, and set aside.

6 To serve, skim any fat off the braising liquid and pour 1⅔ cups/400 ml of it back into the pan in which you cooked the cheeks (reserve the remaining liquid for another use) and add the Madeira jus. Bring to a simmer and cook for 10 to 15 minutes, uncovered, until reduced, to about 1 cup/250 ml. Return the pig's cheeks to the pan, along with the remaining 2 teaspoons/10 g of butter. Simmer for 10 minutes, until the meat is warm, and the jus is thick.

7 Divide the salad among the plates and place the cheeks alongside. Drizzle the remaining jus from the pan over the meat and serve at once.

BRAISED PIG'S CHEEKS WITH CELERY ROOT AND BARBERRY SALAD

Bourbon-glazed spare ribs with smoked corn salad

In recipes like this one, where only half the stock reduction is called for, the remainder can be frozen and used as the base for another sauce or soup, or added to the braising liquid for a dish such as the Braised Pig's Cheeks (page 198). The glaze here is also great for marinating other things: chicken wings for barbecuing, for example, or cubes of tuna or tofu before they're grilled.

Beyond a large saucepan or wok, a roll of foil, and a good ventilator (or open window), you don't need any special equipment to smoke food at home. It's not for everyone, though, so skip this stage if you like. The ribs also work well alongside a salad where the corn kernels are just blanched for a minute and refreshed, before being mixed with the remaining salad ingredients.

If you do make the smoked corn salad, though, it can be used as a side for all sorts of other dishes: some simply grilled tiger prawns and slices of pancetta, for example. It's also delicious just by itself.

If your corn comes with the husks already removed, you can use rice for smoking the kernels instead. Line the bottom of your pan or wok with a big sheet of aluminum foil and spread 2 cups/200 g of uncooked rice (along with the lemon thyme) on top. The initial cooking time, if you do this, will need to be reduced from 5 minutes to 3 minutes. Precise timings for the smoking are important here: just a minute too long and the smoky flavor becomes far too dominant.

Serves 6

2¼ lb/1 kg pork baby back ribs, cut into 12 sections, each with 2 or 3 ribs
¼ cup/80 g coarse sea salt
1½-inch/4-cm piece of ginger, peeled and julienned (1¼ oz/35 g)
1 medium onion, coarsely chopped (4 oz/120 g)
6 cloves garlic, crushed
8 whole star anise
1 cinnamon stick
1 tsp black peppercorns
5½ cups/1.5 liters chicken stock
7 tbsp/100 ml Shaoxing rice wine
7 tbsp/100 ml rice vinegar

Smoked corn salad

4 large ears corn, with husks (2¼ lb/1 kg) or without (2 lb/900 g)
½ oz/15 g lemon thyme sprigs
3 tbsp lime juice
2 tsp maple syrup
¼ cup/60 ml olive oil
1 green chile, seeded and thinly sliced
¾ oz/20 g cilantro leaves
¾ oz/20 g mint leaves
¾ oz/20 g parsley leaves
4 green onions, thinly sliced (1½ oz/45 g)
coarse sea salt

Glaze

3 shallots, thinly sliced (4½ oz/130 g)
1½ cups/350 ml bourbon
¼ cup/60 ml maple syrup
2 tsp Szechuan peppercorns
1½ tbsp lemon juice
2 tbsp sesame oil
3 tbsp ketchup
1½ tbsp rice vinegar
2 dried red chiles
2 cloves garlic, lightly crushed

1 Place the ribs in a large bowl with the salt. Rub it all over the meat and set aside for an hour.

2 Rinse the ribs well under cold water, gently rubbing off all the salt, and pat dry. Put them into a large saucepan for which you have a lid, and add the ginger, onion, garlic, star anise, cinnamon, and peppercorns. Add the stock, along with the rice wine and rice vinegar. Bring to a boil, then reduce the heat to medium-low and simmer gently, covered, for an hour.

3 Lift out the pork and set it aside. If you are not serving them in the next couple of hours, let the ribs cool and store them in the fridge, covered, until ready to use. If you do this, make sure you bring them back to room temperature before you coat them in the glaze before serving.

4 Strain the liquid, discarding the onion, garlic, and spices, and return it to the pan. Place over high heat and cook for 30 to 35 minutes, until the liquid has reduced to just ¾ cup/200 ml. Remove from the heat and set aside. Chill the liquid if you are not serving the ribs in the next 2 hours.

5 To make the salad, remove the husks from the corn and use them to line the bottom of a large saucepan or wok that is deep enough to fit a colander or metal steaming basket inside, and for which you have a lid. Add the thyme sprigs and place the pan over high heat. Once the husks and thyme begin to smoke, after about 6 minutes, place the colander in the pan

and place the ears of corn inside it. Use a lid to seal the pan, then smoke for 5 minutes (or 3, if you are using rice in the bottom of the pan; see headnote page 201). Remove from the heat and set aside, covered, for another 5 minutes. Remove the lid and set aside to cool.

6 Stand each ear of corn on a chopping board and use a large, sharp knife to shave off rows of kernels, cutting from top to bottom. Cut deep enough into the cob so that some of the kernels remain in clusters (this isn't essential; it just looks good). Set the corn kernels aside and discard the cobs.

7 About 45 minutes before you are ready to serve, place all the ingredients for the glaze, along with half of the stock reduction, in a large pan. Bring to a boil, then simmer over medium-high heat for 20 to 25 minutes, until the liquid has reduced to about ¾ cup/200 ml and has the consistency of syrup. Return the pork ribs to the sauce and stir gently so they all get coated. Cook for about 7 more minutes over medium heat, stirring once or twice, until the ribs are warmed through and sticky.

8 Just before serving, finish the salad by placing the lime juice, maple syrup, olive oil, and chile in a large bowl with 1 teaspoon of salt. Whisk to combine, then add the corn kernels, herbs, and green onions and mix together. Place two sections of ribs on each plate—one leaning against the other—and serve with the corn salad alongside.

QUAIL WITH BURNT MISO BUTTERSCOTCH AND POMEGRANATE AND WALNUT SALSA

We went through a miso stage where the sweet, umami-rich white or brown paste found its way into every dish possible. Miso ice cream, miso dressings, miso soup. The inspiration for this particular incarnation was David Chang's *Lucky Peach* magazine, which told how pastry chef Christina Tosi used burnt miso in a banana pie that was so addictive it soon went by the name Crack Pie. The miso is cooked in the oven to the point where it turns almost caramel-like. After a bit of experimenting, we found it worked as well in a savory dish as it did in a sweet incarnation. Boneless chicken thighs also work well here, as an alternative to the quail.

Serves 8 as a starter,
4 as a main

1/2 cup/150 g white miso paste, at room temperature
3 1/2 tsp mirin
2 packed tbsp light brown sugar
2 tsp sherry vinegar
3 tbsp/40 g unsalted butter, at room temperature

2 tbsp sunflower oil
8 whole quail, deboned, with wing tips left on (2 1/2 lb/1.1 kg)
coarse sea salt and black pepper

Salsa
5 1/4 oz/150 g pomegranate seeds (seeds of 1 medium pomegranate)
2 1/2 oz/70 g walnuts, toasted and coarsely chopped

1 1/4 oz/35 g pickled walnuts, rinsed, skins removed, finely chopped (optional)
2 tsp pomegranate molasses
2 tbsp Valdespino sherry vinegar, or another good-quality sherry vinegar
1 tbsp olive oil
3/4 oz/20 g parsley, finely chopped

1 Preheat the oven to 320°F/160°C (280°F/140°C convection).

2 Use a rubber spatula to spread the miso paste thinly and evenly onto a parchment-lined baking sheet. Place the baking sheet in the oven and roast for 20 to 25 minutes, until the miso has turned to dark caramel: the edges should look burnt and the middle dark golden brown. Remove from the oven and set aside to cool. Scrape the burnt miso off the parchment, breaking it as you go, and transfer the pieces to a food processor, along with the mirin, sugar, vinegar, butter, and 1 tablespoon of water. Blitz well for 5 minutes to form a smooth, aerated paste.

3 Place all the ingredients for the salsa, apart from the parsley, in a medium bowl with 1/4 teaspoon of salt and 3 tablespoons of water. Mix well and set aside until ready to use, stirring the parsley in just before serving.

4 When you are ready to serve, set the broiler to its highest setting.

5 Place a large sauté pan over high heat and add the sunflower oil. Season the quail with 1 teaspoon of salt and a good grind of pepper and, once the pan is hot, add them, breast side down, in batches. Sear for 5 minutes, turning once so that both sides get some color. Transfer the quail to a foil-lined baking sheet and spread 1 tablespoon of miso butterscotch evenly over the skin of each bird. Broil for 1 to 2 minutes, until the miso starts to bubble and caramelize. Serve at once, with the salsa spooned on top or alongside.

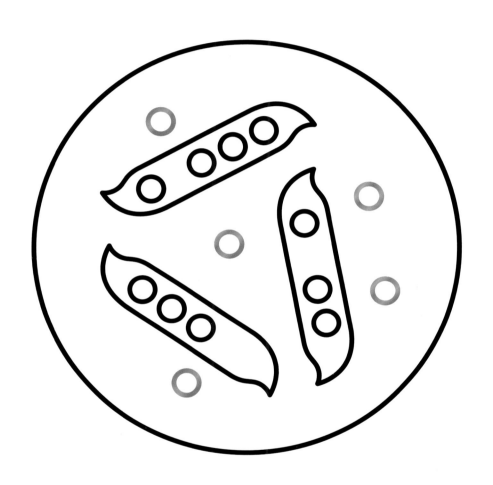

Vegetables

CORN CAKES WITH BEET AND APPLE SALAD

These manage to pull off the trick of being totally light but utterly creamy at the same time. Other cheeses also work instead of the feta: Gorgonzola, for example, if you want something a bit punchier.

If you want to go for restaurant-style presentation, use the corn husks rather than parchment paper to line the muffin pans. They look lovely—like little bamboo baskets. To do this, peel off the husks: you should have about 18 pieces. Discard any stringy bits and place the husks in a bowl, well covered with water. Set aside for 30 minutes, for the husks to soften, then trim them with scissors to make them shorter and easier to line the muffin cups.

If you are looking for a shortcut, just serve the corn cakes with a crisp green salad rather than the beets and apple. Fresh radishes are also lovely, halved and tossed in some olive oil, with a good pinch of coarse sea salt.

If you use a regular muffin pan—where the cups are 2 inches/5 cm wide at the bottom and 1¼ inches/3 cm deep—you'll make 12 cakes, so everyone gets served two. You can also use a larger muffin pan, with cups 3 inches/7 cm wide 1¾ inches/4½ cm deep—to make 6 larger cakes, so that everyone has one.

Serves 6 as a generous starter or light lunch

5 medium ears corn, husks removed, or 1 lb 1 oz/500 g frozen corn kernels, defrosted
3 small shallots, finely diced (3½ oz/100 g)
3 cloves garlic, finely chopped
1 tsp fennel seeds, lightly toasted and coarsely crushed
1 tsp ground cumin, lightly toasted
1 tsp celery seeds
½ oz/15 g tarragon leaves, coarsely chopped
1 tsp baking powder

⅓ cup/80 g unsalted butter, melted, plus 2 tbsp/20 g for greasing the muffin pan
2 large eggs, yolks and whites separated
2 tbsp all-purpose flour
2 oz/60 g feta, broken into 6 or 12 chunks (one for each cake)
coarse sea salt and black pepper

Beet and apple salad
7 tbsp/120 g Greek yogurt
2 tsp Valdespino sherry vinegar or another good-quality sherry vinegar
2 tbsp olive oil
2 tbsp lemon juice

½ tsp fennel seeds, roasted and coarsely crushed, plus ½ tsp extra, to garnish
½ tsp celery seeds
½ oz/15 g parsley, coarsely chopped
2 medium raw beets, peeled and julienned (7 oz/200 g)
1 Granny Smith apple, peeled, cored, and julienned (5 oz/140 g), stored in water with some lemon juice

To serve
⅕ oz/5 g baby basil or small regular basil leaves

1 Preheat the oven to 390°F/200°C (360°F/180°C convection). Grease six or twelve muffin cups (see headnote, page 209) very well with the 2 tablespoons/ 20 g of butter and line with squares of parchment paper, cut large enough so that the sides rise about 1 inch/2.5 cm above the muffin pan.

2 Stand each ear of corn on your chopping board and use a large, sharp knife to shave off the kernels: you should have about 1 pound 1 ounce/500 g. Discard the cobs and transfer the kernels to a food processor along with the shallots and garlic. Pulse for 3 to 4 seconds, until the mixture is coarsely processed but has not turned to a wet purée. Add the fennel seeds, cumin, celery seeds, tarragon, baking powder, butter, and egg yolks, along with 1½ teaspoons of salt and a very good grind of black pepper. Blitz a few more times, to combine—some of the corn kernels will still be whole—then transfer to a medium bowl. Fold the flour in by hand and set aside.

3 Place the egg whites in a separate medium bowl and whisk to form firm peaks. Fold a third of the whites gently into the corn mixture—you don't want to overwork the batter—and then, once incorporated, continue with the next third, and then the next. Once fully incorporated, divide the mixture among the muffin cups, and then insert a chunk of feta into each. Push it halfway down into the batter; the cakes will puff up around the cheese when they cook. Bake for 25 to 40 minutes, depending on the size of your muffin cups, until the cakes have risen and are golden and fluffy; the cakes will still be a bit wet at this point. Remove from the oven and set aside for 10 minutes before lifting each one out of the pan.

4 While the corn cakes are in the oven, place all the ingredients for the salad, apart from the beets and apple, in a medium bowl. Mix well and set aside until ready to serve.

5 Just before serving, add the beets and apple to the salad dressing and mix together gently. Serve the warm cakes with the salad alongside, sprinkled with the remaining fennel seeds and the basil leaves.

Baked blue cheesecake with pickled beets and honey

This is one of a handful of dishes that our customers won't let us take off the menu.

Scully was inspired to make this by his good friend Tim Standing. Tim didn't give him the recipe; he just put the idea out there and told Scully to experiment when they were cooking together in Australia. The original version had a cheesy biscuit base made from biscuits you can only get in Australia. Thinking through the logistics of importing one particular brand of biscuit from one hemisphere to the next for the sake of the dish at NOPI, Yotam suggested that a digestive-biscuit-and-Parmesan variation could be made to work instead. (Find digestive biscuits at British-import shops and in many supermarkets.)

We've made a few changes from the restaurant version to make it easier to re-create at home. First, we've suggested using just Stilton cheese rather than the mix of Gorgonzola and Valdeón that we use at NOPI. Valdeón is a brilliantly bold and salty Spanish blue with a distinctive strength, spice, and complexity. It's not as easy to come by as Stilton, but do get hold of some if you can.

Second, this was first served at NOPI with the pickled shimeji mushrooms mentioned in the headnote for Jerusalem Artichoke Soup (page 36); these were only later replaced by beets. Play around with the pickles: they both work, so just see what you prefer.

The pickled beets need to be made the day before. They keep for a few weeks in the fridge, so can be made well ahead of time. You'll make more than you need for this recipe, so keep any leftovers in the fridge to spoon alongside grilled fish or cheese. If you are short on time or just looking for a shortcut, dicing some ready-pickled beets is a perfectly good substitute.

The thing that gives this dish its initial "wow" is the individual little copper pan each cake arrives in, freshly baked and perfectly formed. You can bake them in wide ramekins or small soufflé dishes if you don't have copper pans, but it also works well as one large cheesecake. If you go for one large cake, you'll need to double the base mixture quantity and increase the baking time to 45 minutes. Make sure, also, that you grease and line the whole pan (rather than just the base) before the batter gets poured in. Finally, instead of serving it at once, you'll need to let it cool for an hour before releasing it from the pan and reheating. Use an 8 inch/22 cm round pan.

Serves 8

Pickled beets
3 large beets (1½ lb/670 g),
   skin on and scrubbed clean
2 cloves garlic, crushed
1 bay leaf
⅓ oz/10 g thyme sprigs
½ tsp black peppercorns
¼ cup/50 g superfine sugar
2 cups/500 ml red wine vinegar
coarse sea salt

Base
3 tbsp/40 g unsalted butter,
   fridge-cold and cut into
   ¾-inch/2-cm dice

1¾ oz/50 g pumpkin seeds,
   toasted
5 digestive biscuits
   (2½ oz/75 g), crumbled
1½ oz/40 g coarsely grated
   Parmesan

Cheesecake
4 tsp/20 g unsalted butter
1 medium leek, trimmed,
   white and green parts finely
   sliced (4½ oz/125 g)
1½ cups/360 g cream cheese
¾ cup/170 g crème fraîche
⅓ cup/80 ml heavy cream
2 cloves garlic, crushed

¾ oz/20 g chives, finely chopped
1 tbsp chopped basil
3½ oz/100 g Stilton, or a mixture
   of 4 parts Valdeón blue
   to Gorgonzola, crumbled
4 eggs, lightly beaten

To serve
2 tbsp runny honey
   (mixed, optionally, with
   a few drops of truffle oil)
1 oz/30 g hazelnuts, toasted
   and lightly crushed
½ oz/15 g baby basil or
   regular basil leaves

1 Place all the ingredients for the pickled beets in a medium saucepan for which you have a lid, and add 1 tablespoon of salt. Pour over 3½ cups/800 ml of water—the beets should be submerged, so add a little bit more water, if you need to—and bring to a boil. Reduce the heat to medium and cook, covered, for 35 to 40 minutes, until soft. Remove from the heat and set aside until completely cool. Lift out the beets, then peel and cut them into ⅓-inch/1-cm dice. Strain the pickling liquid and discard the bay, thyme, and peppercorns. Return the liquid to the pan and simmer over medium heat for about 25 minutes, until reduced to about 2½ cups/600 ml. Set aside to cool, then pour the liquid over the beets. Keep in the fridge for 24 hours before using.

2 Preheat the oven to 390°F/200°C (360°F/180°C convection). Lightly grease eight ramekins or soufflé dishes, each measuring 4½ inches/12 cm-wide, and place a circle of parchment paper in the bottom of each.

3 Place all the ingredients for the cheesecake base in a food processor with ½ teaspoon of salt. Blitz well to form fine crumbs, then divide among the ramekins, pressing down evenly and firmly. Set aside until ready to use.

4 Place the butter for the cheesecake in a small pan and add the leek. Cook over medium heat for about 7 minutes, stirring from time to time, until the leek is soft but still retains its color. Set aside to cool, then transfer to a large mixing bowl, along with the cream cheese, crème fraîche, heavy cream, garlic, chives, basil, ½ teaspoon of salt, and a good grind of black pepper. Mix well to form a smooth paste before adding the blue cheese and eggs. Fold gently, then pour the mixture into the individual ramekins. Bake for 25 to 30 minutes, until a skewer inserted into the middle of one of the cakes comes out clean. Remove from the oven and serve at once, in the ramekins or soufflé bowls, with a drizzle of the honey and the hazelnuts and basil sprinkled on top. The pickled beets, drained, can be spooned on top of the cheesecakes before the garnishes, or served alongside.

FIVE-SPICED TOFU WITH STEAMED EGGPLANT AND CARDAMOM PASSATA

Before a busy lunch or evening service, chefs spend hours prepping everything they're going to need once the action starts and the food orders come in thick and fast. This preparation is known as *mise en place*: the putting in place of everything you need to cook a dish efficiently from beginning to end. Cooking at home is (thank goodness!) a very different experience from cooking in a restaurant, but some dishes do still benefit from this placing in line of everything you need once the stove goes on. Getting your shallots chopped, ginger grated, and lemongrass and red chiles finely chopped in advance will make cooking this a much more relaxed process.

There are three elements here that are all good enough to stand alone as separate dishes. The tofu and the eggplant work well, by themselves or together, with either Sticky Sesame Rice (page 83) or Cardamom and Clove Rice (page 81), and the passata is fantastic spooned over roast beef. The combination of the three together, though—the tofu, the eggplant, and the passata—is a punchy one we love. If you go for the whole dish, you'll still need some sticky, clove, or plain steamed rice to serve alongside.

If you don't have a steamer, you can just as easily steam the eggplant wedges in a colander over a pan of boiling water. Make sure the water is not touching the bottom of the colander and that you are using a pan for which you have a lid. You'll need the help of a big sheet of foil, as well as the lid, when covering the pan, to make sure that all the edges are completely sealed and no steam can escape. Tomato passata is strained, pureed raw tomatoes. If you cannot find it, puree canned tomatoes in a food processor or pass them through a food mill.

Steamed eggplant

2 large eggplants (2¼ lb/1 kg), cut in half lengthwise, then widthwise, then each section cut into 1¼-inch/3-cm wedges

1½ tsp sunflower oil

1 tbsp sesame oil

2-inch/5-cm piece of ginger, peeled and finely grated (1½ oz/40 g)

5 cloves garlic, thinly sliced

7 tbsp/100 ml light soy sauce

¼ cup/60 ml Shaoxing rice wine

⅓ cup/80 ml rice vinegar

3½ tbsp mirin

1 tsp superfine sugar

coarse sea salt

Tomato cardamom passata

1 tbsp sunflower oil

3 Thai (red) shallots or regular shallots, finely diced (1¼ oz/35 g)

4 cloves garlic, crushed

1½-inch/4-cm piece of ginger, peeled and finely grated (1 oz/30 g)

2 stalks lemongrass, tough outer leaves and stalks removed and discarded; finely chopped

2 red chiles, seeded and finely chopped

2 tsp ground cardamom

1 tbsp tomato paste

2½ cups/600 g tomato passata

1 tbsp superfine sugar

Tofu

7 tbsp/60 g all-purpose flour

7 tbsp/60 g cornstarch

1½ tsp ground black pepper

1½ tsp ground white pepper

1 tbsp Chinese five-spice

14 oz/400 g firm tofu, cut into 1-inch/2.5-cm squares

sunflower oil, for frying

To serve

2 tbsp black sesame seeds, or toasted white sesame seeds (optional)

2 small green onions, green and white parts thinly sliced

1 Place the eggplant in a colander with 1 teaspoon of salt. Mix well and leave to drain in a sink or bowl for an hour. Shake well, pat dry, then transfer to a steaming pan and steam for 10 to 15 minutes, or until cooked through. Remove from the heat. Place a medium saucepan over medium-low heat, with the sunflower oil and the sesame oil. Add the ginger and garlic and sauté for 1 to 2 minutes, until fragrant. Add the soy sauce, Shaoxing rice wine, rice vinegar, mirin, sugar, and about 7 tablespoons/100 ml of water. Increase the heat, bring to a boil, then reduce to medium-low again to simmer gently for 10 to 12 minutes, until the liquid has reduced by half. Stir in the eggplant, along with ¼ teaspoon of salt, and continue to simmer for another 8 to 10 minutes, until the sauce is shiny and the eggplant is glazed and starting to break down. Set aside somewhere warm until ready to use.

2 Place the sunflower oil for the passata in a medium saucepan for which you have a lid, and place over medium-low heat. Add the shallots, garlic, and ginger and sauté for 2 to 3 minutes, until soft and fragrant. Add the lemongrass and chile and cook for 2 to 3 minutes. Stir in the cardamom and tomato paste and cook for another 2 minutes. Pour in the passata, stir well, and bring to a boil. Reduce the heat to low and simmer, covered, for about 12 minutes, until the sauce is thick. Add the sugar along with 1½ teaspoons of salt, and cook for a final 2 to 3 minutes. Remove from the heat and set aside somewhere warm, until ready to serve.

3 For the tofu, grind 1 tablespoon of salt with a mortar and pestle until smooth. Transfer to a large bowl with the flour, cornstarch, black and white peppers, and the five-spice and mix well. Just before serving, toss the tofu in the flour mixture until all sides are coated. Pour enough oil into a medium sauté pan so that it rises ¾ inch/2 cm up the sides. Place over high heat and, when hot, add the tofu in batches. Fry for 2 to 3 minutes, until golden brown. Use a slotted spoon to remove the tofu to a paper towel–lined colander, sprinkle lightly with salt, and continue with the remaining tofu.

4 To serve, spoon the eggplant into shallow bowls or plates. Place the tofu on top, followed by the passata. Sprinkle over the sesame seeds and green onions and serve at once.

SNAKE BEAN AND PEANUT ACHAR

Achar is a pickled Malaysian salad that Scully grew up eating. With the help of his nine aunties—all on his Malaysian mother's side!—it's a dish he's also grown pretty adept at making. It keeps well in the fridge (for up to 3 months) and tastes better a day or so after it is made. Just hold back on the snake (or French) beans and peanuts, and stir these in before serving. Remove the *achar* from the fridge 2 hours before you are going to eat it: you want it room temperature rather than fridge-cold. If serving it with the egg, it's best to warm it through before stirring in the peanuts.

The poached egg is enough to accompany the *achar*, but if you are looking for an extra something to make it into a whole meal, serve it with Farinata (page 82). Any other sort of eggs—an omelete, for example, or eggs that have been scrambled or fried—also work well.

Snake beans, as their name suggests, are longer than French beans. They are dark green, thin, and long—up to 3 feet/90 cm!—with a slightly sweet flavor and crunchy texture. Also known as Chinese long beans, they are commonly used in Asian dishes. There's no need to go out of your way to get them, though: French beans or slender green beans also work very well.

Serves 4 to 6

1 small green cabbage, outer
  leaves discarded, cut in
  half lengthwise, cored,
  and thinly sliced widthwise
  (1 lb 5 oz/600 g)
coarse sea salt

Achar paste
5 tbsp/75 ml sunflower oil
1 small onion, finely chopped
  (4½ oz/120 g)
2 small celery stalk, finely
  diced (3½ oz/100 g)
2 large red chiles, seeded
  and finely sliced
½ tsp ground turmeric
1 tsp ground cumin
1 tsp celery seeds
¼ tsp ground cloves
¼ tsp ground cinnamon
¼ tsp ground allspice
¼ cup (packed)/60 g soft light
  brown sugar
½ cup/120 ml cider vinegar

2 tbsp yellow mustard seeds
5 stems fresh curry leaves
  (⅓ oz/10 g)
7 oz/200 g snake beans,
  trimmed and cut into
  4-inch/10-cm lengths, or
  French beans, trimmed
2 oz/60 g skinless roasted
  peanuts
6 freshly poached eggs,
  to serve (optional)

1 Place the cabbage in a medium bowl and sprinkle over 1 tablespoon of salt. Mix well and set aside for 30 minutes. This helps removes the bitterness from the cabbage. Rinse under cold water, then drain, pat dry, and set aside.

2 Put 3 tablespoons of the sunflower oil into a large saucepan and place over medium-high heat. Add the onion, celery, and chiles and cook for 5 to 6 minutes, stirring from time to time, to soften. Add the turmeric, cumin, celery seeds, cloves, cinnamon, and allspice and stir for another minute. Pour over 7 tablespoons/100 ml of water and cook for 1 to 2 minutes, stirring to form a paste. Add the sugar and vinegar, cook for a minute, then add the cabbage. Mix well so that the cabbage is coated, then reduce the heat to medium. Simmer for 25 minutes, stirring from time to time, until the cabbage has softened but still retains a bite and you have about 3 tablespoons of liquid left in the pan. Remove from the heat and set aside.

3 Put the remaining 2 tablespoons of oil into a small frying pan and place over high heat. Add the mustard seeds and curry leaves and fry for a minute, until the curry leaves are crisp and bright green and the mustard seeds have started to pop. Pour this over the cabbage *achar*, mix well, and set aside until completely cool.

4 Bring a large pan of salted water to a boil. Add the snake beans and blanch for 3 to 4 minutes, until al dente. Drain, then refresh well under cold water and pat dry very well. When ready to serve, add the beans to the cabbage mix, along with half the peanuts and ¾ teaspoon of salt. If serving without the egg, just mix well, transfer everything to a large serving platter or individual plates, sprinkle with the last of the peanuts, and serve. If you are poaching the eggs, warm the cabbage through before adding the peanuts and beans, and then serve an egg over each portion.

Urad dal purée with hot and sour eggplant

This is served as a fish dish in NOPI, with the addition of a panfried gray mullet fillet perched on top. We've reduced the number of components to make at home—the combination of the dal purée and eggplant is substantial and delicious enough to work alone as a veggie main—but return the fish element if you are pushing the boat out (to sea).

Dalna means "to split" in Hindi, so urad dal is simply the split and smaller version of the dull black-colored urad bean (just as chana dal is the split and smaller version of the chickpea). Known also as split black lentils, the hulled and split urad dal are creamy white. It all sounds far more complicated than it actually is: just know you are looking for the white insides of black-skinned beans.

Serves 4

3½ oz/100 g tamarind pulp

about 4 cups/1 liter sunflower oil, for frying the eggplant, plus ⅓ cup/80 ml

2 large eggplants, cut in half widthwise and again lengthwise, then each section cut into ¾-inch/2-cm wedges (2 lb/900 g)

3 tbsp/50 g ghee

8 cloves garlic, crushed

1½-inch/4-cm piece of ginger, peeled and coarsely chopped (1½ oz/40 g)

1½ cups/300 g urad dal, rinsed

7 tbsp/100 ml lemon juice

2 large onions, thinly sliced (10½ oz/300 g)

1 tbsp whole aniseed

2 long red chiles, seeded and finely sliced

5 stems fresh curry leaves, stems removed (⅓ oz/10 g)

1½ tbsp mild curry powder

1 tsp ground turmeric

3 tbsp soft light brown sugar

2 small cinnamon sticks

30 cardamom pods lightly bashed

1 tbsp whole cloves

1 oz/30 g cilantro, coarsely chopped

about 6 tbsp/120 g Greek yogurt, to serve

coarse sea salt

1 Place the tamarind pulp in a medium bowl and pour over about 2 cups/450 ml of boiling water. Leave to soak for half an hour, then squeeze the tamarind and mix so that the pulp has completely softened into the water. Strain the tamarind water, discard the pulp, and set aside; you should have about 1½ cups/370 ml of liquid.

2 Pour enough oil into a medium pan so that it rises 1¼ inches/3 cm up the sides. Place over high heat and, once hot, add a quarter of the eggplant wedges; you don't want to overcrowd the pan. Fry for 6 to 8 minutes, until golden brown, then use a slotted spoon to transfer them to a paper towel–lined colander. Set aside to drain while you continue with the remaining batches (you can re-use the oil).

3 Place the ghee in a medium pan over medium-low heat. Add the garlic and ginger and sauté for 3 to 4 minutes, until soft and fragrant. Add the dal, stir well, and cook for 1 minute. Increase the heat to medium-high, pour over 3⅓ cups/800 ml of water and cook for about 12 minutes, until the dal is tender but still retains a bite. Remove from the heat and carefully transfer to a food processor, along with

the lemon juice and 2½ teaspoons of salt. Blitz well to form a paste—it should be smooth but still have a bit of texture—then return to a clean pot. Cover the surface with plastic wrap—it needs to touch the surface to prevent a skin forming—and set aside somewhere warm until ready to use.

4 Place the ⅓ cup/80 ml of sunflower oil in a medium saucepan over medium-high heat. Add the onions, along with the aniseed and a pinch of salt. Sauté for 7 to 8 minutes, until soft, then add the chiles and curry leaves. Cook for another minute, then add the curry powder, turmeric, and sugar. Cook for a minute, stirring until dissolved, then pour over the tamarind water. Wrap the cinnamon, cardamom, and cloves in muslin and add to the pan. Cook for 9 to 10 minutes, until thick and glossy. Discard the wrapped spices and stir in the eggplant, along with 1 teaspoon of salt. Keep somewhere warm until ready to serve.

5 Spread the warm dal on serving plates—you might need to add a few tablespoons of water or lemon juice if it has become too firm—and spoon the eggplant on top. Serve at once, with the cilantro sprinkled on top and a spoonful of yogurt to finish.

Spiced chickpea patties with coconut and curry leaf paste

At NOPI we serve these with an extra condiment of sliced cherry tomatoes, grated orange zest, and shredded parsley, with a dressing of Dijon mustard, lemon juice, and oil. They're also lovely with store-bought or home-made fried shallots (see page 110) sprinkled on top. Pile on the extras as you like, but the patties are more than brilliant with just the coconut and curry leaf paste suggested here, with a spoonful of Greek yogurt alongside and a squeeze of fresh lime.

If you're looking for a shortcut, skip the coconut and curry leaf paste and make a simple lime and cardamom yogurt to serve with the patties instead. To do this, mix about 6 tablespoons/120 g of Greek yogurt with 1½ teaspoons of olive oil, ½ teaspoon of ground cardamom, finely grated zest of half a lemon, and 1½ teaspoons lime juice.

Don't be alarmed by not having to boil the chickpeas before they get puréed. As when we make falafel, this is part of the process, and they get all the cooking they need, first in the pan, and then when the patties are warmed through in the oven.

This is not a quick recipe but it can be prepared in advance. The paste can be made up to 3 days before you want to eat it and it also freezes well. The patties can be made the day before serving, then kept in the fridge ready to be tossed in flour and fried.

Serves 4

1¼ cups/250 g chickpeas, soaked
  overnight in plenty of water
  with ½ teaspoon baking soda
1½ tbsp ghee, plus 7 tbsp/100 g
  for frying
1 medium onion, finely chopped
  (4½ oz/130 g)
3 cloves garlic, crushed
¼ cup/50 g mung dal, rinsed
5 stems fresh curry leaves
  (⅓ oz/10 g)
1½ tbsp coriander seeds,
  lightly toasted and ground
1½ tbsp cumin seeds,
  lightly toasted and ground
1 tsp chile flakes

1¾ oz/50 g cilantro,
  finely chopped
3 or 4 large tomatoes, quartered,
  seeds discarded, cut into
  ¾-inch/2-cm dice (8 oz/230 g)
3½ tbsp lime juice
finely grated zest of 1 small lime
1⅓ cups/120 g chickpea flour
coarse sea salt and black pepper

Coconut and curry leaf paste
coarsely grated flesh of 1 large
  coconut (8 oz/250 g)
1 medium onion, coarsely
  chopped (4 oz/120 g)
¾-inch/2-cm piece of
  ginger, peeled and coarsely
  chopped (⅓ oz/10 g)

2 dried chiles, seeded
¾ oz/20 g seedless tamarind
  pulp or 1½ tbsp tamarind
  paste (see page 316)
2 tbsp sunflower oil
1 tbsp yellow mustard seeds
⅓ cup/75 g urad dal, rinsed
½ medium onion, thinly
  sliced (2 oz/60 g)
2 stems fresh curry leaves
  (⅕ oz/5 g)
1⅔ cups/400 ml coconut milk
1 tsp ground turmeric
1½ tbsp lime juice

To serve
about 6 tbsp/120 g Greek yogurt
1 lime, cut into 4 wedges

1 Drain and rinse the chickpeas and pat them dry with a clean kitchen towel. Transfer to a food processor and blitz until finely ground.

2 Put the 1½ tablespoons of ghee into a medium sauté pan and place over medium-high heat. Add the onion and garlic and cook for 5 to 6 minutes, until soft. Add the mung dal and curry leaves and cook for another 3 to 4 minutes, until fragrant, then add the ground coriander and cumin seeds, chile, cilantro, and a good grind of black pepper. Fry for 30 seconds, stirring constantly, then pour over ¾ cup/175 ml of water. Mix well, cook for 2 minutes, then add the tomatoes. Sauté for a minute, then remove from the heat. Add the ground chickpeas, lime juice, lime zest, and 1 tablespoon of salt. Mix well, then set aside to cool before forming the mixture into 3-ounce/80-g patties that are 2 inches/5 cm wide and ⅔ inch/1.5 cm thick: you should have enough mixture to make 12 patties. Set aside in the fridge for an hour, to firm up.

3 To make the paste, place the coconut, onion, ginger, chiles, and tamarind pulp in the bowl of a food processor, along with ½ teaspoon of salt. Add a scant ½ cup/120 ml of water, blitz to form a thick wet paste, and set aside.

4 Place a large saucepan over medium heat with 1 tablespoon of oil. Add the mustard seeds and dal and cook for about 2 minutes, until light golden brown and fragrant. Transfer the seeds and dal to a separate

bowl, then return the pan to medium-high heat and add the remaining tablespoon of oil. Add the onion and cook for 3 minutes, stirring from time to time, then reduce the heat to medium. Add the curry leaves, fry for a minute, and then pour over the coconut milk, along with the coconut paste and the turmeric. Return the yellow mustard seeds and urad dal to the pan, mix well, bring to a boil, then simmer over medium heat for 30 to 40 minutes, until thick. Transfer half of the sauce to a food processor, along with the lime juice, ½ cup/120 ml of water, and 1½ teaspoons of salt. Blitz until smooth and return to the pan with the remaining sauce in it. Stir, and keep somewhere warm until ready to serve.

5 Preheat the oven to 375°F/190°C (340°F/170°C convection).

6 Place a large frying pan over medium-high heat and add the 7 tablespoons/100 g ghee. Toss the chickpea patties in the chickpea flour and add them to the hot pan in batches, so as to not overcrowd them. Fry for 5 to 6 minutes, turning once halfway through, until golden brown on both sides. Transfer to a paper towel–lined plate to drain, and then put on a large baking sheet. Fry the remaining patties, then place them in the oven for about 5 minutes, or until warmed through.

7 To serve, divide the warm coconut paste among four shallow bowls and top with the patties. Serve at once, with spoonfuls of yogurt on top and the lime wedges.

SPICED CHICKPEA PATTIES WITH COCONUT AND CURRY LEAF PASTE

Pearl barley risotto with watercress, asparagus, and pecorino

We know that the use of the word *risotto* here should be in big quotation marks. People get very protective about the rules of their culinary heritage. Yotam's opinion about what is and what isn't allowed to go into the making of hummus, for example, is as unwavering as an Italian chef's rules for the ingredients list in a risotto. Disclaimers aside, making risotto with pearl barley adds bite and texture that work very well with the smooth, green watercress purée.

Start with thick-stemmed asparagus for this, if you can: it'll make it far easier to shave each spear with a vegetable peeler and get the ribbons you're after. Don't be put off from making this if asparagus is not in season; thin ribbons of zucchini—shaved raw with a vegetable peeler—work well as an alternative. One medium zucchini will be enough to produce about 6½ ounces/180 g of shaved ribbons.

Serves 4

1½ cups/300 g pearl barley
2½ quarts/2.4 liters
  vegetable stock
3½ oz/100 g baby spinach leaves
7 oz/200 g watercress
6 tbsp/90 ml olive oil
½ cup/120 g unsalted butter
  (two-thirds cut into ⅓-inch/1-cm
  dice, one-third in one piece)

1 medium shallot, finely diced
  (2½ oz/70 g)
2 cloves garlic, finely chopped
3 thyme sprigs
1 bay leaf
4 portobello mushrooms, stems
  and caps thinly sliced (8 oz/250 g)
1 medium leek, green and white
  parts thinly sliced (6½ oz/180 g)
2 tbsp lemon juice
coarse sea salt and black pepper

Asparagus and pecorino salad
7 oz/200 g asparagus (10 thick
  spears), woody stems trimmed
2 oz/60 g pecorino cheese
½ tsp olive oil
1½ tsp lemon juice

1 Place the barley in a medium saucepan and add 7 cups/1.8 liters of the stock. Bring to a boil over high heat, then reduce the heat to medium and simmer for 30 to 35 minutes, uncovered, until the barley is tender but still retaining a bite. Drain and set aside.

2 Wash out the saucepan and fill it with water. Bring to a boil, add the spinach, and blanch for 30 seconds, then use a slotted spoon to transfer the leaves to a colander. Rinse well under cold water—this will help prevent discoloration—then squeeze out the excess moisture and set aside. Keeping the pan of water at a boil, add the watercress, and blanch for 30 seconds. Transfer to a colander, rinse under cold water, and squeeze out the excess moisture. Add to the spinach leaves, coarsely chop, and set aside.

3 Wipe out the saucepan and add 2 tablespoons of the olive oil, along with the undiced butter. Place over medium heat, add the shallot and garlic, and cook for 6 to 7 minutes, stirring often, until soft but taking on no color. Add the thyme and bay leaf, pour over 2 cups/500 ml of the stock, and bring to a boil over high heat. Cook for 10 minutes, for the stock to reduce down to a quarter, so that you have about 3½ tablespoons left in the pan. Add the spinach and watercress and cook for a final 2 minutes. Remove from the heat, lift out and discard the bay leaf and thyme, then, while still hot, carefully transfer to a blender with ½ teaspoon of salt and a few cracks of black pepper. Turn on the blender and blitz, adding the diced butter a few cubes at a time, waiting until one batch has been incorporated before adding the next. Set aside.

4 Put 2 tablespoons of the olive oil in a large sauté pan and place over high heat. Add the mushrooms and cook for 3 minutes, until softened but not colored. Remove the mushrooms, along with any liquid in the pan, and set aside. Return the sauté pan to medium-high heat with the remaining 2 tablespoons of olive oil. Add the leek and cook for 3 minutes, until softened but having taken on no color. Leave in the pan and set aside.

5 To make the salad, run a vegetable peeler from the base to the tip of each asparagus stalks to make long, thin ribbons. Place them in a mixing bowl, then do the same with the cheese, running the vegetable peeler along it to create thin ribbons. Add these to the asparagus, along with the olive oil, lemon juice, a pinch of salt, and a crack of black pepper. Use your hands to mix gently and set aside. Don't make this salad too far before serving—it won't improve with sitting around.

6 When ready to serve, add the barley and mushrooms to the pan of leeks and pour over the remaining 1 cup/120 ml of stock. Mix well, then place over medium-high heat and cook for 3 to 4 minutes. Add the watercress and spinach purée and stir for a final minute to warm through. Add the lemon juice, 1 teaspoon salt, and a grind of black pepper. Mix well and serve at once, with the asparagus and pecorino salad on top.

PERSIAN LOVE RICE WITH BURNT BUTTER TZATZIKI

This might well be called Persian labor-of-love rice. The parcels take a little time to prepare, but it's no bad thing, in matters of love, to put some time aside. They can be made well in advance though, taken right up to the point before they are grilled in the pan, so all preparation can be at your leisure.

Speed-dating is always an option, however, and there are lots of shortcuts if you want them. You can skip on the tzatziki, for example, and just serve the parcels with a spoonful of Greek yogurt and a squeeze of lemon. The sauce is rather special and well worth making, though, and any leftovers make a great dip to have with meatballs. The rice itself is also so good that you can do without the grape leaves entirely, if you like, and just serve the rice on its own, with or without the sauce. As with all good relationships, the possibilities are endless.

You'll make more Persian spice mix than you need here, but it will keep for a month in a sealed jar, to be used in your next batch of rice. It's also a lovely way to season fish, lamb, or roasted quail, and can be sprinkled on top of roasted root vegetables once they've been cooked.

Mulberries are fruits that taste rather like blackberries. They're difficult to get hold of as they are so perishable once they fall from the tree. Mulberries can be either black or white and are much more easily available dried. We use the dried white variety at NOPI, but use golden raisins, if that's what you have.

Serves 4

Persian spice

1 tbsp dried rose petals,
  ground to a fine powder
1 tbsp coriander seeds,
  toasted and finely ground
  (or 2¼ tsp ground coriander)
¾ tsp ground cardamom
¼ tsp freshly grated nutmeg
¼ tsp ground cinnamon
¼ tsp coarse black pepper

Tzatziki

2 small zucchini, trimmed and
  coarsely grated (6½ oz/190 g)
½ cup/140 g Greek yogurt

2 tsp lemon juice
⅕ oz/5 g finely chopped chives
⅕ oz/5 g finely chopped
  mint leaves
3½ tbsp/50 g unsalted butter

Love rice

2½ tbsp/30 g dried mulberries
  or golden raisins
¼ cup/40 g barberries
  (see page 198)
24 large jarred grape leaves
  (5 oz/140 g)
1 tbsp olive oil
1 small onion, finely diced
  (4 oz/120 g)
2 cloves garlic, crushed

1¼-inch/3-cm piece
  of ginger, peeled and finely
  grated (¾ oz/20 g)
a pinch of saffron, soaked in
  1 tbsp boiling water
⅔ cup/125 g basmati rice
1¼ cups/300 ml hot
  vegetable stock
1 medium carrot, peeled and
  coarsely grated (3½ oz/100 g)
1½ oz/40 g sliced
  almonds, toasted
1½ oz/40 g shelled
  pistachios, toasted
1 tbsp sunflower oil
1 tsp dried rose petals,
  to serve (optional)
coarse sea salt and black pepper

1 Mix together all the ingredients for the Persian spice and store in an airtight container until ready to use.

2 Place the zucchini in a colander with ¼ teaspoon of salt. Set aside for 15 minutes to drain, then squeeze out the excess moisture. Transfer to a medium bowl and add the yogurt, lemon juice, chives, mint, ¼ teaspoon of salt, and a grind of black pepper. Place the butter in a small saucepan and melt over medium-high heat. Cook for about 2 minutes, until the butter has turned brown and smells nutty. Remove from the heat, strain through a fine-mesh sieve, then stir it into the zucchini yogurt. Cover and keep in in the fridge until serving.

3 Pour ⅔ cup/150 ml of hot water over the mulberries and barberries and leave to soak for 10 minutes. Drain and set aside.

4 Carefully separate and rinse the grape leaves and put them in a medium saucepan. Cover with water and simmer over medium-low for about 15 minutes, until completely soft. Drain, refresh under cold water, cut off the tough stalks, and set aside to dry.

5 Place the olive oil in a large sauté pan for which you have a lid, over medium heat. Add the onion and sauté for 3 to 4 minutes, until translucent. Add the garlic and ginger and continue to cook for 2 to 3 minutes, stirring from time to time. Reduce the heat to low, then add 1 tablespoon of the spice mix and the saffron-infused water. Cook for 1 minute, stirring, then add the rice. Stir to coat all the grains, then pour over the hot stock. Mix well, increase the heat, and bring to a boil. Reduce to a gentle simmer and cook, covered, for 12 minutes, until the rice is just tender. Remove from the heat and stir in the strained berries, carrot, almonds, and pistachios, along with 2 teaspoons of salt and a good grind of black pepper. Set aside.

6 To form the grape leaf parcels, line each of four 4-inch/10-cm cookie cutters (or small bowls at least 2 inches/5 cm deep) with a square of plastic wrap large enough to hang over the edge. Lay 4 leaves, shiny side down, around the edges of the mold, slightly overlapping and hanging over the edges, then place one in the bottom of each mold. Divide the rice among the four molds, pressing it down to make sure the rice is compact, and place a final leaf on top, shiny side up. Fold in the overhanging leaves so that the parcel is sealed, then draw up the plastic wrap to wrap it into a bundle. Set aside in the fridge for an hour to firm up.

7 Preheat the oven to 390°F/200°C (360°F/180°C convection). When ready to serve, place a large ovenproof sauté pan over high heat. Unwrap the plastic wrap from the parcels and brush them all over with the sunflower oil. Place them in the pan and cook for 5 to 6 minutes, turning once so that both sides get charred. Transfer the pan to the oven to warm for 10 minutes and then serve, with the tzatziki alongside and the rose petals sprinkled over the parcels.

PERSIAN LOVE RICE WITH BURNT BUTTER TZATZIKI

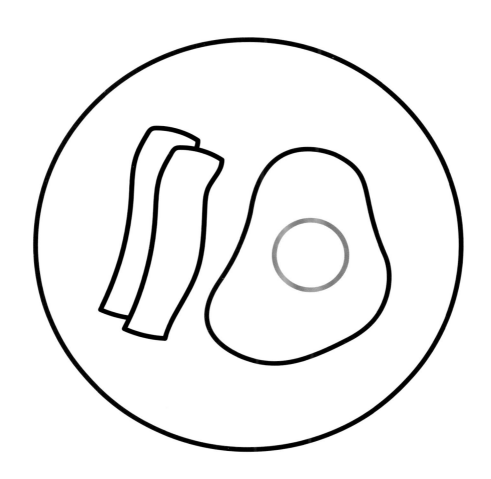

BRUNCH

Ham hock with baked beans, fried egg, and sourdough

A weekend fry-up, NOPI-style. The flavors of the ham and beans benefit hugely from sitting around together for a day or two, so make this at least a day before you plan to eat it, if you can. With the work all done, it really can then be easy-like-Sunday-morning.

You can skip out on blanching the ham, if you like. We tend to do it so that we can control the salt levels of the dish more precisely. It's not absolutely necessary—just make sure that you taste and assess the dish before adding any seasoning if you start with an unblanched ham.

If you're looking for a decadent little upgrade, try frying duck eggs, which are bigger and richer than eggs from hens.

Serves 6

1²/₃ cups/300 g lima beans, soaked overnight in plenty of water with 1 tsp baking soda

1 large ham hock (about 3 lb/1.4 kg)

1/3 cup/80 ml olive oil

4 cloves garlic, peeled and lightly crushed

1 medium onion, cut into 1/3-inch/1-cm dice (5 oz/140 g)

1 medium carrot, cut into 1/3-inch/1-cm dice (3½ oz/100 g)

2 large celery stalks, cut into 1/3-inch/1-cm dice (3½ oz/100 g)

1/4 tsp black peppercorns

1/2 tsp ground allspice

1/2 tsp ground cloves

1/2 tsp dried chile flakes

1½ tsp English mustard powder

1½ tsp dried oregano

1 tsp sweet smoked paprika

1 tbsp tomato paste

2 cups/500 ml beef stock

2 (14-oz/400-g) cans whole peeled tomatoes, including the juices

2 strips shaved orange rind

2 rosemary sprigs, 6 thyme sprigs, and 2 bay leaves, tied together with kitchen twine

To serve

6 slices sourdough bread, 3/4 inch/2 cm thick

2 tbsp olive oil, plus extra to fry the eggs

6 eggs, fried just before serving

1/3 oz/10 g parsley, finely chopped

coarse sea salt and black pepper

1 Drain and rinse the lima beans and place them in a large saucepan. Cover with plenty of water—it should rise 2½ inches/5 cm above the beans—then bring to a boil over high heat. Reduce the heat to medium and simmer for 30 to 45 minutes, skimming the froth off the surface a few times, until the beans are almost tender but still retain a bite. The cooking time for beans can vary greatly, so bite into one to see if it's ready. Drain, refresh under cold water, and set aside until required.

2 Fill a medium pot half full of water and bring to a boil. Lower in the ham hock—it should be fully submerged in the water—and return to the boil. Simmer for 30 minutes over medium-high heat, skimming the surface of any froth. The ham needs to stay submerged in water the whole time, so top up with water if you need to. Lift the ham hock out of the water and set aside to cool. The water can be discarded.

3 Preheat the oven to 425°F/220°C (390°F/200°C convection).

4 Place the olive oil and garlic in a large, deep casserole—about 8 inches/21 cm wide and 7½ inches/19 cm deep—for which you have a lid, and place over medium-low heat. Cook for 5 to 6 minutes, stirring from time to time, until the garlic is golden brown. Lift out the garlic cloves and set aside. Increase the heat to medium-high, add the onion, and cook for 4 minutes. Add the carrot and celery and cook for another 4 minutes, then add the peppercorns, allspice, cloves, chile flakes, mustard powder, oregano, and paprika. Fry for 1 minute, until fragrant. Add the tomato paste

and stir for a minute before adding the beef stock, canned tomatoes, orange rind, cooked garlic cloves, tied-up herbs, and 2 cups/500 ml of water. Stir well, bring to a boil, and simmer for 5 to 6 minutes before adding the blanched ham and the beans. Stir well, then place a cartouche on top of the beans (a round of parchment paper the same size as the pot). Cover the pot with a lid and place in the oven for 2½ hours, until the beans are tender, checking halfway through to make sure the meat is still covered and the beans aren't sticking; you might need to add a bit more water—around 1 cup/250 ml—at this stage. Remove from the oven and set aside, covered, for an hour, until completely cool. This will allow the beans to soak up the flavors from the ham.

5 Once cool, lift out the ham hock and pick the meat off the bone. Discard the fat, skin, and bone and use your hands to pull the meat into about sixteen large pieces. Lift out and discard the herbs from the beans, then return the meat to the pan. Stir well and put back over medium-low heat to warm through. You might need to add a bit of water or stock to loosen the beans if they have been left overnight and become too firm.

6 Just before serving, preheat the broiler and lightly drizzle each slice of bread with 1 teaspoon of oil. Broil for 1 minute on each side, then slice in half diagonally and place two pieces on the side of each plate. Place the ham hock pieces alongside the toast, with the beans spooned on top. Finish with the eggs and serve at once, with a light pinch of salt and pepper and a sprinkle of the parsley.

BROILED GRAPEFRUIT WITH STAR ANISE SUGAR AND ELDERFLOWER YOGURT

Scully finds it hard to conceive of a sweet dish without the addition of some star anise. Yotam is generally of the opinion that there are few desserts that are not improved by the addition of a tablespoon or two of alcohol. The combination of the two, here, works to great effect. But leave out the Grand Marnier, if you prefer.

Make more of the star anise sugar than you need here—it's a great addition to desserts such as the Ricotta Fritters on page 273, or sprinkled on breakfast dishes such as French toast and thin crêpes. The best way to grind the star anise is with a spice or coffee grinder. If you don't have one, you'll need to work hard with a mortar and pestle to break the anise down and then pass it through a fine-mesh sieve.

Thanks to Jim Webb, who recruited Scully to Ottolenghi all those years ago.

Serves 6

Star anise sugar
10 whole star anise
3 tbsp superfine sugar

Yogurt mixture
1 tsp superfine sugar
2 tbsp Grand Marnier (optional)
3 tbsp elderflower cordial
3½ tbsp grapefruit juice
¾ cup/200 g plain yogurt
Finely grated zest of 1 grapefruit

6 grapefruits (4¾ lb/2.2 kg)

---

1 Place the star anise in a spice or coffee grinder and blitz to form a fine powder. Pass through a fine-mesh sieve to remove any chunky bits, then place the fine powder in a small bowl. Add the sugar, mix together, and set aside.

2 Place the sugar for the yogurt mixture in a small saucepan with the Grand Marnier, elderflower cordial, and grapefruit juice. Bring to a boil, then simmer over medium heat for about 8 minutes, stirring frequently, to form a thick syrup; you should have about 3 tablespoons. Set aside to cool, then mix in the yogurt and zest. Keep in the fridge until ready to use.

3 Use a paring or grapefruit knife to trim the bottom ⅕ inch/5 mm off the base of the grapefruit so that they sit flat on your work surface and won't roll. Slice all of the grapefruits in half horizontally, then work the knife around the inside of all the grapefruit halves, where the flesh meets the skin. Cut out all the flesh, avoiding the bitter white pith, remove it from the shell, and dice it into ¾-inch/2-cm cubes. Discard the six untrimmed hollowed-out grapefruit halves, along with all the white pith and seeds, and return the cubed flesh to the six halves that sit flat.

4 Preheat your broiler to its highest setting. Sprinkle 1 tablespoon of star anise sugar over the top of each grapefruit half and place on a foil-lined baking sheet. Broil for 4 to 5 minutes, until the sugar has caramelized. Serve at once, with the yogurt on the side.

FRENCH TOAST WITH ORANGE YOGURT

Having sold the Super French Toast that appeared in Yotam's *Plenty More* as pretty much the definitive word on the matter, we momentarily questioned the inclusion of another French toast recipe here. It's such a brunch favorite of our NOPI regulars, though, that we weren't allowed to leave it out.

Serves 6

Orange yogurt
1/2 cup/150 g Greek yogurt
finely grated zest of 1/2 orange
1 tbsp orange juice
1 tbsp confectioners' sugar

Mixed berries
10 1/2 oz/300 g mixed frozen
   berries
1/3 cup/70 g superfine sugar
2 tsp lemon juice

Star anise sugar
8 whole star anise, blitzed in a
   spice grinder into a fine powder
1/4 cup/50 g superfine sugar

French toast
5 eggs
3/4 cup/200 ml whole milk
14 oz/400 g brioche loaf,
   ends trimmed, cut into six
   (1 1/4-inch/3-cm) slices
1/3 cup/80 g unsalted butter,
   fridge-cold, cut into
   3/4-inch/2-cm dice

1 Fold together all the ingredients for the orange yogurt in a small mixing bowl and keep in the fridge, covered, until required.

2 Place the berries in a medium saucepan with the sugar and lemon juice. Place over high heat and cook for 6 minutes, stirring from time to time, until the sugar has dissolved and the compote is shiny and thick. Remove from the heat and set aside for an hour to come to room temperature; the compote will thicken slightly.

3 Mix together the star anise and sugar, then spread out on a small plate—ready for the toast to get dusted—and set aside.

4 Place the eggs in a medium bowl and whisk well, until pale, light, and fluffy. Continue to whisk as you slowly pour in the milk, then transfer to a dish that is large enough to fit the 6 slices of brioche in a single layer—use two dishes if you need to. Add the brioche slices and set aside for 5 minutes, turning them once or twice. It will seem like a lot of liquid for the bread to absorb, but it will do; just be careful when you are turning it, as it gets very soft.

5 Preheat the oven to 465°F/240°C (425°F/220°C convection).

6 Place a large nonstick frying pan over medium-high heat with 4 teaspoons/20 g of butter. When the butter starts to foam, lay 3 pieces of brioche in the pan and fry for 1 to 2 minutes. Flip the slices over, add 4 teaspoons/20 g more butter to the pan, and continue to fry for another 1½ minutes, until golden. Remove the slices from the pan and set aside on a baking sheet while you wipe the pan with some paper towels and repeat with the remaining brioche and butter. Once all the brioche is on the baking sheet, transfer to the oven and bake for a final 4 minutes, until the toast has puffed up and is golden brown. Remove from the oven and dip each slice in the star anise sugar one at a time, flipping so that both sides get coated.

7 Serve at once, with the berry compote alongside and the orange yogurt spooned on top.

Sweet potato pancakes with yogurt and date syrup

This is far from being a dish that is lacking in any way. However, as with most things sweet potato-, pancake-, or brunch-related, the addition of some bacon will never be short of takers once the pancakes are served. You can make the pancake batter a day ahead, if you like, up to the point just before the egg whites are whisked and stirred in.

Serves 4, generously

2 medium sweet potatoes, unpeeled (1 lb 9 oz/700 g)
1 1/2 cups/200 g all-purpose flour, sifted
2 tsp baking powder
1 tsp grated nutmeg
1 tsp ground cinnamon
3 eggs, yolks and whites separated
2/3 cup/150 ml whole milk
3 1/2 tbsp/50 g unsalted butter, melted, plus 1/3 cup/80 g extra, cut into dice, for frying
1 tsp vanilla extract
1 tbsp honey
coarse sea salt

To serve
1/2 cup/150 g Greek yogurt
3 tbsp date syrup
1 tsp confectioners' sugar, for dusting

---

1 Preheat the oven to 465°F/240°C (425°F/220°C convection).

2 Place the sweet potatoes in a small parchment-lined baking pan and roast for an hour, until completely soft and browned. Remove from the oven, set aside to cool, then peel off the skin. Discard the skin and place the flesh in the middle of a clean muslin square. Draw up the sides, roll into a ball, and squeeze out the liquid from the flesh. The drained weight of the sweet potato should be around 11 oz/320 g. Reduce the oven temperature to 360°F/180°C (320°F/160°C convection).

3 Mix together the flour, baking powder, nutmeg, and cinnamon in a medium bowl with 1 1/2 teaspoons of salt. Place the egg yolks, milk, melted butter, vanilla, and honey in a separate bowl and whisk well to combine. Fold the liquid ingredients into the dry ingredients and stir to combine before adding the sweet potato flesh. Whisk well, until completely smooth.

4 Place the egg whites in a separate bowl and whisk until stiff: this should take 3 to 4 minutes if whisking by hand, or 1 to 2 minutes if using an electric mixer. Gently fold the beaten whites into the sweet potato mixture and set aside.

5 When ready to serve, put 4 teaspoons/20 g of the diced butter into a large frying pan and place over medium heat. When the butter starts to foam, ladle about 2 heaped tablespoons of pancake batter into the pan; you should be able to cook 3 pancakes at a time. Cook for 3 to 4 minutes, turning once halfway through, once the edges of the pancake are brown and the mixture starts to bubble in the middle. The pancakes are quite soft, so be careful as you turn them over. Transfer to a parchment-lined baking sheet and set aside while you continue with the remaining batter, wiping the pan clean before adding 4 teaspoons/20 g more butter with each batch. You should make 12 pancakes. Transfer to the oven for 5 minutes, just to warm everything through.

6 To serve, place 3 pancakes in the middle of each plate and spoon the yogurt on top. Drizzle with the date syrup, dust with the confectioners' sugar, and serve.

BLACK RICE WITH MANGO AND COCONUT CREAM

Although black glutinous rice was a staple of Scully's childhood breakfasts, it was Yotam who got hooked on the rice during his travels in Malaysia. The rice, contrary to what its name suggests, is a very deep burgundy color and gluten-free. It tastes nutty, looks striking, and has a texture that is both starchy and slightly al dente at the same time, with each grain retaining its identity when cooked.

For the best results, soak the rice overnight, and stir often while it's cooking to help release the starch and increase its creamy softness. The widely available Nerone Italian black rice works fine but, really, it's the Southeast Asian black glutinous variety you should be seeking out.

Pandan leaves are used widely in both sweet and savory Southeast Asian cooking, infusing dishes with a coconutty, almost grassy fragrance. You'll have to go to an Asian food store to find them, but if you do, you'll be rewarded with a big bunch that you can freeze for future use. They can be substituted with a vanilla bean, slit open and seeds scraped.

Serves 6

2 1/2 cups/400 g black glutinous rice, soaked in plenty of water overnight
3 1/2 oz/100 g pandan leaf (10 large leaves), tied in a knot, or 1 vanilla bean, slit open lengthwise and seeds scraped

1 medium mango, peeled and diced into 3/4-inch/2-cm cubes (7 oz/200 g)
2 medium bananas, peeled and sliced 1/3 inch/1 cm thick (5 1/4 oz/150 g)
1/2 cup/120 g coconut cream
coarse sea salt

Palm sugar syrup
7 oz/200 g palm sugar, coarsely grated if starting with a block
2 3/4 oz/80 g pandan leaf (8 large leaves), or 1 vanilla bean, slit open lengthwise and seeds scraped

1 Drain and rinse the rice and place it in a large saucepan with the pandan leaves, 5 cups/1.2 liters of water, and 1 tablespoon of salt. Bring to a boil, then cook over medium heat for 30 to 35 minutes, stirring every few minutes, until the rice is cooked through but still retains a bite and has the consistency of thick, wet porridge. Discard the pandan leaves and keep the rice somewhere warm until ready to serve.

2 While the rice is cooking, make the syrup. Place the palm sugar and pandan leaves in a small saucepan with 2/3 cup/150 ml of water. Bring to a boil, then cook over medium-high heat for 20 minutes, until it has the consistency of maple syrup and has reduced by half. Remove and discard the pandan leaves and add 3 1/2 tablespoons of the syrup to the rice. Stir, then divide the rice among six bowls. Top with the mango and banana and drizzle over the coconut cream. You want the cream to have a pouring consistency, so thin it out with a little bit of water, if needed. Serve at once, with the remaining palm sugar syrup drizzled on top.

Zucchini and Manouri Fritters

These were first developed for the NOPI breakfast menu by Sarit Packer and John Meechan, during the restaurant's early days. Rumor spread and, due to popular demand, they quickly made their way onto the lunchtime and supper menus as well, where they've remained ever since. They make a lovely light lunch or impressive starter and are also great as a snack or canapé with drinks. If you are serving them as a snack, make them slightly smaller—1 heaped teaspoon rather than the 1 heaped tablespoon needed for the larger portion.

These are shaped into quenelles in the restaurant. They look like little rugby balls—three-sided oval shapes—made by passing the mix between two spoons, scraping the sides down as you go. They look great, but the method, though very simple, is a little cheffy. We've therefore changed the shape to the easier round fritters here, for the home cook—but feel free to don the chef's whites if you like. All you need is two spoons and some hot water for dipping them, so that the mixture does not stick. You'll need to deep-fry (rather than shallow-fry) the quenelles, so add enough oil to the pan so that it rises 2 inches/5 cm up the sides. Cook them for 3 to 4 minutes, and then finish off in a 425°F/220°C (390°F/200°C convection) oven for 5 minutes, so that the mixture is cooked through.

We use manouri cheese in our fritters at NOPI. It's a Greek semihard creamy ewe's milk cheese that's fantastic for frying or grilling. It's not easy to source, unfortunately, so you might need to use feta or halloumi instead.

Makes 12 fritters, to serve 4 for breakfast, or 24 smaller fritters, to serve 8 as a snack

Lime and cardamom sour cream
scant 1 cup/200 g sour cream
1/5 oz/5 g cilantro, coarsely chopped
1/2 tsp ground cardamom
finely grated zest and juice of 1 lime

3 medium zucchini, trimmed and coarsely grated (1 1/4 lb/580 g)
2 small shallots, finely chopped (3 1/2 oz/50 g)
2 cloves garlic, crushed
finely grated zest of 2 limes
1/2 cup/60 g self-rising flour
2 eggs, lightly beaten
2 1/2 tsp ground coriander
1 1/2 tsp ground cardamom

5 1/4 oz/150 g manouri, or halloumi or feta, broken into 1/2-inch/1 to 2-cm chunks
about 2/3 cup/150 ml sunflower oil, for frying
coarse sea salt and black pepper

1 Mix together all the ingredients for the sour cream sauce in a small bowl, along with 1/4 teaspoon of salt and a grind of black pepper. Set aside in the fridge until ready to serve.

2 Place the grated zucchini in a colander, sprinkle over 1 teaspoon of salt, and toss well. Set aside for 10 minutes, then squeeze the zucchini to remove most of the liquid: you want to keep a little bit of moisture, so don't squeeze them completely dry. Transfer to a large bowl and add the shallots, garlic, lime zest, flour, eggs, ground coriander, cardamom, and a grind of black pepper. Mix well to form a uniform batter, then gently fold in the cheese so it doesn't break up much.

3 Pour enough oil into a large frying pan so it rises 1/8 inch/3 mm up the sides and place over medium heat. Once hot, add 4 heaping tablespoons of the batter to the pan, spacing them well apart and flattening each fritter slightly with the flat side of a slotted spoon as they cook. Cook for 6 minutes, turning once halfway through, until the fritters are golden and crisp on both sides. Transfer to a paper towel–lined plate and keep somewhere warm while you continue with the remaining batter in two batches. Place 3 fritters on each plate and serve at once, with the sauce alongside or in a bowl on the side.

CORN BREAD WITH ROASTED PEACHES AND MAPLE CREAM

Customers at Ottolenghi Upper Street have been asking for our corn bread recipe for years. We've kept the recipe under wraps until now—some trade secrets are allowed—so this is "the big reveal." Some of the savory aromatics from the original recipe are missing here, so that it works as a brunch, but the basic recipe is the same.

We love to use white peaches for this—their sweetness is almost floral and they don't have any of the acidity that yellow peaches can have—but don't worry if you can't get hold of any. Yellow peaches also work well, as do nectarines or plums. Just make sure you keep the net amount the same.

To make this already substantial brunch into something even more substantial, serve it with some smoked bacon that has been lightly brushed with maple syrup and sprinkled with a bit of cayenne pepper.

Serves 4

Corn bread

3 oz/80 g corn kernels, fresh or frozen (shaved kernels from 1/2 medium ear of corn)

2/3 cup/85 g all-purpose flour, sifted

1/2 cup/75 g instant polenta

2 1/2 tsp baking powder

2 tbsp superfine sugar

4 1/2 tbsp/65 g unsalted butter, plus extra for greasing the loaf pan

5 tbsp/75 ml whole milk

1/4 cup/70 g Greek yogurt

3 eggs, yolks and whites separated

1 1/2 tsp runny honey

coarse sea salt and black pepper

Maple cream

1/2 cup/120 ml heavy cream

1 1/2 tsp maple syrup

1/2 cup/120 g cream cheese, room temperature

Ginger-vanilla syrup

1 1/2 cup/375 ml Sauternes

2-in/5-cm piece of ginger, peeled and thinly sliced widthwise (1 3/4 oz/50 g)

1/4 cup/84 g honey

1 vanilla bean, halved lengthwise and seeds scraped

Roasted peaches

4 large, juicy white peaches, yellow peaches, nectarines, or plums (1 1/2 lb/650 g), halved and stones removed

2 tsp demerara sugar

---

1 Preheat the oven to 425°F/220°C (390°F/200°C convection).

2 Place a large frying pan or wok over high heat and, when hot, add the corn kernels. Char for 2 minutes, shaking the pan from time to time, until golden brown all over. Remove from the heat and set aside to cool.

3 Lightly grease a loaf pan, about 3 1/2 by 9 1/2 inches/ 9 by 22 cm, with butter and line it with parchment paper. Place the flour, polenta, baking powder, and sugar in a medium bowl with 1 teaspoon of salt and a good grind of black pepper. Mix well and set aside. Melt about 2 tablespoons/25 g of the butter and put this into a separate bowl with the milk, yogurt, egg yolks, honey, and the roasted corn. Mix well, then gently fold this into the flour mixture, until well combined. Use an electric mixer or whisk to beat the egg whites until they form soft peaks. Carefully fold a third of the whites into the corn mixture, followed by the second third and then the last, taking care not to overwork the batter (it's fine to have streaks of egg white at this stage). Pour the batter into the prepared loaf pan and bake in the oven for 25 to 30 minutes, until a skewer inserted into the middle of the bread comes out clean and the top is golden brown. Remove from the oven and, after 10 minutes, tip the bread out of the loaf pan and set aside on a cooling rack to cool completely.

4 To make the maple cream, place the cream and maple syrup in a medium bowl and whisk until firm peaks are formed. Continue to whisk gently as you add the cream cheese, stopping as soon as it is combined. Keep in the fridge, covered, until ready to use.

5 To make the ginger-vanilla syrup, place a medium saucepan over medium-high heat with the Sauternes, ginger, honey, and vanilla bean and seeds. Bring to a boil and cook for 5 to 6 minutes, until about 1 cup/ 250 ml is left in the pan. Remove from the heat and set aside until ready to serve.

6 Set the broiler to high and lay the peach halves on a small foil-lined baking pan, skin side down and fitting together snugly, so that they poach as well as broil. Brush the cut side of the peaches with 2 teaspoons of the ginger syrup each and sprinkle over the demerara sugar. Place under the broiler, leaving about 6 inches/ 15 cm between the broiler and the pan—and cook for 8 to 10 minutes, basting with more syrup every couple of minutes or so. Remove the pan from the broiler once the peaches are nicely caramelized and set aside to cool. You'll have about 1/2 cup/130 ml of syrup left, which will be used when serving.

7 When ready to serve, trim the ends off the bread and cut 8 slices, each 3/4 inch/2 cm thick. Place a large frying pan over medium-high heat with 4 teaspoons/ 20 g of the remaining butter. Cook for 1 to 2 minutes, until the butter starts to foam, then add 4 slices of corn bread to the pan. Fry for 5 to 6 minutes, turning halfway through, until golden brown on both sides. Remove the bread from the pan and keep somewhere warm while you continue with the remaining bread and butter. Divide the bread among four plates and place two peach halves alongside. Top with a spoonful of maple cream and serve at once, with a strip of vanilla bean laid on top and a final drizzle—1 or 2 tablespoons— of the syrup.

CORN BREAD WITH ROASTED PEACHES AND MAPLE CREAM

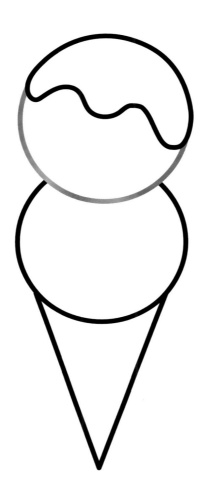

DESSERTS

Baked chocolate ganache with spicy hazelnuts and orange oil

Chocolate, orange, and cream: some combinations are just classic. So much so that not even our playful additions—hazelnuts, coriander, cardamom, salt—make a dent on this idyllic combination.

For a quick and fun alternative to the spicy hazelnuts, a line of popping candy can be used instead. It's a delight to watch people's faces as they are taken by the surprise of little balls exploding in their mouths.

If you want a restaurant-style extra, shape the chocolate into quenelles, rather than just spooning it onto the plate. The term describes the three-sided oval shape that results from smoothing a mixture between two tablespoons that have been dipped in hot water. Scooping up, then passing the mixture between two spoons like this, scraping the sides as you do, results in something that looks like a little rugby ball. It's a nice touch, but don't worry if you're not feeling cheffy: it's certainly not essential to the dish.

Either way, you'll need to start a day ahead for the chocolate to set in the fridge. You'll have a little of the chocolate ganache left over, which can be saved as a snack to have with coffee or served warm with some ice cream.

Serves 8

Chocolate ganache
9 oz/250 g dark chocolate
   (70 percent cocoa solids),
   broken into ¾-inch/2-cm pieces
⅔ cup/150 g unsalted butter,
   cut into ¾-inch/2-cm dice, plus
   extra for greasing the dish
1 egg, plus 3 egg yolks
5 tbsp/60 g superfine sugar
coarse sea salt, to serve

Spice mix
2 tsp coriander seeds
¾ tsp black peppercorns
1 small cinnamon stick
1 whole star anise
8 cardamom pods
¾ tsp superfine sugar
1½ oz/40 g hazelnuts, toasted,
   skins removed and roughly
   chopped

Crème fraîche
10½ oz/300 g crème fraîche
2½ tsp confectioners' sugar,
   sifted

Orange oil
finely grated zest of ½ orange
1 tbsp olive oil

1 Preheat the oven to 375°F/190°C (340°F/170°C convection).

2 Place the chocolate and butter for the ganache in a heatproof bowl and place over a saucepan half full of simmering water: take care that the water is not touching the bottom of the bowl. Keep on the heat for about 5 minutes, stirring and folding the mixture every now and then, until the chocolate is melted and shiny. Remove from the heat and set aside until completely cool.

3 Place the egg, egg yolks, and superfine sugar in a stand mixer bowl and whisk for 5 to 6 minutes, until thick, light, and foamy. In stages, carefully fold the beaten eggs into the chocolate by hand, taking care not to overwork the mixture, then transfer to a lightly greased and parchment-lined 8½ by-3 inch/ 22 by 8-cm loaf pan. Place in the oven and bake for about 10 minutes, until the surface is opaque but the middle has a slight wobble. Remove from the oven and set aside to cool. Cover and refrigerate until set, preferably overnight. You don't want the ganache to be too firm when serving, so remove it from the fridge 2 hours before serving.

4 To make the spice mix, place the coriander seeds, peppercorns, cinnamon stick, star anise, and cardamom pods in a frying pan and toast for 2 to 3 minutes, until fragrant. Transfer to a spice grinder or a mortar and pestle and grind until completely fine. Transfer to a medium bowl, mix in the sugar and hazelnuts, and set aside.

5 Mix together the crème fraîche and confectioners' sugar and keep in the fridge until ready to use.

6 To make the orange oil, mix together the orange zest and olive oil and set aside.

7 To serve, arrange the hazelnut spice mix in a straight line down the middle of eight plates. Scoop a tablespoon-size portion of chocolate onto each plate (dipping the spoon in hot water will help keep things neat) and place on an angle across the nuts. Place a spoonful of crème fraîche next to the chocolate and drizzle the orange oil on top. Finish with a tiny pinch of salt and serve at once.

Poached quince with raspberry and quince jelly and mascarpone sabayon

---

We find it hard to think of a dessert more suited to the feasting that surrounds Christmas than one that combines quince, jelly, and booze! The combination of pieces of quince with jelly that has been made from the fruit's cooking juices showcases the festive fruit tremendously well. Commercial quinces today have, unfortunately, been bred to cook in a matter of minutes rather than the hours they used to take, so, as a result, have much less flavor than they used to. To redress the balance, we've added a fair amount of aromatics to the cooking syrup.

To make the raspberry purée, simply crush some fresh or thawed frozen raspberries and pass them through a fine sieve. You'll need to start a day in advance here with the jelly and fruit for the jelly to set. Serve this with biscotti or a similar hard cookie.

With thanks to John Meechan and Sarit Packer, who got this—along with so many other sweet things—off the ground in the early NOPI days.

Serves 8

3 medium quinces (1³/4 lb/800 g in total)
2 tbsp lemon juice

Poaching liquor
3/4 cup/150 g superfine sugar
3 tbsp lemon juice
8 whole star anise
15 cardamom pods, crushed
10 whole cloves

4 cinnamon sticks
1 vanilla pod, sliced lengthwise and seeds scraped

Jelly
5 gelatin leaves, weighing about ¹/3 oz/9 g, soaked in cold water for 3 minutes
1/4 cup/60 ml Vin Santo, or another sweet dessert wine
2 tbsp raspberry purée from 12 medium raspberries (see headnote, page 257)

Sabayon
6 egg yolks
7 tbsp/90 g superfine sugar
1/2 cup/120 ml Vin Santo, or another sweet dessert wine
2²/3 oz/75 g mascarpone, at room temperature

To serve
1 oz/30 g pistachio nuts, slivered or coarsely chopped (optional)

1 Peel the quinces (reserving the skins) and quarter them lengthwise. Use a small, sharp knife to remove the core, which you also need to keep. Place the quince quarters in a medium bowl, cover with water, add the lemon juice, and set aside. Put the quince cores and skins into a medium saucepan, along with all the ingredients for the poaching liquor and 4¹/2 cups/1 liter of water. Bring to a boil, then simmer over medium heat, uncovered, for 10 minutes. Drain the quince quarters and add them to the pan. Place a small heatproof plate on top of the quinces to hold them down and continue to simmer over medium heat for 10 to 15 minutes, until the fruit is soft but not falling apart; this may take longer, depending on your quince. Remove from the heat and drain the quinces in a fine sieve and over a bowl so that the poaching liquid is preserved. Discard the skins, cores, and aromatics and cut the quince quarters into ¹/2-inch/1.5-cm dice. Set aside in the fridge.

2 To make the jelly, return the strained syrup to the pan and boil over high heat for 10 to 12 minutes, until the liquid has thickened and you have 1²/3 cups/400 ml left in the pan. Set aside for 5 minutes, so that it is hot rather than boiling, then pour the reduced liquid into a medium bowl. Squeeze the water out of the gelatin leaves and whisk these into the hot liquid. Once dissolved, add the Vin Santo and 1¹/2 tablespoons of the raspberry purée, keeping

the remaining 1¹/2 teaspoons aside to serve. Stir well, then pour the syrup into a shallow bowl or small rimmed baking pan. Set aside in the fridge for at least 4 hours or, preferably, overnight, for the jelly to set. You'll need to remove the jelly from the fridge 1 hour before serving so that it is not set too hard. Remove the diced quince at the same time so that it is not fridge-cold.

3 Make the sabayon just before serving. Fill a medium saucepan with enough water so that it rises a third of the way up the sides. Bring to a boil over medium heat, then place a heatproof bowl on top of the saucepan; it needs to fit snugly in the pan without touching the water. Put the egg yolks in the bowl, along with the sugar and Vin Santo, and whisk constantly over the bubbling water for about 10 minutes, until the mixture is thick, shiny, and hot (you can whisk by hand or, more easily, use a hand-held mixer if you have one). Remove from the heat, add the mascarpone, and whisk until smooth.

4 To serve, divide the diced quince among eight wine glasses or glass bowls. Cut the jelly into 1-inch/2- to 3-cm dice and spoon on top. Pour over the sabayon (warmish or at room temperature) and serve with the remaining raspberry purée drizzled on top and the pistachios sprinkled over, if using.

Roasted pineapple with tamarind and chile, and coconut ice cream

Some desserts—just like some cocktails—will always be just a little bit '80s, particularly those where tropical fruit gets cooked. And none the worse for it, we say. This is Scully's tribute to the decade of his youth, to piña coladas, and also to the now-closed Danks Street Depot in Sydney, where he used to eat brunch.

You can buy ready-made tamarind paste but, as ever, we recommend making your own, starting with the pulp. In order to make 2 tablespoons of tamarind paste, soak 1 ounce/30 g of tamarind pulp in 1/4 cup/60 ml of water for about half an hour, squeezing from time to time so that all the pulp and tamarind disperses through the water. Strain through a fine-mesh sieve, discarding the pulp.

Serves 6

Ice cream

2/3 cup/150 ml heavy cream

1 2/3 cup/400 ml coconut milk

1 cup/250 ml coconut cream

12 kaffir lime leaves

1 vanilla bean, halved lengthwise and seeds scraped

2 egg yolks

7 tbsp/90 g superfine sugar

1 1/2 tbsp lime juice

Spiced syrup

2 1/2 cups/600 ml water

7 tbsp/90 g superfine sugar

16 whole cloves

1 large cinnamon stick, broken into quarters

1 large red chile, seeded and coarsely chopped

1 vanilla bean, halved lengthwise and seeds scraped

2-inch/5-cm piece of ginger, peeled and thinly sliced (1 1/2 oz/40 g)

2 tbsp tamarind paste (see headnote, page 260)

1 very large pineapple, peeled, quartered lengthwise, tough core removed (1 3/4 lb/800 g)

6 small Thai basil sprigs, to garnish (optional)

1 First make the ice cream. Place the cream, coconut milk, coconut cream, kaffir lime leaves, and vanilla bean in a medium saucepan. Place over medium-high heat and cook for 6 to 7 minutes, until just coming to a boil. Remove from the heat and set aside to infuse for 5 minutes.

2 Place the egg yolks and sugar in a large mixing bowl and whisk until creamy and pale. Using a ladle, spoon a little bit of the hot cream mixture into the eggs and sugar, whisking continuously as you pour. Continue with the remaining cream until everything is incorporated. Wipe your saucepan clean and pour in the custard. Place over medium heat and cook for 15 minutes, stirring continuously with a rubber spatula, until the mixture is thick enough to coat the spatula and leaves a gap if you draw a line through it with your finger; don't overcook or the custard will curdle. Strain into a bowl, discarding the leaves and vanilla beans, and store in the fridge until well chilled, or place in an ice bucket to speed up the cooling process. Pour the chilled custard into an ice cream machine, along with the lime juice. Churn for about 35 minutes, until semifrozen but still creamy. Transfer to a cold plastic container and freeze until ready to use. Remove from the freezer 5 minutes before serving.

3 Preheat the oven to 465°F/240°C (425°F/220°C convection).

4 Place all the ingredients for the spiced syrup in a medium saucepan over medium-high heat. Bring to a boil, then reduce the heat to medium and simmer gently for 5 minutes to let the flavors infuse. Place the pineapple wedges in a high-sided 9 by 12-inch/ 22 by 30-cm baking pan, and then pour the syrup evenly over the pineapple. Place it in the oven for 40 to 50 minutes, basting every 10 minutes or so, until the pineapple is cooked through and caramelized, and a knife inserted goes in without any resistance. Keep an eye on the liquid level in the pan; you might need to add a little bit more water and stir it in if the liquid has evaporated. Remove from the oven and set aside to cool slightly in the syrup for about 5 minutes. Remove the pineapple from the pan and serve with 1 1/2 teaspoons of syrup per portion drizzled on top. Dot with a few of the cloves and cinnamon pieces from the syrup, garnish with the Thai basil, and serve a spoonful of ice cream alongside.

Popcorn ice cream with caramelized popcorn and black pepper

Scully had been working away for months on his idea to infuse ice cream with popcorn. Excitement levels were high: it was one of those magical moments when a new flavor combination is discovered. It was with a wry smile, therefore, that Scully looked upon the rows and rows of salted caramel popcorn ice cream in Waitrose, developed by Heston Blumenthal, that had come on to the shelves just at the same time. D'oh!

You'll need to start this a day ahead for the cream to infuse and really get the sweet popcorn flavor. You'll have some popcorn left over but it will keep well in a sealed container for some happy snacking. Save the egg whites for making meringues.

Serves 4

4 tbsp/60 g unsalted butter
5¼ oz/150 g uncooked
  popcorn kernels

2 cups/500 ml heavy cream
3 cups/700 ml whole milk
2 vanilla beans, split open
  lengthwise and seeds scraped
4 egg yolks

¾ cup/160 g superfine sugar
1½ tbsp liquid glucose
½ tsp freshly ground black
  pepper
coarse sea salt

1 Place the butter in a large saucepan for which you have a lid, and set over medium-high heat. Heat for 4 to 5 minutes, until the butter is frothing and starting to turn brown. Add the popcorn kernels and stir so that they are coated in the butter. Cover the pan and cook for 3 minutes, shaking the pan very frequently as you hear the kernels pop open. Remove from the heat when the popping sound stops. Transfer 5 ounces/140 g of the cooked popcorn to a medium bowl and keep the remaining 1½ ounces/40 g separate to caramelize.

2 Pour the cream and milk into the same saucepan in which you cooked the popcorn and add the vanilla beans and seeds. Place over low heat and cook for 8 minutes. Remove from the heat just before it comes to a boil, pour over the 5 ounces/140 g portion of popcorn and stir well. Cover the bowl with plastic wrap, set aside to cool, and leave in the fridge to infuse overnight.

3 The next day, bring the mixture back to room temperature and strain it through a fine-mesh sieve into a separate bowl, squeezing all the flavor out of the popcorn into the milk before discarding the popcorn and vanilla pod.

4 Place the egg yolks in a large bowl with ½ cup/100 g of the superfine sugar. Whisk until light and fluffy, then use a ladle to spoon the cream mixture into the eggs, continuously whisking as you pour. Return the custard to a large saucepan with ¼ teaspoon of salt. Place over medium heat and cook for 5 to

7 minutes, stirring continuously with a rubber spatula, until the mixture is thick enough to coat the spatula and leaves a gap if you draw a line through it with your finger. You don't want to overcook and curdle the custard but, if you do, just pass it through a fine-mesh sieve. Remove from the heat and transfer to a bowl to cool. Store in the fridge until well chilled, or place in an ice bucket to speed up the cooling process. Pour the custard into an ice cream machine and churn for 35 minutes, until semifrozen. Transfer to a plastic container and keep in the freezer, covered, until required. You can do this in advance, but bring the ice cream out of the freezer for 5 minutes before serving.

5 Place the remaining ¼ cup/60 g of superfine sugar and glucose in a clean, medium nonstick saucepan over medium heat. Cook for 6 to 7 minutes, slowly swirling the pan from time to time but without stirring, until the sugar is golden brown. Reduce the heat to medium and carefully add the remaining popcorn, along with the freshly ground black pepper and ½ teaspoon of salt. Stir once, then brush the sides of the pan with a wet pastry brush. Cook for 1 minute, stirring constantly, until all the popcorn is covered in the caramel. Remove from the heat, spread out on a wax paper–lined baking sheet and set aside to cool. The popcorn will be all stuck together at this stage but you can break it up before serving.

6 To serve, divide the ice cream among bowls and serve with the caramelized popcorn sprinkled on top.

Caramel peanut ice cream with chocolate sauce and peanut brittle

This combination of caramel, roasted peanuts, and chocolate sauce is, basically, just a seriously sophisticated Snickers ice cream. It's both as familiar as you'd want it to be and even more delicious than you imagine it could be.

Making caramel is one of those things that can seem a bit daunting if you've not done it before. There's nothing complicated about it, though, so don't be put off. You just have to hold your nerve as the sugar turns and darkens, at the same time keeping a close eye out so that you don't take it too far. It might take a practice or two before you perfect it, but the prospects of your turning into a caramel pro are pretty good.

Double the quantities for the chocolate sauce and brittle, if you like. They both keep well and are lovely to have around as leftovers for the days ahead. See photos on the preceding pages.

Serves 6

Ice cream
5 oz/140 g raw skinless peanuts
7/8 cup/175 g superfine sugar
2 3/4 cups/650 ml whole milk
2/3 cup/150 ml heavy cream
1 tbsp liquid glucose
7 egg yolks
coarse sea salt

Chocolate sauce
6 tbsp/90 ml heavy cream
1 tbsp whole milk
1 1/2 oz/40 g dark chocolate
   (70 percent cocoa solids),
   coarsely chopped
2 2/3 oz/75 g Nutella spread
   or milk chocolate
1 tsp hazelnut oil

Peanut brittle
1 3/4 oz/50 g raw skinless peanuts
7 tbsp/85 g superfine sugar
2 tbsp/30 g unsalted butter, plus
   extra for greasing the pan

1 Preheat the oven to 390°F/200°C (360°F/180°C convection).

2 Place the peanuts for both the brittle and the ice cream (6³/4 ounces/190 g in total) in a small baking pan. Roast for 12 to 15 minutes, until golden brown, then remove from the oven. Set aside the 1³/4 ounces/50 g needed for the brittle and place the remaining 5 ounces/140 g for the ice cream in the small bowl of a food processor with ¼ cup/50 g of the sugar for the ice cream and 1 teaspoon of salt. Blitz for 4 to 5 minutes—do this while the nuts are still warm—to form a wet sticky paste, and then set aside.

3 Place a medium saucepan over medium-high heat and pour in the milk and cream for the ice cream. Cook for about 4 minutes, until the mixture comes to a boil. Reduce the heat to medium, add the peanut paste, and whisk for about 1 to 2 minutes, until combined. Remove from the heat and keep warm.

4 Place a separate medium saucepan over medium heat with the remaining 10 tbsp/125 g of sugar for the ice cream, along with the glucose and 1 tablespoon of water. Cook for about 6 to 8 minutes, swirling slightly but resisting the urge to stir, until a dark golden brown caramel stage is reached. Remove from the heat and slowly, from a distance, pour the warm peanut cream mixture into the caramel—it's very important that the pan is not on the heat, as the mixture will bubble vigorously—whisking constantly but carefully until all the caramel is dissolved in the liquid.

5 Place the egg yolks in a large bowl and add a tablespoon of the peanut-caramel cream. Whisk to combine, then slowly pour in a third of the cream, whisking constantly as you do. Pour in another third, and then the remainder, whisking the whole time, until the mixture is glossy and thick. Return this mixture to the same saucepan over medium heat and cook for 3 to 4 minutes, stirring constantly with a rubber spatula, until the mixture is thick enough to coat the spatula and leaves a gap if you draw a line through it with your finger. If you have a thermometer, the temperature should be 185°F/85°C. Remove from the heat and transfer to a bowl to cool. Store in the fridge until well chilled, or place in an ice bucket if you want to speed up the cooling process.

6 Pour the chilled custard into your ice cream maker, churn for 30 to 35 minutes, then place in the freezer for at least 4 hours. Make sure you bring it out of the freezer about 10 minutes before serving.

7 To make the chocolate sauce, pour the cream and milk into a small saucepan and place over medium-high heat. Bring to a boil, then remove from the heat. Place the chocolate pieces and Nutella in a separate bowl and pour in the hot milk and cream, whisking constantly until combined. Add the oil, along with ⅛ teaspoon of salt, and whisk until shiny and glossy. Set aside until ready to use. The sauce can be served hot or at room temperature.

8 To make the peanut brittle, grease a small baking sheet and set aside. Place the sugar in a medium saucepan over medium heat. Cook for 7 to 8 minutes, gently swirling the pan, until the sugar starts to caramelize and has an even golden brown color. Carefully add the butter, then increase the heat to medium-high and use a wooden spoon to stir gently for 1 minute, until the butter dissolves. Add the roasted peanuts and fold them in so that they are coated with the caramel. Cook for another 30 seconds, stirring constantly, then tip the nuts out on to the baking sheet. Set aside for at least 1 hour, to cool and harden, then chop into ⅓-inch/1-cm pieces. Store in an airtight container until ready to use.

9 To serve, spoon 3 small scoops of ice cream into each bowl, followed by 2 tablespoons of chocolate sauce drizzled on top. Top each portion with 1½ table-spoons of brittle and serve.

TAPIOCA WITH COCONUT JAM AND CARAMELIZED RUM BANANAS

We're regressing by another decade here: from Scully's Roasted Pineapple of the '80s (see page 260) to Yotam's flambéed bananas of the '70s. A (modern-day) shortcut can be taken by just chopping up some fresh banana, instead, or leaving out the banana altogether. If you do this, just put a bit more of the coconut milk on top, along with a squeeze of lime.

For anyone who has been through the British school system and has memories of school lunches from the '70s and '80s, don't be put off by your memories of tapioca. Talking to our friends, it seems that a whole generation has been ruined, calling the little pearls of cassava flour "frogspawn." Although they do indeed turn translucent and jellylike when cooked, it's precisely their consistency and texture that we like so much and that we urge all doubters to try again.

The tapioca can be made in advance—up to the point where the coconut cream has been stirred in and then set aside—then just warmed through before serving. This is delicious the day after it is made, so any leftovers can either be eaten at room temperature or served warm. The coconut jam, cream, and bananas are also heaven in a crêpe, if any or all of these elements need using up.

Serves 8

Kaffir lime cream
1²/₃ cups/400 ml coconut cream
1³/₄ oz/50 g palm sugar, coarsely
   grated if starting with a block
10 fresh kaffir lime leaves

Tapioca
1¹/₃ cups/200 g tapioca

2 whole vanilla beans, sliced open
   lengthwise and seeds scraped
coarse sea salt

Coconut jam
3¹/₂ oz/100 g palm sugar, coarsely
   grated if starting from a block
7 oz/200 g coarsely grated
   coconut flesh (the flesh from
   1 medium coconut)

Caramelized bananas
2 large bananas, peeled
   (9 oz/260 g)
1 tbsp light brown sugar
3 tbsp/40 g unsalted butter
¼ cup/60 ml rum

To serve
¹/₃ cup/80 ml coconut milk

1 First make the lime leaf–infused cream. Place the coconut cream, palm sugar, and kaffir lime leaves in a small saucepan. Bring to a boil over medium heat, then reduce the heat to medium-low. Simmer for 5 minutes, remove the pan from the heat, and set aside to cool.

2 Place the tapioca in a medium saucepan with the vanilla bean and seeds and ¹/₂ teaspoon of salt. Add 4¹/₂ cups/1 liter of water and bring to a boil. Reduce the heat to medium-low and simmer for 12 to 14 minutes, stirring constantly, until the tapioca is transparent but still retains a bite. Pour in the infused coconut cream, discarding the lime leaves. Heat the tapioca through for 1 minute, then set aside somewhere warm until ready to serve. You want it to have the consistency of a thick porridge, so you might need to add 2 or 3 more tablespoons of water to the tapioca before serving.

3 While you are cooking the tapioca, make the coconut jam. Place the palm sugar in a medium saucepan with ²/₃ cup/150 ml of water. Bring to a boil, then reduce the heat to medium and add the coconut, along with ¹/₂ teaspoon of salt. Stir well, then cook for 15 minutes, stirring from time to time, to get a thick, sticky consistency. Remove from the heat and set aside.

4 Cut the bananas in half lengthwise, and again in half widthwise. Spread them out cut side up, and sprinkle with the brown sugar. Place the butter in a large frying pan over medium-high heat and, once it starts to foam, add the banana sections to the pan, sugared side down. Reduce the heat to medium and cook for 4 to 5 minutes, until the bananas have turned golden brown and are beginning to caramelize. Gently flip the bananas, add the rum to the pan, and very carefully light with a match to flame up: there is a lot of rum here, so take care to stand back and have a lid at the ready to put out the flames if they flare up. Otherwise, allow the alcohol to cook for a minute and for the flames to naturally subside before removing the pan from the heat.

5 To serve, divide the tapioca among eight glass bowls and place a piece of banana on each portion. Spoon 2 tablespoons of coconut jam on top and serve warm or at room temperature, with 2 teaspoons of coconut milk drizzled over each portion.

RICOTTA FRITTERS WITH BLACKBERRY SAUCE AND CHOCOLATE SOIL

This is an impressive way to round off a meal, with the wow factor made easier by the fact that much of the preparation can be done in advance. The chocolate soil (so called because of the way it looks!), the blackberry sauce, the star anise sugar, and the batter for the fritters can all be made well in advance—2 days for the batter and blackberry sauce; much longer for the soil and sugar—so you'll just need to fry and bake the fritters before serving.

You'll have some leftover chocolate soil here, but it will keep in a sealed container for a week, and is a treat to have around to sprinkle on ice cream and milkshakes.

Serves 6

Chocolate soil
6 tbsp/45 g all-purpose flour
1/2 tsp cornstarch
3 tbsp/40 g superfine sugar
1/3 cup/30 g cocoa powder
3 tbsp/40 g unsalted butter, melted
coarse sea salt

Ricotta fritters
2 1/2 tbsp/20 g confectioners' sugar, sifted
3/4 cup/100 g all-purpose flour
1/2 tsp baking powder
1 lb 1 oz/500 g firm ricotta
finely grated zest of 2 large oranges
scraped seeds of 1 vanilla bean
2 eggs, plus 1 egg yolk
about 2 cups/450 ml sunflower oil, for frying

Blackberry sauce
1/4 cup/50 g superfine sugar
1 1/2 lb/700 g fresh (or thawed frozen) blackberries
1/2 cup/120 ml sloe gin or 6 tbsp/90 ml regular gin

Star anise sugar
2 whole star anise, finely ground (or 2 tsp ground star anise; see page 237)
1/3 cup/70 g superfine sugar

1 Preheat the oven to 320°F/160°C (280°F/140°C convection).

2 First make the chocolate soil. Place the flour, cornstarch, sugar, and cocoa powder in a bowl, along with 1/2 teaspoon of salt. Mix together, then slowly pour in the melted butter. Use a wooden spoon, then the tips of your fingers, to mix until a crumble-like texture is formed, then spread out on a parchment-lined baking sheet. Bake for 15 to 20 minutes, stirring once halfway through, until the consistency is that of a crumbly cookie. Don't worry if some of the mix clumps together; you'll be able to break it back into crumble once it has cooled and set. Remove from the oven—the mixture will still be moist but will firm up as it cools—and set aside until ready to use.

3 To prepare the fritters, sift the confectioners' sugar, flour, and baking powder into a large mixing bowl. Add the ricotta, orange zest, vanilla seeds, and 1/4 teaspoon of salt and use a wooden spoon to mix and combine. Place the eggs and egg yolk in a separate bowl and whisk together well, until pale and tripled in volume—about 3 minutes using an electric mixer. Fold this into the ricotta mixture to combine. Store in the fridge for at least 4 hours to firm up. The mixture will keep, covered, for up to 2 days.

4 Place the superfine sugar for the blackberry sauce in a small saucepan with 2 tablespoons of water. Bring to a boil over medium-high heat, stirring to help the sugar dissolve, then set aside for the sugar syrup to cool. Place 1 pound 1 ounce/500 g of blackberries in a blender and blitz to form a purée. Pass the mixture through a fine-mesh sieve and into a bowl to strain out the seeds. Pour over the sugar syrup and gin, mix to combine, and set aside in the fridge for at least 1 hour—you want it to be very cold—until ready to serve.

5 Place the star anise in a medium mixing bowl, stir in the sugar, and set aside.

6 When you are ready to serve, preheat the oven to 425°F/220°C (390°F/200°C convection).

7 Pour the sunflower oil into a medium saucepan—it should rise about 1 1/4 inches/3 cm up the sides of the pan—and place over medium-high heat. Once hot, use two tablespoons to shape the ricotta mixture into irregular balls, each weighing about 1 3/4 ounces/50 g; use one spoon to scoop the mixture up and the other spoon to scrape it off into the hot oil. Fry in batches of four—you don't want to overcrowd the pan—for 3 to 4 minutes, constantly turning so that all sides are golden brown. Use a slotted spoon to lift the fritters out of the oil and transfer to a paper towel-lined plate to drain while you continue with the remaining two batches. Transfer all the fritters to a parchment-lined baking pan and bake for 8 minutes, until cooked through. Remove from the oven and, while still hot, roll them in the star anise sugar to coat.

8 To serve, divide the blackberry sauce among six shallow bowls. Place the hot fritters in the sauce, sprinkle over a teaspoon of chocolate soil per portion, and garnish with the reserved blackberries. Serve at once.

RICOTTA FRITTERS WITH BLACKBERRY SAUCE AND CHOCOLATE SOIL

COFFEE AND PECAN FINANCIERS

NOPI regulars voice their unhappiness when these come off the menu for a due break, and are equally jolly to see them return. What makes the little sponges so popular, in our mind, is the fact that they are irresistibly fresh (they are baked to order)—plus the pecan coffee cream, which is culinary sorcery if ever there was such a thing.

Everything can be prepared in advance here—the flavor in both the pecan coffee cream and the cake batter intensifies and improves overnight—but the cakes should be eaten fresh out of the oven.

What makes a financier a financier is the *beurre noisette* element: the nutty brown butter. They should, traditionally, be made in little rectangular molds so that they look, as their name suggests, like little bars of gold. We've changed their shape here, presuming home cooks have muffin pans, but use financier or madeleine molds, if you have them.

Makes 20 cakes, to serve 10

Financiers
3¹/2 oz/100 g pecans
²/3 cup/150 g unsalted butter,
    cut into ³/4-inch/2-cm dice, plus
    extra for greasing the muffin
    pans

1²/3 cups/200 g confectioners'
    sugar
3¹/2 oz/100 g ground almonds
³/4 cup/100 g all-purpose flour
¹/2 cup/65 g malted milk powder
1 tsp baking powder
2 tsp ground coffee
8 egg whites (10¹/2 oz/300 g)

2 shots of espresso (¹/4 cup/60 ml)
coarse sea salt

Pecan coffee cream
3¹/2 oz/100 g pecans
3 shots of espresso (6 tbsp/90 ml)
2¹/4 cups/530 ml heavy cream
5 packed tbsp/75 g light brown
    sugar

1 Preheat the oven to 375°F/190°C (340°F/170°C convection). Spread the pecans for both the financiers and the cream out on a parchment-lined baking sheet and place in the oven for 12 to 15 minutes, until they have taken on a bit of color. Use the flat side of a large knife to lightly crush them. Set aside half of the pecans for the financiers and half for the cream.

2 To make the financiers, put the butter into a medium saucepan and place over high heat. Once it starts to foam, cook for 3 to 4 minutes, until it turns golden brown and smells nutty. Strain through a muslin-lined sieve and set aside for about 15 minutes to cool slightly.

3 Place the confectioners' sugar in a large bowl with the ground almonds, flour, malted milk powder, baking powder, ¹/2 teaspoon of salt, and the ground coffee. Mix together and set aside. Place the egg whites in a separate bowl and whisk to form soft peaks: this should take about 3 minutes if you are whisking by hand and just 1 minute with an electric mixer. Fold the whites into the dry ingredients by hand, followed by the espresso. Next, pour in half the browned butter, continuing to fold by hand as you pour in the remaining butter. Finally, fold in the pecans. Set aside in the fridge—with some plastic wrap placed on the surface to prevent it forming a skin—for at least 2 hours or overnight.

4 Next, make the pecan coffee cream. Place the espresso in a medium saucepan. Bring to a boil and then cook for about 1¹/2 minutes over high heat, swirling the pan to reduce by half. Add the pecans, cream, and brown sugar and return to a boil. Cook for 4 minutes, until the cream thickens, then remove from the heat. Set aside to cool for at least 2 hours or overnight, in the fridge. If you leave it overnight, the cream will thicken in the fridge, so you will need to return it to a low heat in the saucepan for 1¹/2 minutes, to loosen it up. Pass the mixture through a fine-mesh sieve into a medium bowl and set aside to cool. The nuts can be discarded at this stage (you can eat them if you like, but they don't look attractive). Whisk the cream mixture for about 4 minutes with a hand-held electric mixer, until thickened to soft peaks with the consistency of a soft mousse. It is very easy to over-whip, so keep a close eye on it here. If you do over-whip it, just add a little bit of milk to bring it back. Set aside in the fridge until ready to serve.

5 Preheat the oven to 425°F/220°C (390°F/200°C convection).

6 Grease two muffin pans with cups 2 inches/5 cm in diameter, and line the bottom of each cup with a round of parchment paper. You will have enough mix to make 20 financiers, so if you have 12 cups in each tray, you can leave 4 ungreased. Spoon in the batter until each cup is three-quarters full and bake for 10 to 12 minutes, until the cakes are golden brown on top and just cooked through: a knife inserted should come out with a tiny amount of batter on it. Remove from the oven and set aside to rest for 5 minutes before removing the cakes from the pan. Serve warm or at room temperature, with the pecan coffee cream alongside.

Farro pudding with caramelized orange, tahini, and pistachios

_____

The difference in consistency and taste among various types of tahini is enormous. Our strong preference is for one of the several good Arabic brands—Al Yaman and Al Arz are two favorites—rather than the Greek varieties, which we find to be rather sticky. Arabic tahini (mainly Lebanese and Palestinian), by contrast, is wonderfully smooth, creamy, and nutty. After one taste, you'll be converted and addicted, finding ways to spoon it into every meal. Spread on morning toast; mixed with honey and swirled through porridge; mixed with a little soy sauce, honey, and cider vinegar and drizzled over broccoli: there's a whole tahini cookbook out there, waiting to be written. Don't worry if you only have the Greek variety, though, it will still work fine.

Yotam made a version of this for his previous book, _Plenty More_, using pot barley instead of farro. Both have the attraction of being ultimately comforting; at the same time, each grain retains its own identity and doesn't becomes at all mush-like. Either spelt or pearl barley also work well, if that's what you have.

You can make this as one large pudding rather than transferring the mixture to individual ramekins, as suggested here. If doing this, remove the foil from the baking dish after 40 minutes, as instructed, and continue cooking for a final 15 minutes with the foil off.

Serves 6 to 8

1½ cups/300 g farro, rinsed well
  under plenty of cold water
¾ cup/150 g superfine sugar
2½ cups/600 ml whole milk
¾ cup/200 ml heavy cream

Finely grated zest of ½ lemon,
  plus 1 tbsp lemon juice to serve
½ vanilla bean, sliced open bean,
  and seeds scraped
2 tbsp/30 g unsalted butter
coarse sea salt

Caramelized orange
2 large oranges
½ cup/100 g superfine sugar

To serve
4 tbsp tahini paste
2 oz/60 g shelled pistachios,
  roasted and coarsely chopped
½ tsp orange blossom water

1 Preheat the oven to 340°F/170°C (300°F/150°C convection).

2 Put the farro into a medium saucepan with the sugar, milk, cream, lemon zest, vanilla bean and seeds, butter, and 1 teaspoon of salt. Mix well and place over medium-high heat. Bring to a boil—this should take about 5 minutes—then transfer to an 8 by 10-inch/20 by 24-cm baking dish. Cover with foil and bake for 40 minutes, stirring once halfway through, until the consistency is that of runny rice pudding. Spoon the mixture into individual ramekins. They need another 15 minutes in the oven, until the farro is soft and swollen but still retains a bite, so you can either set them aside at this point (if making them in advance) or transfer them to the oven, uncovered, for their final stage of cooking.

3 Now make the caramelized orange. Finely zest half of one of the oranges, set the zest aside, then use a small sharp knife to slice off the top and bottom of both oranges. Cut down the side of each orange, following its natural curve, to remove the skin and white pith.

Over a small bowl, cut in between the membranes to remove the individual segments, collecting all the juice along the way and squeezing the remaining membranes: you should get about ¼ cup/60 ml of juice and 7 ounces/200 g of orange segments. Keep the juice and orange segments separate.

4 Spread out the sugar in a small saucepan and place over medium heat. Cook for about 8 to 10 minutes, resisting the urge to stir until the sugar has melted and turned to a rich golden caramel. Off the heat, carefully pour in the orange juice, stirring vigorously as you pour. Return to the heat and carry on stirring until any caramel lumps have dissolved. Remove from the heat and add the orange segments and zest. Carefully mix—you don't want the segments to break up—and set aside until ready to use.

5 When ready to serve, drizzle each portion of hot pudding with some of the tahini and spoon orange segments on top. Mix the pistachios with the lemon juice and orange blossom water, spoon over the puddings, and serve.

STRAINED RICOTTA WITH BLACKCURRANT COMPOTE AND RHUBARB

You'll need to get the ricotta mixture hanging 2 days before you want to serve this. Beyond having to think ahead, though, there's actually very little to do here, and the result is wonderfully rewarding. The curled rhubarb—deceptively simple to do, given how composed and "restaurant-like" it looks—is particularly impressive.

If you can't get blackcurrants, then blackberries, raspberries, plums, or juicy, ripe strawberries also work.

Serves 4

9 oz/250 g ricotta
1/2 cup/120 g crème fraîche

scraped seeds of 1/2 vanilla bean
2 egg whites
3/4 cup/140 g superfine sugar
1 medium rhubarb stalk
(2 3/4 oz/80 g)

4 1/4 oz/120 g fresh or
frozen blackcurrants
coarse sea salt

1 Two days before serving, place the ricotta, crème fraîche, and vanilla seeds in a medium bowl and mix by hand until smooth. Add a pinch of salt and set aside.

2 Place the egg whites in a separate bowl and whisk until stiff. Add 1/2 cup/100 g of the sugar and continue to whisk until combined and the peaks are stiff and glossy. Gently fold the egg whites into the ricotta mixture, then transfer to the middle of a clean muslin square. Draw up the sides to form a ball, tie together with string, and hang it in the fridge overnight, for the liquid to drip out. (Slotting a chopstick through the string and placing it horizontally over a container that is deep enough to let the ball hang free is a good way of catching and containing the liquid that gets released.)

3 After 12 to 24 hours, divide the ricotta mixture into 4 balls—they should weigh about 2 1/2 ounces/75 g each—and place each one in a separate clean muslin square. Twist them tightly, tie with string, and hang, as before, with the help of a chopstick held over a container deep enough for them to hang free. You

can hang all 4 balls on one chopstick, to save space. Leave in the fridge overnight, twisting them for a final time and wiping the balls dry before removing them from the cloth.

4 Fill a small bowl with iced water and set aside. Using a vegetable peeler, peel long, thin strips of rhubarb. Cut each strip widthwise into 4-inch/10-cm pieces, and then transfer the strips straight into the iced water. Sit the bowl in the fridge for at least an hour, for the rhubarb to curl. Drain and dry just before serving.

5 To make the compote, place the blackcurrants in a small pan with the remaining 1/4 cup/40 g of sugar and 1 1/2 tablespoons of water. Bring to a boil over medium heat, stirring gently so that the sugar dissolves, then remove immediately. Set aside to cool for 5 minutes, then keep in the fridge until required.

6 To serve, place a ball of ricotta in the middle of each plate and spoon some blackcurrant compote on top. Place the rhubarb strips alongside and serve.

STRAWBERRY AND ROSE MESS

This is both a wow of a dessert and—given that all the elements can be made in advance and just put together at the last minute—is also a very relaxing one to make and serve to friends. The dried rose petals look lovely sprinkled on top, but don't worry if you can't get hold of any: the advantage of having a dessert with the word "mess" in its title is that there is very little pressure to perform on the presentation front. You'll have a little bit of sorbet left over here, which can be saved for another day. You can also buy good-quality strawberry sorbet and save yourself much of the work.

Serves 6

Strawberry sorbet
3 tbsp superfine sugar
1/3 cup/40 g confectioners' sugar
1 1/2 tbsp liquid glucose
7 oz/200 g strawberries, hulled and blitzed into a purée

5 1/2 oz/160 g mascarpone
1 1/8 cups/270 g crème fraîche
2 tbsp confectioners' sugar, sifted
1 1/4 tsp rose water
3 tbsp superfine sugar
2 tbsp pomegranate molasses
1 tsp sumac
7 oz/200 g strawberries, hulled and chopped into 3/4-inch/ 2-cm pieces

2 oz/60 g meringues (store-bought is fine), broken roughly into 3/4-inch/2-cm pieces
seeds of 1 medium pomegranate (3 1/2 oz/100 g)
2 tsp dried rose petals (optional)

1 Place all the ingredients for the sorbet in a small saucepan with 1/4 cup/60 ml of water. Warm through over low heat, stirring so that the sugar and glucose dissolve. Transfer to a bowl to cool and store in the fridge until well chilled, or place in an ice bucket to speed up the cooling process. Pour into an ice cream machine and churn for about 20 minutes, until firm but not completely set. Place in a container and freeze until needed.

2 Place the mascarpone and crème fraîche in a medium bowl and whisk until smooth. Add the confectioners' sugar and rose water and continue to whisk, just until combined. Keep in the fridge until required.

3 Mix the superfine sugar with 2 1/2 tablespoons/ 40 ml of boiling water and stir until the sugar dissolves. Add the pomegranate molasses and sumac, stir to combine, and set aside.

4 When ready to serve, divide the strawberries among four bowls or glasses, followed by the meringues, rose water cream, and half the sumac syrup. Top with the pomegranate seeds and a tablespoon of sorbet. Finish with the remaining syrup and the rose petals and serve at once.

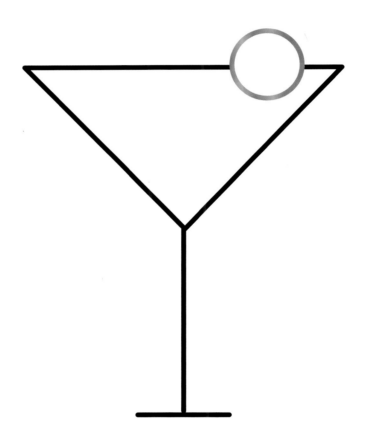

COCKTAILS

Cocktail Equipment

You really don't need a lot of fancy equimpent to make cocktails at home. If you don't have a Boston shaker with a glass top, for example, use a clean jam jar with a lid. If you don't have a muddler, use a small whisk or the end of a rolling pin (the kind without handles). A tea strainer or fine-mesh strainer can work well instead of a Hawthorne strainer, if that's what you have. Ice crushers are all well and good, but the result will be just the same if you wrap some cubes in a clean kitchen towel and bash them with a rolling pin. Making cocktails at home should be an enjoyable and relaxed kind of activity (just like cooking, actually).

If you do want to get going with the equipment, however, the list opposite is a guide to what would be useful to have. We've tried to help by putting the icons for what each cocktail needs, gear-wise, if you are not improvising with the alternatives, along with the glasses we recommend serving from.

TOOLS

SHAKER
(16 oz/450 ml)

FINE-MESH STRAINER
(OR MUSLIN-LINED)

DOUBLE-ENDED JIGGER

HAWTHORNE STRAINER

ICE CRUSHER
(OR ROLLING PIN)

PLASTIC SPRAY BOTTLE
(THE KIND USED TO DAMPEN
CLOTHES WHEN IRONING WORKS WELL)

BAR SPOON

MIXING GLASS

GLASSES

MARTINI GLASS

TUMBLER OR ROCKS GLASS

CHAMPAGNE FLUTE

CORIANDER AND GINGER MARTINI

You can make sugar syrup in either a saucepan or mason (or jam) jar. If making it in a saucepan, mix together equal amounts of superfine sugar and water and place over medium heat for about 5 minutes, stirring from time to time, just until the sugar has completely dissolved. If making it in a mason or jam jar, mix the sugar and water together in the jar, seal the lid tightly, and shake hard every 10 minutes or so, until the sugar has dissolved. As with all our sugar syrups, you'll make a lot more than you need, but store it in an airtight container and it will keep well in the fridge or freezer for future use.

We like to use the wheat-based Ketel One vodka here. It comes from a family-run Dutch distillery and is as cool and crisp as most Dutch designs. Also cool and crisp, but not at all Dutch (although she could be mistaken for being so, given her over-six-foot height), this was conceived by Georgie Thorp, ex head bartender at NOPI.

Serves 2

Ginger syrup
3-inch/8-cm piece of ginger, peeled and coarsely chopped (2 oz/65 g)
3/4 cup/150 g superfine sugar

1¼ oz/40 ml ginger syrup
3½ oz/100 ml Ketel One vodka
1¾ oz/50 ml lime juice
1 tsp coriander seeds, lightly toasted
10 cilantro leaves

---

1 To make the ginger syrup, place the ginger and sugar in a blender with ¾ cup/200 ml of water. Blitz for about 45 seconds, until fully combined. You will make about 1¼ cups/300 ml of syrup, which can be kept in the fridge, or frozen, for future use.

2 When ready to serve, place the ginger syrup in a cocktail shaker, along with all the remaining ingredients and plenty of cubed ice. Shake hard for about 20 seconds, then double-strain (through a Hawthorne strainer and into a fine-mesh sieve) into two prechilled martini glasses. Serve at once.

CHILE FINO OLD-FASHIONED

Sotol is like the grown-up sibling of tequila and mezcal, the two more rowdy distilled spirits from Mexico. *Añejo* means "aged," and añejo sotol is matured in French oak barrels for two years. There's a distinct family resemblance between tequila and sotol—they both have a gentle, fruity sweetness—but the sotol is a bit more gentle and nuanced than the more lip-smacking tequila can be. The sotol needs infusing for at least 24 hours to get the heat of the chile.

With thanks to Georgie Thorp for creating this.

Serves 2

Chile-infused añejo sotol
1 long red chile, sliced lengthwise but stem still intact
1 (700 ml) bottle of Añejo Sotol

2¹/₂ oz/75 ml chile-infused añejo sotol

³/₄ oz/25 ml fino sherry
³/₄ oz/25 ml hazelnut liqueur
4 dashes Angostura bitters
4 julienned strips of lemon zest, to garnish
2 julienned strips of red chile, to garnish

---

1 To infuse the sotol, drop the sliced chile into the bottle. Replace the lid and set aside for at least 24 hours. The longer you leave it, the spicier it will become. When ready to use, strain the sotol through a fine-mesh sieve, discarding the chile and the seeds.

2 When ready to serve, fill up a mixing glass with ice cubes and add all the ingredients, apart from the julienned lemon zest and chile. Stir for about 30 seconds, then strain through a Hawthorne strainer into two rocks glasses filled with ice. Garnish with the lemon zest and chile and serve at once.

BANANA AND CARDAMOM

Some cocktails just *do* fit the tropical-Caribbean-cliché. Anything involving Velvet Falernum—a longtime staple in the bars of Barbados— is going to transport you straight there. The liqueur is made from sugar cane, lime, almond, and cloves. Coupled with the rum and cardamom, you're pretty much ready to set up shop under a coconut tree. Don't worry if you can't get hold of the banana leaves to garnish: they're a nice touch but they're not essential.

Bob's Bitters is a brand of bespoke bitters that have one single flavor, rather than a mix of spices. Bartenders love the control these bitters allow over the flavors going into a cocktail. You can get them online, but don't worry if you don't have any: just increase the number of cardamom pods used instead.

With thanks to Lukasz Rafacz, head bartender at NOPI, whose recipe this is.

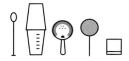

Serves 2

Cardamom honey
15 cardamom pods, well crushed
  with a mortar and pestle
3/4 oz/200 ml honey

1/2 small banana, peeled and cut
  widthwise into 1/3-inch/1-cm
  wide slices
16 cardamom pods (or 20, if you're
  not using the cardamom bitters),
  lightly crushed with a mortar
  and pestle
8 drops of Bob's cardamom
  bitters (optional)
2 1/2 oz/75 ml Flor de Caña
  white rum

3/4 oz/25 ml Velvet Falernum
  liqueur
2/3 oz/20 ml cardamom honey
1 3/4 oz/50 ml unfiltered apple
  juice
1 1/4 oz/40 ml lime juice
2 small banana leaves, to serve
  (optional)

1 To make the cardamom honey, place the cardamom pods and honey in a glass with 7 tablespoons/100 ml of hot water. Stir with a muddler, and then set aside for 12 hours. Strain out and discard the cardamom pods, then transfer the honey syrup to a jar in the fridge. It will keep for up to 2 weeks.

2 When ready to serve, place 2 slices of banana and 10 cardamom pods (or 14 if you are not using the Bob's Bitters) in the jar of a shaker. Muddle together, making sure the cardamom pods break open, then add the remaining ingredients. Top with ice cubes and shake hard for 10 to 15 seconds. Double-strain (through a Hawthorne strainer and into a fine-mesh sieve) into two rocks glasses filled with ice cubes. Insert the remaining cardamom pods in 2 slices of banana to garnish and finish with a banana leaf, if using.

KUMQUAT AND PASSION FRUIT

We use Tapatio Reposado tequila in our NOPI cocktails. *Reposado* means "rested" in Spanish. Having aged for about 4 months in ex-Bourbon oak barrels, the resulting drink is indeed a very chill one. With its agave-sweet and slightly woody tones, it's a more subtle tequila than the drink—with its salt-and-lemon-shot reputation—is often given credit for. There are lots of tequilas to choose from, but it's worth seeking out a *reposado*, if you can: Patrón, Herradura, and Don Julio all have good varieties.

This is all about the tartness of the kumquat, whose sharp flesh and sweet skin make for an incredibly refreshing drink. This is a cocktail with both the gentle punch of tequila and the delicacy of rose water. It's essentially a margarita, NOPI-style. We serve it in a rocks glass but you can serve it in a martini-style glass, if you like.

You'll make more syrup than you need for this recipe, but it can be frozen for future cocktails or stored in the fridge, where it will keep for up to 2 weeks, to have at the ready to pour over muesli, ice cream, or yogurt.

With thanks to Niall Downey, whose creation this is.

Serves 2

Kumquat syrup
8 kumquats
1¼ cups/250 g superfine sugar

6 kumquats
2 passion fruits, halved
¾ oz/25 ml kumquat syrup

2½ oz/75 ml Tapatio Reposado tequila (or another reposado tequila)
¾ oz/25 ml Cointreau
¾ oz/25 ml lemon juice
a spray of rose water, to serve

---

1 First make the kumquat syrup. Cut the 8 kumquats in half and place in a medium saucepan with the sugar. Add 1 cup/250 ml of water and place over medium heat. Bring to a simmer and continue to cook for 2 minutes, stirring from time to time, crushing the kumquats as they soften. Remove from the heat and set aside to cool before straining into a mason jar (or another jar you can seal) through a fine-mesh or muslin-lined sieve.

2 Cut the 6 kumquats in half widthwise, and divide them between two rocks glasses. Set aside one of the passion fruit halves, then spoon out the seeds from the other three halves and add to the glasses. Muddle everything together, then fill the glasses with crushed ice. Divide the kumquat syrup between the glasses, followed by the tequila, Cointreau, and lemon juice. Give everything a good stir and top up with more crushed ice. Cut the remaining passion fruit half into thin slices and place one slice on top of each glass. Spray with the rose water and serve at once.

Rooibos old-fashioned

Fernet Branca is a bitter, black, sharp Italian spirit. It's made up of 27 herbs from 4 different countries. Rumors and myths abound about its ability to magically cure ills. With an alcohol content of about 40 percent, however, it's more likely to be dulling the short-term senses than fixing anything in the long term. Medicinal analogies continue for those who think it tastes something like Listerine mixed with black licorice. Either way, we love it. So much so that, when Lukasz Rafacz was approached by the Diageo Reserve world-class cocktail-making competition to submit an entry for the competition, this was it.

Again, you'll make more syrup than you need here, but it will keep in the fridge for up to 3 weeks, to be used for future drinks or to drizzle on yogurt, porridge, or ice cream.

Serves 2

Rooibos tea syrup
1¼ cups/250 g superfine sugar
10 rooibos teabags
1 whole star anise
1 small cinnamon stick
4 black peppercorns
3 tbsp honey 3½ oz/100 ml

Woodford Reserve bourbon (or Bulleit bourbon)
⅓ oz/10 ml Fernet Branca
⅔ oz/20 ml rooibos tea syrup
4 dashes of Mozart chocolate bitters
2 shaved strips of orange peel, avoiding the bitter pith, to serve

1 Place all the ingredients for the rooibos tea syrup in a small saucepan with 1 cup/250 ml of water. Bring to a simmer over medium heat and simmer for about 20 minutes, until the liquid has reduced by a third. Remove from the heat and set aside to cool before straining through a fine-mesh or muslin-lined sieve and transferring to a sealed bottle or jar. The aromatics can be discarded. Keep in the fridge until ready to use.

2 When ready to serve, fill a mixing glass with ice cubes and add all the cocktail ingredients, apart from the orange peel. Stir for about 30 seconds, then strain through a Hawthorne strainer into two rocks glasses filled with ice. Roll up the orange peel and squeeze it above the cocktail, to extract the essential oils before placing it on top of the drink as a garnish. Serve at once.

SAFFRON CHASE

Anything that involves champagne needs to be served in an ice-cold glass. In order to get it as cold as it needs to be, you can either pop your flutes into the freezer for a couple of hours or, as we do in NOPI, simply fill the glasses with crushed ice and leave for 2 minutes before tipping the ice out into the sink.

Chase is a single-estate English distiller based in Herefordshire producing gin, vodka, and various liqueurs that, in our search for the finest, we love to use. There are other brands out there which are good, though—St-Germain elderflower, for example.

This is a nice and easy cocktail to make. You don't even have to stir the ingredients in a mixing glass, if you don't want to; you can just pour the ingredients straight into a chilled glass.

With thanks to Niall Downey.

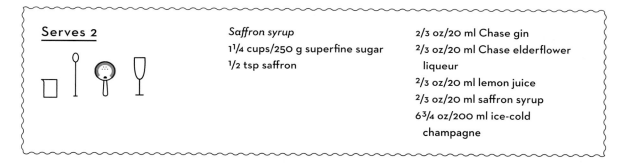

Serves 2

Saffron syrup
1¼ cups/250 g superfine sugar
½ tsp saffron

⅔ oz/20 ml Chase gin
⅔ oz/20 ml Chase elderflower
  liqueur
⅔ oz/20 ml lemon juice
⅔ oz/20 ml saffron syrup
6¾ oz/200 ml ice-cold
  champagne

1 First make the saffron syrup. Place the sugar in a small saucepan with 1 cup/250 ml of water. Place over medium-high heat and bring to a gentle simmer. Add the saffron and continue to simmer for 2 minutes. Remove from the heat and set aside to cool before transferring into a mason jar or another sealed jar. Store in the fridge until ready to use—it will keep for up to 3 weeks.

2 Place the gin, elderflower liqueur, and lemon juice in a mixing glass. Fill the glass half full with ice cubes and stir five times to the left and five times to the right with a spoon. It's important to get the stirring right here—not too much and not too little—so that you don't bring too much dilution to the drink. Strain into the chilled champagne flutes. Stir ⅓ oz/ 10 ml of saffron syrup into each glass, top with the champagne, and serve at once.

PINEAPPLE AND SAGE MARTINI

This was the first ever cocktail to get on the menu when NOPI opened. It was created by Niall Downey, who was living with Scully at the time. The cloves make it particularly well suited to festive parties. Its constant presence on our menu, however, hints at its suitability for drinking throughout the whole year.

You'll make more of the pineapple purée than you need, so you can either freeze the remainder in batches, to be used when needed, or eat it as a delicious purée, swirled into semi-whipped cream or spooned on top of some plain yogurt for breakfast. The remaining clove syrup can be kept in the fridge for a few weeks or frozen for longer.

Serves 2

Pineapple purée
1 large pineapple, unpeeled, leaves trimmed and discarded (3 lb/1.4 kg)

Infused gin
4 cardamom pods, roughly crushed by hand or in a mortar and pestle
20 sage leaves, plus 2 extra to serve
1 (750 ml) bottle of Tanqueray London dry gin

Clove syrup
1 1/4 cups/250 g superfine sugar
4 whole cloves

3 1/2 oz/100 ml infused gin
1 3/4 oz/50 ml pineapple purée
3/4 oz/25 ml lemon juice
2/3 oz/20 ml clove syrup

---

1 Preheat the oven to 390°F/200°C (360°F/180°C convection).

2 Wrap the pineapple in foil and roast in the oven for 3 hours. Remove and set aside to cool. Peel the pineapple and cut it lengthwise into 4 wedges. Cut out and discard the core, then place the flesh in a blender. Blitz to form a purée and set aside.

3 Add the crushed cardamom pods and sage leaves to the bottle of gin and set aside for at least 3 hours, swirling the bottle from time to time. Strain through a fine-mesh sieve, discard the cardamom and sage, and return the gin to the bottle.

4 To make the clove syrup, place the sugar in a medium saucepan with 1 cup/250 ml of water. Bring to a boil, then reduce the heat to low. Add the cloves and simmer for 10 minutes, stirring from time to time. Lift out and discard the cloves, then set the syrup aside until completely cool.

5 Pour the infused gin into a shaker with the pineapple purée, the lemon juice, and the clove syrup. Add ice, shake vigorously for 10 to 15 seconds, and strain into prechilled martini glasses. Garnish each with a fresh sage leaf and serve at once.

Sotol and mezcal

Ilegal mezcal joven is a small-batch mezcal from the Oaxaca region of Mexico. For anyone wondering about the legality of the drink, rest assured there's only one "l" in the spelling, rather than two! The *joven* is not as sweet or smoky as the more mature *reposado* or the even more mature *añejo*, which both see the inside of an oak barrel for much longer than the young *joven*. All are 100 percent agave and 80 percent proof, though—none of them are mucking around.

Use tequila instead of the sotol, if you can't get hold of the latter. The *reposado*—or rested—sotol has more nuance than its younger cousin, but the rowdier member of the spirit family can act as stand-in, if need be.

Any leftover jalapeño salt is great to have around in the kitchen, at the ready to sprinkle on roasted meat, grilled fish, or freshly fried chips. With thanks to Lukasz Rafacz, whose creation this is.

Serves 2

Jalapeño agave
2 green jalapeño chiles, finely chopped
1 1/4 cups/300 ml agave nectar

Jalapeño salt
4 green jalapeño chiles, coarsely chopped with seeds
1/3 oz/10 g coarse sea salt

2 pink grapefruit segments, plus 2 slices to serve
2 1/2 oz/75 ml Hacienda de Chihuahua sotol reposado
3/4 oz/25 ml Ilegal mezcal joven
2/3 oz/20 ml lemon juice

3/4 oz/25 ml pink grapefruit juice
2/3 oz/20 ml jalapeño agave
4 dashes of grapefruit bitters (or Angostura bitters)
a pinch of jalapeño salt, plus an extra pinch to serve

---

1 To make the jalapeño agave, place the jalapeños—along with all the seeds—in a container with the agave syrup. Top it up with 7 tbsp/100 ml of hot water and stir everything together. Set aside for 6 hours, then strain through a fine-mesh sieve into an empty container. Seal and store in the fridge until ready to use—it will keep for up to a month.

2 Preheat the oven to 230°F/120°C (210°F/100°C convection).

3 To make the jalapeño salt, place the jalapeños in a spice grinder with the salt. Blitz to combine, then spread out on a parchment-lined baking sheet. Place in the oven and cook for 1 1/2 hours, until completely dry. Peel the jalapeño mixture off the parchment paper and place the pieces in a spice grinder. Grind to a powder, transfer to a sealed container, and set aside until ready to use.

4 When ready to serve, muddle the grapefruit segments in the bottom of a shaker. Add the remaining ingredients and top up with cubes of ice. Shake well for 10 to 15 seconds, then double-strain (through a Hawthorne strainer and into a fine-mesh sieve) into two rocks glasses filled with cubes of ice. Top each with a slice of grapefruit, sprinkle with jalapeño salt, and serve at once.

Spiced pumpkin

The recipe for Bénédictine liqueur has been, ever since the drink was developed in nineteenth-century France by Alexandre Le Grand, a closely guarded secret. It's apparently known to only three people at any given time, so there are, as a result, lots of copycat recipes. Every bottle of Bénédictine has the initials D.O.M. on the label, which stands for "Deo Optimo Maximo" ("To God, most good, most great"). This coctail recipe, on the other hand, is much more accessible. It's a cocktail particularly suited to autumn and winter, pretty much designed for any Halloween, Thanksgiving, or Christmas party. The spiced rum needs 48 hours to infuse. You'll have plenty of rum and syrup left to keep for the next occasion for celebration. This is another creation from Lukasz Rafacz.

Serves 2

Allspice syrup
1¼ cups/250 g demerara sugar
2 whole star anise
1 vanilla bean, sliced lengthwise and seeds scraped
5 whole black peppercorns, plus a pinch of freshly ground black pepper
a pinch of freshly grated nutmeg

2 allspice berries, roughly crushed in a mortar and pestle
shaved peel of 1 orange
1 small cinnamon stick

Spiced rum
1 (750 ml) bottle of Goslings Black Seal rum
1 cinnamon stick
1 vanilla bean, sliced open lengthwise
1 slice shaved orange peel
2 allspice berries
4 whole cloves
6 black peppercorns

a pinch of freshly ground nutmeg
1 thin slice of ginger

2½ oz/75 ml spiced rum
¾ oz/25 ml allspice syrup
¾ oz/25 ml Bénédictine liqueur
1¼ oz/40 ml lime juice
2 tbsp pumpkin purée (we use Libby's 100 percent natural brand)
freshly grated nutmeg, to serve

1 Place all the ingredients for the allspice syrup in a medium saucepan with 1 cup/250 ml of water. Bring to a simmer over medium heat and cook for 30 minutes, until the mixture thickens and reduces by a quarter. Remove from the heat, set aside to cool, then strain through a fine-mesh or muslin-lined sieve. Transfer to a sealed jar and keep in the fridge, where it will last for up to a month.

2 Place all the spices and the ginger for the spiced rum in the bottle of Black Seal. Seal the bottle and set aside for 48 hours, for the flavors to steep. Strain out the aromatics through a fine-mesh seive and discard, then return the spiced rum to the bottle, ready to use.

3 When ready to serve, place all the ingredients apart from the nutmeg in a shaker with some cubed ice. Shake for 10 to 15 seconds, then double-strain (through a Hawthorne strainer and into a fine-mesh sieve) into two chilled martini glasses. Grate some nutmeg on top and serve at once.

Sumac martini

For anyone who thinks they don't like cocktails because they are too sweet, this is for you. Sumac—the dark red spice with a sharp, astringent kick—is one that we love to sprinkle over food. It has a musty, lemony flavor that, as Lukasz Rafacz discovered when creating this drink, works just as well in a cocktail.

Serves 2

Sumac-infused Ketel One vodka
3 tbsp sumac
1 (750 ml) bottle Ketel One vodka

2 oz/60 ml sumac-infused Ketel One vodka
1¼ oz/40 ml Velvet Falernum liqueur
1¾ oz/50 ml lime juice
1¼ oz/40 ml pomegranate juice
a pinch of sumac, to garnish

---

1 To make the infused vodka, place the sumac in a large glass or ceramic bowl and pour over the vodka. Cover and set aside for 2 hours, stirring from time to time, then strain back into the bottle through a fine-mesh or muslin-lined sieve.

2 When ready to serve, place all the ingredients in a shaker with some cubed ice. Shake really hard for 10 to 15 seconds, then double-strain (through a Hawthorne strainer and into a fine-mesh sieve) into two chilled martini glasses. Serve at once, with a sprinkle of sumac on top.

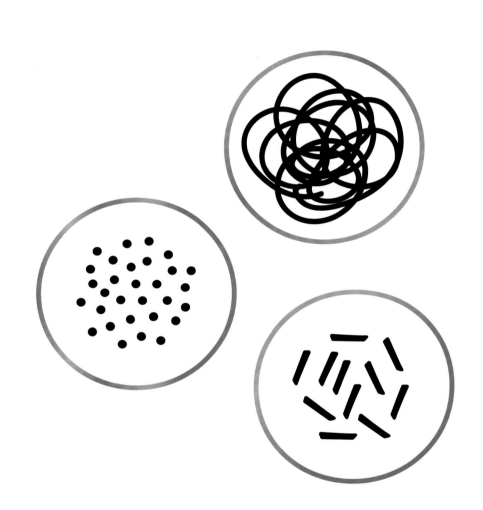

Condiments

Asian Master Stock

This is the secret behind two of our signature main course meat dishes: the Twice-Cooked Baby Chicken (page 167) and the Beef Brisket Croquettes (page 180). The list of ingredients is pretty much a roll call of Scully's favorite ingredients. Don't worry if you can't get to a speciality shop, though; the more mainstream alternatives suggested also work well. The stock can be used more than once, so don't throw it away once the chicken has been poached in it: the flavor only improves second time around.

If making the stock for the beef brisket, use a light soy sauce. If making it for the twice-cooked chicken, use a dark soy. If the stock is to be used for both dishes, though, don't panic: dark soy will be absolutely fine.

Makes about 5 cups/1.2 liters

5 1/4 cups/1.25 liters chicken stock

2/3 cup/150 ml dark or light soy sauce (see headnote)

3/4 cup/200 ml Shaoxing rice wine

2 1/3-inch/6-cm piece of ginger, peeled and julienned (1 2/3 oz/45 g)

4 cloves garlic, peeled and lightly crushed

1 1/2 oz/40 g cassia bark or cinnamon sticks

1/2 oz/15 g dried mandarin peel (or 1 long strip of shaved orange zest)

1 1/2 tsp Szechuan peppercorns

8 whole star anise

1/2 cup/100 g demerara sugar

1 Place all the ingredients in a large saucepan. Bring to a boil, then reduce the heat and simmer gently for 30 minutes. Remove from the heat and leave to cool. If the stock is for the beef brisket, it will need to be strained before storing in the fridge. If it is for the chicken dish, it can go straight into the fridge, without straining. Master stock can be frozen for up to 3 months.

CHILE JAM

We serve this with the Seared Scallops (page 40), but it's a hugely versatile condiment to have around. It's great spooned over roasted root vegetables—try it instead of the ginger tomatoes in Butternut Squash, for example (page 22) or served alongside some white fish or a roasted bird. It's delicious with anything, really: spooned inside a cheese sandwich or used as a dip for Truffled Polenta Fries (page 27), instead of the garlic aioli.

Don't be put off by the smell of the dried shrimp when it's cooking! It's difficult to think of another ingredient where the difference between how it smells and how it tastes is so great.

Makes about 1²/₃ cups/400 ml

2 cups/500 ml sunflower oil
30 Thai (red) shallots, thinly sliced (7 oz/200 g)
24 cloves garlic, thinly sliced (2³/₄ oz/80 g)

³/₄ oz/20 g galangal, peeled and thinly sliced
¹/₃ oz/10 g long red dried chiles, seeded
1³/₄ oz/50 g dried shrimp, rinsed and patted dry

3¹/₂ oz/100 g palm sugar, coarsely grated
1¹/₂ tbsp fish sauce
¹/₃ cup/80 ml tamarind water (see page 316)

---

1 Pour the sunflower oil into a large saucepan and place over medium-high heat. Add the shallots and fry gently for 6 to 7 minutes, until golden brown. Use a slotted spoon to remove the shallots and transfer them to a paper towel–lined plate while you continue frying. Add the garlic and fry for 2 minutes, until golden brown. Transfer to the paper towel–lined plate and add the galangal and chiles to the pan. Fry for just 1 minute, then remove. Finish with the shrimps: these will need just 30 seconds in the oil before being removed. Set everything aside to cool, then transfer to a food processor. Add 6 tablespoons/90 ml of the frying oil and blitz well until a smooth paste is formed. Add the paste to a medium saucepan along with the sugar, fish sauce, and tamarind water. Place over low heat and cook for about 15 minutes, stirring from time to time, until a jamlike consistency is formed.

2 Cool before storing in a jar in the fridge, where it will keep for up to 3 months.

LEMONGRASS CURRY PASTE

Roasting the shrimp paste in foil in the oven takes off the bitter edge that can sometimes spread through a dish. You can get lots of good ready-made curry pastes in Asian stores and other supermarkets (the Maesri Prik Khing variety is a NOPI favorite—steer clear of anything with preservatives, artificial flavors, or MSG), but we have yet to find one that is as good as making your own. This paste works well with white meats and most fish and seafood varieties, as well as with tofu and root vegetables.

Makes about 10 1/2 oz/300 g

1 tsp shrimp paste
4 small shallots, peeled and quartered (1 3/4 oz/50 g)
3 large cloves garlic, crushed
2-inch/5-cm piece of ginger, peeled and coarsely chopped (1 3/4 oz/50 g)

7 bird's-eye chiles (or 2 large red chiles), seeded and coarsely chopped
5 lemongrass stalks, trimmed, lightly bruised with a rolling pin and coarsely chopped
18 fresh kaffir lime leaves

1 tsp ground turmeric, or 3/4 oz/20 g fresh turmeric, peeled and coarsely chopped
1 tbsp coriander seeds, toasted
3/4 tsp ground cumin
1 tsp ground cardamom
3 tbsp sunflower oil
1/3 cup/75 ml coconut milk
coarse sea salt

1 Preheat the oven to 425°F/220°C (390°F/200°C convection). Wrap the shrimp paste in a small parcel of foil, place on a baking sheet, and roast for 8 minutes, until the aroma of fish is strong. Remove from the oven and transfer to the small bowl of a food processor with 1/2 teaspoon of salt, along with all the remaining ingredients apart from the coconut milk. Blitz well to form a coarse but uniform paste. Add the coconut milk and blend again until smooth. Store in the fridge until ready to use.

DUKKAH

This is to go with Lobster, Fennel, and Grilled Grapes Salad (page 102) but should be a pantry staple. It's fantastic to have at hand to sprinkle over a range of things. Leafy salads, platters of roast vegetables, hummus and other legume spreads, simply cooked rice, or lentils—they all benefit from a sprinkle of this aromatic Egyptian seed and nut mix. You can prepare *dukkah* in advance and store it in an airtight container for a month or so. Take care not to burn the seeds when you are making this: as soon as they begin to pop in the pan they are ready to be removed from the heat. Texture is also important here: the mixture should be quite coarse, so don't process the nuts and seeds much with the mortar and pestle.

Makes about 3 1/2 oz/100 g

2 1/2 oz/70 g hazelnuts, with skins
2 tbsp sunflower seeds
1 tsp fennel seeds

1 tbsp cumin seeds
1 tbsp dried green peppercorns
  (or white peppercorns)
3 tbsp coriander seeds

1 1/2 tbsp sesame seeds
1/2 tsp nigella seeds
1 tsp sweet paprika
coarse sea salt

---

1 Preheat the oven to 320°F/160°C (280°F/140°C convection).

2 Spread the hazelnuts on a baking sheet and place in the oven for 20 minutes. Add the sunflower seeds after 10 minutes, keeping them apart from the nuts. Remove both from the oven and leave to cool.

3 Put a cast-iron pan or heavy-bottomed frying pan over medium heat and leave for 5 minutes to heat up well. Spread the fennel seeds in the pan and dry-roast them for 30 seconds. Add the cumin seeds and cook for another 30 seconds, or until they start to pop, then transfer them both to a little bowl. Keeping the pan on the heat, add the green peppercorns and cook until they start to pop, about 30 seconds. Transfer to a separate bowl. Toast the coriander seeds for up to a minute, until they start to pop. Keep separate.

4 Reduce the heat to low and cook the sesame and nigella seeds together, stirring occasionally, until the sesame seeds turn light brown, then remove from the pan.

5 Rub the hazelnuts between the palms of your hands to remove and discard some of the skin. Use a mortar and pestle to coarsely break them, then transfer to a medium bowl. Lightly crush the cumin and fennel seeds and add to the hazelnuts. Do the same with the coriander seeds, followed by the green peppercorns, then the sunflower seeds. Add them to the rest, along with the sesame and nigella seeds, paprika, and 1/2 teaspoon of salt. Mix well, then store in an airtight container, where it will keep for about a month.

MEAL SUGGESTIONS

Creating a good meal at home often relies on choosing a good combination of different elements. To help you when planning your meals, here are some suggestions for dishes you might want to put together for a whole NOPI-style meal.

Starters or Salads	Mains + Sides	Desserts
Tomatoes with Wasabi Mascarpone *page 59*	**Lamb Rump + Jerusalem Artichokes with Tarragon** *page 155 + page 80*	**Popcorn Ice Cream** *page 263*
Burrata with Blood Orange *page 17*	**Pepper-Crusted Beef Tenderloin + Potato and Celery Root Gratin** *page 186 + page 94*	**Poached Quince with Raspberry and Quince Jelly** *page 257*
Sea Trout and Bulgur Tartare *page 43*	**Roasted Pork Belly + Wilted Kale with Fried Chile** *page 192 + page 95*	**Baked Chocolate Ganache** *page 255*
Grilled Asparagus with Romesco *page 18*	**Baked Blue Cheesecake + Green Salad with Sumac** *page 211 + page 87*	**Coffee and Pecan Financiers** *page 276*
Fondant Rutabaga Gratin *page 75*	**Spiced Pork Roast + Mixed Chinese Vegetables** *page 195 + page 88*	**Tapioca with Coconut Jam** *page 270*
Roasted Eggplant with Black Garlic *page 5*	**Gurnard + Sticky Sesame Rice + Wilted Kale with Fried Chile** *page 121 + page 83 + page 95*	**Strawberry and Rose Mess** *page 284*
Mixed Cauliflowers *page 60*	**Bourbon-Glazed Spare Ribs + Paprika Oven Fries** *page 201 + page 91*	**Broiled Grapefruit with Star Anise Sugar** *page 237*
Sharp and Spicy Watermelon Soup *page 31*	**Sea Bream with Mango and Papaya Salad + Sticky Sesame Rice** *page 109 + page 83*	**Tapioca with Coconut Jam** *page 270*
Baby Carrots and Mung Beans *page 24*	**Spiced Buttermilk Cod with Dal + Cardamom and Clove Rice** *page 112 + page 81*	**Roasted Pineapple** *page 260*

Starters or Salads	Mains + Sides	Desserts
Burnt Green Onion Dip with Kale *page 13*	Quail + Sticky Sesame Rice + Roasted Carrots *page 204 + page 83 + page 92*	Caramel Peanut Ice Cream *page 268*
Truffled Polenta Fries *page 27*	Urad Dal Purée with Eggplant + Mixed Chinese Vegetables *page 221 + page 88*	Poached Quince with Raspberry and Quince Jelly *page 257*
Pea Soup *page 33*	Lemon Sole + Purple Sprouting Broccoli with Skordalia *page 124 + page 21*	Coffee and Pecan Financiers *page 276*
Sharp and Spicy Watermelon Soup *page 31*	Lobster, Fennel, and Grilled Grape Salad *page 102*	Ricotta Fritters *page 273*
Celery Root Purée *page 7*	Grape Leaf Beef Pie + Green Salad with Sumac *page 190 + page 87*	Poached Quince with Raspberry and Quince Jelly *page 257*
Butternut Squash with Ginger Tomatoes *page 22*	Persian Love Rice + Black Radish, Red Endive, and Apple Salad *page 229 + page 68*	Roasted Pineapple *page 260*
King Prawns *page 101*	Twice-Cooked Baby Chicken + Paprika Oven Fries + Green Salad with Sumac *page 167 + page 91 + page 87*	Popcorn Ice Cream *page 263*
Fried Baby Artichokes *page 10*	Venison Fillet with Date Labneh + Whole Roasted Celery Root *page 161 + page 97*	Strained Ricotta with Blackcurrant Compote and Rhubarb *page 282*
Seared Scallops with Pickled Daikon *page 40*	Roasted Pork Belly + Wilted Kale with Fried Chile *page 192 + page 95*	Strawberry and Rose Mess *page 284*

We also thought it would be helpful to highlight some of the dishes that can be served on their own or, at most, with some plain bread, rice, or a green salad. The list below gives just a few suggestions, rather than being comprehensive.

For a lunch or light supper

Watermelon Soup *page 31*

Jerusalem Artichoke Soup *page 36*

Pea Soup *page 33*

Baby Squid *page 39*

King Prawns *page 101*

Pistachio and Pine Nut–Crusted Halibut *page 118*

Lobster Salad *page 102*

Scallops with Corn and Merguez Salsa *page 129*

Baked Blue Cheesecake *page 211*

Fondant Rutabaga Gratin *page 75*

Corn Cakes with Beet and Apple Salad *page 209*

For a more substantial meal

Lamb Meatballs *page 147*

Chicken Supremes *page 163*

Chicken Pastilla *page 172*

Roasted Duck Breast *page 179*

Lamb Rump *page 155*

Pepper-Crusted Beef Tenderloin *page 186*

Grape Leaf Beef Pie *page 190*

Basil Spätzle *page 126*

Sea Bass *page 105*

Buttermilk Cod *page 112*

Tuna Skewers *page 138*

Five-Spiced Tofu *page 214*

Snake Bean and Peanut Achar *page 217* **+ Farinata** *page 82*

Pearl Barley Risotto *page 227*

Persian Love Rice *page 229*

OUR INGREDIENTS A TO Z

Ajwain seeds These have a distinct taste: slightly bitter and pungent, at the same time as being very welcoming. We use them in our watermelon soup but they also work well lightly crushed and sprinkled over roasted root vegetables or a legume-based dish. If you can't find them, use celery seeds instead.

Ancho chile Mild on heat, big on smoky flavor, we use these to add a background heat to a range of stews, soups, sauces, and marinades. They tend to come whole and dried, but if you can't find any, use other whole or flaked dried chiles instead, reducing the quantity, as they will probably be much hotter than anchos.

Anchovies (dried) Also known as *ikan bilis*, these are tiny salt-cured and dried anchovies, often fried, which are served as snacks in Malaysia, Singapore, and Burma, alongside peanuts. They are also key ingredients in *sambals* and various sauces, introducing a wonderful umami flavor.

Annatto seeds Also known as achiote, these seeds are mainly used in Mexican and Caribbean cooking as a yellow-orange food coloring. The taste is not a particularly strong one but it is nonetheless unique: slightly peppery with a hint of nutmeg.

Arak This anise-flavored spirit traditionally accompanies mezze in the Arab world. It's affectionately called "lion's milk" because it turns cloudy when water and ice are added. We like to use it throughout our cooking—the aniseed works well with fish and is also great in desserts. Ouzo, Pernod, or raki can be used as an alternative.

Banana leaves These are often used in Keralan cooking as a way to wrap, protect, and cook fish. They look stunning and are a good way of keeping the fish moist, but if you can't get hold of any, use parchment paper instead.

Barberries These dried Iranian berries have a sweet-and-sour flavor that we love. They can be stirred into a rice and herb salad or a *kuku* (an Iranian-style frittata), adding small bursts of color and flavor. Dried sour cherries, coarsely chopped, can be used as an alternative. Little dried blackcurrants, soaked in a little lemon juice, also work well.

Black cardamom This is dried over an open fire so has a distinct smoky aroma, subtly reminiscent of bacon. It has a much bolder flavor than green cardamom, but they share minty and ginger notes, so just use the green variety, if that's what you have.

Black garlic This has the texture of a gummy candy and the flavor of balsamic licorice. It is, essentially, white garlic that's been treated over a long period and allowed to ferment and turn completely mellow and sweet. It's sold either as a whole bulb, whose cloves you then need to peel, or in a small jar of slightly smaller cloves, already separated and peeled. It's a unique ingredient: one that's hard to replicate with an alternative.

Black rice (Thai glutinous rice) This is a very popular rice in Southeast Asian cooking, where it is often cooked in coconut milk and served for breakfast, topped with fresh fruit. Like other short-grain rice, it's nutty, chewy, soft, and starchy. It looks stunning on the plate and can be used in sweet or savory dishes. If you can't find it, use the Italian Nerone rice instead.

Burrata This is a fresh, round Italian cheese. The outer shell is pure mozzarella and the softer inside is a mixture of mozzarella and cream, which starts to ooze out when the ball is sliced open. Burrata means "buttered" in Italian, and it has a creamy smoothness that is second to none. If you can't find it, though, use buffalo milk mozzarella instead.

Cardamom (ground) This gives an aromatic and distinctive sweetness to all sorts of desserts as well as to many savory dishes. We love to add a pinch to our green chile sauce called *zhoug*. If you can't buy it already ground, just blitz whole green cardamom pods in a spice grinder until they're as fine as powder.

Chipotle chiles (dried) These ripe smoke-dried jalapeño chiles add a meaty and smoky depth of flavor to any soup or stew. They vary in heat, so assess how hot yours are before adding it to a dish. If you can't get hold of any, substitute fresh chile and smoked paprika.

Curry leaves The difference between dried and fresh curry leaves is huge, the latter having a lot more strength and aroma. We always use fresh, and they are increasingly available in the fresh herb section at supermarkets. If you need to use dried, however, just double the number required.

Dukkah This is a mix of toasted and crushed hazelnuts and a mix of seeds—sunflower, sesame, and nigella seeds, fennel seeds, cumin, and coriander seeds—with sweet paprika. It's an Egyptian condiment whose name comes from the Arabic meaning "to pound." We love to sprinkle it on leafy salads, roast vegetables, hummus, fish, and meat. You can buy it ready-made but, to make your own, see page 307.

Farro This ancient wheat is from the same family as spelt. It has a nutty al dente texture that, like spelt, allows each grain to retain its own identity when cooked. It's a versatile wheat, happy to be paired with robust flavors. Farro is sold whole, semi-pearled or pearled, which affects the amount of time it takes to cook. As well as spelt, pearl barley can also be used, if you can't find farro.

Freekeh This Middle Eastern-grown wheat comes either whole grain or cracked. It often has a smoky flavor—the result of being picked unripe and roasted over wood fires to burn off the husks—which we love. It's as simple to cook as couscous or bulgur but has a more complex, nutty flavor. It's available in specialty shops, health food shops, and online.

Galangal A key ingredient in Thai cooking, this comes from the same family as ginger. It's a lot more aromatic and lemony, though, so while ginger can be used as an alternative, the result will be different and a dish tends to be able to take more ginger than it can galangal.

Ghee This is butter that has been clarified and evaporated, commonly used in north Indian cooking. Its taste is rich and slightly nutty. You can get it in specialty shops and a lot of supermarkets. It's also easy to make your own by melting butter in a heavy-bottomed saucepan over low heat for about 45 minutes. Once the sediment settles on the bottom of the pan, strain and transfer to a sterilized jar.

Glutinous rice flour Also known as sweet rice flour, this has a very sticky feel due to its high starch content. You can get it in Asian stores and health food shops. It's not sweet but, as well being used in savory dishes, it's often used as a binding agent in gluten-free baking.

Gochujang red pepper paste This scarlet-red Korean chile paste is made from hot red peppers, fermented soy beans, and glutinous rice flour. It's got a distinct taste—sweet and savory, almost like Marmite, at once. You can find it in Asian stores but, if you want to make a version of your own, see page 183 for the recipe.

Harissa or rose harissa This paste is a key ingredient in north African cooking. It's made from rehydrated dried chiles, with lots of herbs and spices—over 40!—mixed in. The addition of rose petals gives a special sweetness and softens the chile kick.

Kaffir lime leaves As with curry leaves, the difference in vibrancy between the fresh and dried leaves is huge. The fresh freeze well, so grab a bag whenever you see one to freeze for future use. As with curry leaves, if you need to use dried, just double the number of leaves.

Mirin This sweet, viscous rice wine isn't a hard to find ingredient, but the difference between some supermarket brands and what you can buy from specialty shops is huge. Try to use one with as few ingredients added as possible. It should be made from rice, water, and *koji*—a cultured rice used to spur fermentation. Brands with added preservatives and sugar or corn syrup should be avoided.

Miso paste White, brown, and barley miso are all widely available in supermarkets, health food stores, and specialty stores. Made from fermented soy beans and rice, wheat, or barley, miso has a sweetness and intensity that is a great way of infusing tons of savory flavor into a dish.

Moscatel vinegar This Spanish wine vinegar has a sweet and deep taste. There's a lot going on flavor-wise—it's fruity and rich but also lightly acidic. A good-quality white wine vinegar can be used as an alternative.

Mulberries These clustered fruits taste rather like blackberries. They're hard to get hold of fresh, as they are so perishable once picked, and they are more easily available dried. We like to use the dried white (rather than black) variety. Golden raisins can be used as an alternative.

Nanami togarashi Also known as *shichimi togarashi*, this Japanese spice mix is made from a blend of various ingredients—recipes vary—but the dominant notes come from ground red chiles, dried orange, ginger, nori, and ground *sansho*. It's available in Asian stores and in a number of mainstream supermarkets but, if you're looking for an alternative, a good pinch of regular chile flakes will be fine.

Nori seaweed Sheets of dried green nori seaweed are best known for the role they play in sushi-making. We also love to grind the sheets up to form the base of a dressing for a fresh salad or a dipping sauce for cubes of fried tofu. It's great, too, in a simple sauce to spoon over white fish.

Oolong tea This tea, grown in the mountains of Taiwan, has the strength of black tea but the aromatic and flowery flavors of a green. When we are smoking food—anything from balls of labneh cheese to a side of salmon to lamb chops—a sprinkle of oolong leaves generally features. It's expensive, though, so use lapsang souchong if you prefer.

Palm sugar This comes either in block form (from specialty shops and some supermarkets) or as small crystallized granules (from most supermarkets). We prefer the block form, *gula jawa*, named after Java in Indonesia, where it's a staple ingredient in the country's cooking. Whether coarsely grated into curries, used in sauces like our Chile Jam (page 305) or in a number of sweet dishes, it has a distinct depth and sweetness.

Pandan leaves These are widely used in Southeast Asian cooking—in both sweet and savory dishes—infusing everything with a lightly sweet, grassy, and coconut-like fragrance. Their smell and flavor are distinct, but you'll need to go to a specialty Asian food shop to find them. They are worth seeking out, though, and freeze well for future use. If you are looking for an alternative, though, a vanilla bean—slit open lengthwise and seeds scraped—works well.

Pedro Ximénez sherry vinegar This is as sweet as vinegar comes: it's dark, viscous and almost molasseslike in its richness. We love to drizzle it on ice cream. It's widely available, but other good sweet vinegars can be used as a substitute.

Ras el hanout This means "top of the shop" in Arabic and, rather than there being one definitive list of ingredients, it's a North African blend of sweet and hot spices that are then finely ground. Flavors tend towards ginger, cardamom, allspice, nutmeg, cloves, black pepper, and cinnamon. It's widely available and you can always tweak it to your liking: a bit more cinnamon, perhaps, or some powdered dried rose petals stirred through.

Rice vinegar As with mirin, tamarind paste, Shaoxing rice wine, and so forth, the shorter the list of ingredients for these Asian ingredients, the better the product will be. We like to use Mizkan rice vinegar—it's less acidic and slightly sweet compared to other vinegars—but use a supermarket variety, if that's what you have. Always taste it before adding it to a dish, though, so that you can decide whether a pinch of sugar will work well or if you should be adding slightly less than recommended.

Rose petals We like using dried Iranian rose petals in baking or to give an extra finishing touch to desserts and cakes, even to spicy fish. They look stunning and have a floral and fragrant aroma.

Shaoxing rice wine Made from brown glutinous rice, this amber-colored Chinese spirit has a distinctive nutty taste. You can get it in specialty shops and supermarkets but, as an alternative, a good dry or pale dry sherry can also work well.

Shrimp (dried) These are what they say on the package. Don't be put off by the smell when they are cooking! As with anything fermented, they add a particular flavor which is very difficult to replace by using another ingredient. They are available in specialty shops and online.

Shrimp paste Don't judge this intensely savory and aromatic paste by its smell. It delivers its flavorsome rewards in the final dish! If you're finding a bitterness in your cooking when using shrimp paste, wrap it in some foil and roast it for 10 minutes in a hot oven before adding it to your dish. It's widely available in specialty stores and Asian supermarkets.

Sorrel This startlingly sour green leaf gives a great lemony kick to any soup or salad. It's not always easy to get hold of, though, so use a mix of mâche, arugula, and grated lemon zest as an alternative.

Sumac The dark red crushed berries of the sumac shrub bring an astringent and citrusy kick to any dish they are sprinkled over. Scrambled eggs, grilled chicken, and roasted vegetables can be quickly enlivened with a pinch. The spice is widely available in both specialty shops and supermarkets.

Szechuan peppercorns These are used in cooking as much for the experience they bring to the sensation of eating as for their citrus flavor. They have a medium heat, but it's the numbing tingle left on the lips and tongue that marks these red dried berries out.

Tamarind Tamarind provides the backbone to much Asian cooking. It brings a sweet and sour depth—at once sharp and acidic but also fruity and soothing—to a range of dishes. Ready-made pastes are widely available, but they taste very different from (and not nearly as good as) the version you make yourself. In order to make 2 tablespoons of tamarind paste, soak 1 ounce/30 g of tamarind pulp with 1/4 cup/60 ml of water for about half an hour, squeezing from time to time so that all the pulp and tamarind disperses through the water. Strain through a fine-mesh sieve, discarding the pulp.

Thai basil This variety of basil has a distinctly licorice taste. It's becoming more widely available in supermarkets but you can use regular basil, mixed with a few leaves of chopped tarragon, as an alternative.

Thai (red) shallots These are the small, red, round shallots sold in specialty Asian shops. Their taste is distinct from the bigger golden varieties—they have a lower water content, so their taste is more pronounced—but use another small variety, if that's what you have.

Urad dal "Dal" refers to any bean, pea, or seed that has been split, so this is the split and smaller version of the urad bean (just like chana dal and mung dal are the split and smaller versions of the chickpea and mung bean). They are creamy white and can be either cooked and left whole in curries or blitzed to make a mashlike base upon which to sit a curry. Supermarkets are beginning to stock wider ranges of beans and peas, and they're also available in specialty shops.

Urfa chile flakes These Turkish flakes are mild on heat but big on aroma. They're sweet and smoky, with a fantastic burgundy color. They go well with almost anything and are widely available online, but can, if you like, be substituted with other types of dried chile flakes.

Valdespino sherry vinegar This cask-aged vinegar has a wonderfully sweet and complex taste: rich and mature and fruity and fresh all at once. It's widely available, but other good-quality sherry vinegars also work well.

Verjuice Made from the juice of semiripe wine grapes, this has the tartness of lemon juice and the acidity of vinegar but without the harshness of either. The taste is distinct but, if you can't get hold of it, use a mix of two parts lemon juice to one part red wine vinegar instead.

Yuzu juice Small bottles of the juice from this East Asian citrus fruit are becoming more widely available in supermarkets (as well as in Asian shops). The flavor is very fresh: something between a lime and a mandarin. A squeeze of lime, however, makes an adequate substitute.

Za'atar This is a Middle Eastern spice blend made up of dried and ground sumac, sesame seeds, and dried and ground hyssop. It can be sprinkled on pretty much anything and everything, from hummus to labneh to fried eggs, roast vegetables, and roast meat.

Acknowledgments

Restaurant

We mentioned in our Introduction (page xii) Noam, Cornelia, Basia, and Sarit, the founding mothers and fathers of NOPI with whom we collaborated in setting up the restaurant and getting it off the ground. We'd like to thank them all deeply.

Other key players to whom we are indebted are Sami Tamimi, the top authority in the kitchen; Heidi Knudsen, who's taken over as general manager; and Alex Meitlis, our highly creative designer and dear friend (and the person to whom all complaints about the NOPI ladies' restrooms should be directed).

If we only could, we'd list the name of every person who has ever worked in NOPI since the restaurant opened in 2011. The team is key in so many ways and every single member has added her or his unique contribution to what makes the NOPI experience delightful and extraordinary.

Still, we would like to single out and thank a few people who were with us for a long while or made a particular impact: David Lagonell, Nicole Pisani, Carlos Capparelli, Angelos Kremmydas, John Meechan, Myles Broscoe, Gabriel Camacho Drew, Robert Wainwright, Mark Hannell, Ainars Tapis, Luke Findlay, Adriano Toledo, Marbin Marrero, Donata Orsi, Gena Deligianni, Katie Healy, Saga Ronnbacka, Cami Raben, Gal Zohar, Honami Matsumoto, Niall Downey, Georgie Thorp, Athanasios Athannatos, Chad Canning, Patryk Wakula, Leo Miaskowski, Rebecca Baker, Anton Loxha, Kinga Iwanczyk, Silvia Cortes, Monika Wozinska, Pierre Malouf, Albi Ison, Fabio Izzo, Ludwig Soukup, Huja Bantin, Sarah Steele, Raquel Cegarra Lopez, Matteo Sartore, Aline Ferreira Nunes, Enrico Lecci, Alain Nyobe, Fergus Kealy.

We are also grateful to our devoted customers, who keep on coming, enjoying, and letting the world know about it.

Book

If there is one person who's carried this project on her back and deserves every possible accolade for it, it is Tara Wigley. We are ridiculously lucky to have Tara with us and utterly grateful to her.

We would also like to sincerely thank Esme Robinson, Claudine Boulstridge, and Sarah Joseph, who cooked and assessed the recipes a ridiculous number of times with incredible patience and much insight.

Lukasz Rafacz, head bartender at NOPI, was tremendously generous with both his time and his knowledge, creating our great cocktail list.

Caz Hildebrand, an old-time collaborator and friend, wears two (very beautiful) hats here: one as the creator of NOPI's graphic language and the other as the designer of this book. Caz, thank you for the golden ring!

Jonathan Lovekin has managed to pull yet another rabbit out of his bottomless hat and shed a fresh, enticing new light on our food. Adam Hinton spent time with our team and customers and brilliantly captured NOPI's true spirit. Thanks also to Sanjana Lovekin and Lindy Wiffen for all the stunning plates.

Felicity Rubinstein, Fiona MacIntyre, and Lizzy Gray have been working hard behind the scenes continuously, indulging us and allowing us to make precisely the book that we wanted to make. Across the pond, Aaron Wehner and Sandi Mendelson continuously do an amazing job.

Other colleagues and friends who were, as always, extremely helpful are Maria Mok, Lucy Henry, Mark Hutchinson, Sarah Bennie, Gemma Bell, and Bob Granleese.

Finally, we would both like to dedicate the book to a few family members and close friends and acknowledge their continual presence in our lives.

Scully
Most importantly, thank you to my loving mother, Mary, for everything you have done for me over the years, for instilling in me the drive to push forward and become the man that I am today. Thanks also to my aunties, my cousins, and the rest of the family for showing me the beauty of Malaysian cuisine and teaching me all about it. To Musa Scully, Melissa Scully, Stephen Dickey, Adam Ornowski, Danielle Ornowski, Calvin Von Niebel, David Bravo, Christopher Lyon, Francis Puyat, Nguyo Milcinovic, Ramiro Gasparrotto, Kamil Kliber, Mariouz Gabrys, Oliver Pagani, Sam Wilkinson, Tim Yates, Tim Standing, Tom Cately, Vince Mammone, and Zoe Blackmore.

Yotam
To Karl Allen, Michael and Ruth Ottolenghi, Tirza, Danny and the Florentin family, Pete and Greta Allen, Helen Goh, Shachar Argov, Garry Chang, Alison Quinn, Lingchee Ang, Itamar Srulovich, Tamara Meitlis, Keren Margalit, Yoram Ever-Hadani, Itzik Lederfeind, Ilana Lederfeind and Amos, Ariela, and David Oppenheim.

Index

Originally published in slightly different form in Great Britain by Ebury Press, an imprint of
Ebury Publishing, Penguin Random House Ltd., London.

Library of Congress Cataloging-in-Publication Data is on file with the publisher.

Hardcover ISBN: 978-1-60774-623-2
eBook ISBN: 978-1-60774-624-9

Printed in China

Design by Here Design

10 9 8 7 6 5 4 3 2 1

First U.S. Edition